The Rise of Western Journalism,
1815–1914

The Rise of Western Journalism, 1815–1914

Essays on the Press in Australia, Canada, France, Germany, Great Britain and the United States

Edited by ROSS F. COLLINS and E.M. PALMEGIANO

McFarland & Company, Inc., Publishers
Jefferson, North Carolina, and London

LIBRARY OF CONGRESS CATALOGUING-IN-PUBLICATION DATA

The rise of western journalism, 1815–1914 : essays on the press in Australia, Canada, France, Germany, Great Britain and the United States / edited by Ross F. Collins and E.M. Palmegiano.
    p.   cm.
Includes bibliographical references and index.

ISBN-13: 978-0-7864-3143-4
softcover : 50# alkaline paper ∞

1. Journalism — Developed countries — History —19th century.
2. Journalism — Developed countries — History — 20th century.
I. Collins, Ross F.   II. Palmegiano, E. M.
PN4811.R57   2007
079'.1722 — dc22   2007025598

British Library cataloguing data are available

©2007 Ross F. Collins and E.M. Palmegiano. All rights reserved

No part of this book may be reproduced or transmitted in any form or by any means, electronic or mechanical, including photocopying or recording, or by any information storage and retrieval system, without permission in writing from the publisher.

On the cover: (top) The *New York World* building, 1909; *(left)* New *York Herald* composing room, 1902; *(right)* newsboys at the (Wilmington, Delaware) *Evening Journal,* 1910; *(bottom)* printing press at the 1876 Centennial Exhibition in Philadelphia *(all images from the Library of Congress)*

Manufactured in the United States of America

McFarland & Company, Inc., Publishers
  Box 611, Jefferson, North Carolina 28640
    www.mcfarlandpub.com

Table of Contents

Preface — 1

Introduction — 3

Australia: Shaking Off the Shackles to Earn the Badge of Independence
 Rod Kirkpatrick — 11

Canada's Victorian Press: Influences from Home and Abroad
 David R. Spencer — 42

Traitorous Collaboration: The Press in France, 1815–1914
 Ross F. Collins — 71

Germany: Mass-Circulation Newspapers Shaped by an Authoritarian Setting
 Ulf Jonas Bjork — 106

The "Fourth Estate": British Journalism in Britain's Century
 E.M. Palmegiano — 139

Coming of Age: The Growth of the American Media in the Nineteenth Century
 Carol Sue Humphrey — 173

Notes on Contributors — 203

Index — 205

Preface

This pioneering study focuses on the transformation of print journalism in its golden age, from emergence as an effective though not popular medium of public communication in 1815 to recognition as *the* major medium in the Western world in 1914. Although print currently has competition from other media genres, the format created in the nineteenth century still dominates. Now when we debate "the news," we mean news measured in content and presentation by Western guidelines. When we buy a magazine, we expect and accept a Western version notwithstanding the word's Arabic etymology. The "*makhazin*," or storehouse, as Robert L. Patten suggested in his 2000 essay in *Nineteenth-Century Media and the Construction of Identities*, is an apt linguistic root for the contemporary miscellany.

The following pages offer a cross-cultural record of the journalism that is the basis of the "Western" style. The collection covers Great Britain, France, the United States, Canada, Australia and Germany, countries that developed models for the modern press or adapted those models. These states played roles on the international stage by virtue of empire, cultural sway, natural resources, population and/or military prowess.

No other work treats the journalism of all these areas as they relate to each other. As a further example of neglect, even in a disciplinary approach, no book in English considers the nineteenth-century media in France or Germany. Yet as press theorist William Hachten noted, in *The World News Prism* (sixth edition), the paradigms of the journalistic planet are those that this text outlines. As the press of these countries evolved, journalists interacted. The nature and scope of their interaction explain how a Western standard became an international standard, one that grew to be important and ubiquitous by 1914.

Since today's journalism forms so large a part of everyone's daily media bread, its origins would naturally interest historians. What is so intriguing about nineteenth-century press innovations is that they occurred concurrently with one of the most pivotal revolutions in history, industrialization. As nations industrialized, the press changed. The metamorphosis in journalism, like that in the societies where it thrived, was conceptual and technical. Publications originally aimed at an elite able to read and able to pay. By the First World War, the press was a product that reached millions and cost almost nothing.

In order to understand this shift, the authors examined a variety of primary and secondary sources throughout the world. Owners, editors, reporters, magazine scribes, people who crossed between journalism and politics or other careers are relevant but so too are the cartoons and other illustrations that demonstrate the characteristics of the press. As the bibliographies for each essay indicate, the range of evidence is wide.

These materials confirm cross-pollination in journalism. This sharing was significant, yet scholars have tended to isolate press experiences. By integrating them, this volume reveals how nineteenth-century publishers and their staffs remapped journalism in several and similar ways. In so doing, they pieced together a mosaic that became the prototype for a global press.

Journalists slowly reshaped journalism by expanding its definition, identifying new revenue streams, and embracing technology. Their redefinition is pivotal to the modern idea of the press, but their notions of its funding are hardly collateral. The consequence, which the contributors detail, is a press that prioritizes news but enjoys influence because of its views and depends largely on advertising.

The investigation of the nineteenth-century press raised many questions. Was it an objective bystander recording events? Was it a tool for ideologues and Machiavellians? Was it a voice for otherwise voiceless people? Was it a triumph for capitalism irrespective of intellectual cost? Was it a signal of the blessings or the dangers of machines, perhaps the most telling question in the twenty-first century? The answers to these queries are the essence of this work.

Introduction

The changes in the Western world in the nineteenth century are too vast for overstatement. From agriculture to industry, from superstition to science, from word-of-mouth to wireless, from horse to horseless carriage, the century witnessed a cultural revolution. The person born in Europe or its colonial progeny at the time of Napoleon's Waterloo would not recognize those places at the beginning of the Great War. Indeed, many historians contend that the transformations in this era eclipsed even the cataclysms of the decades that followed when conflict replaced progress as the watchword.

Chronicling the industrial burgeoning of the West and other shifts, as they swept away much of the past, was the press. The press was more than the log of society; it was a social institution. Like other media, from ballads to pulpits, it delivered and interpreted information. Like them, too, it shaped thinking by selection of stories. Unlike other media, however, nineteenth-century print journalism was an emporium where readers could exchange ideas frequently, an activity that formalized "public opinion" and thus enabled the press to be a powerbroker, a status that a growing mass audience reinforced.

To say that this century marked the birth of the Fourth Estate is no exaggeration. Newspapers, which had begun earlier, still had small circulations in 1815. They tended to be local gazettes by printers who had other revenue or partisan papers concerned with national politics. Locals could be chatty or as polemical and pontifical as metros. By 1914 the artisan had given way to the businessman, circulations had soared, and prices had dropped. Magazines, which also antedated Napoleon, were at first the muses of the rich who could afford their cost and comprehend their subtlety. They and the elite reviews, didactic about politics and literature, faced competition as literacy spread and inexpensive journals catered to every taste imaginable.

Essays in this book illuminate this transition in narratives that incorporate analysis where appropriate. They focus on the principal trends and the

Introduction

chief personnel. Although each essay reveals unique journalistic experiences, common themes appear, notably with respect to the newspaper. Among them are the relationship between government and journalism, the impact of technology, the function of advertising and the emergence of a mass press.

The nexus between government and journalism was important in Great Britain and Australia early in the nineteenth century but persisted in France and Germany much longer. The attempts of British ministers and Australian governors to control by libel law, subsidy, stamp duty or official authorization were modest compared to the more stringent restrictions imposed by Paris and Berlin. The press in the United States and that in France exemplify the extremes, one utterly without restraint and the other shadowed by suppression. Canadian colonies, with English and French populations, showed how ethnicity as well as politics tilted the journalistic balance. Irrespective of divergence in the specific relations between rulers and writers, the only distinction between governments that regulated journalism and those that tolerated it was one of degree. Limitations could check or channel the voices from below, but liberty could just as surely neutralize them by encouraging a plethora of publications. Manipulation by bureaucrats in the first scenario was simply more overt than that by politicians in the second. Whether free or fettered, the press was significant to those in authority because it aired material that readers used to judge public issues and it organized those judgments. In so doing, journalism became a force that could constrain leaders otherwise unaccountable or accountable only to a few. They could not ignore the press, particularly as suffrage widened.

Technology was sometimes coincidental, always consequential for the press of every country discussed in this book. The invention of telegraphy transformed news-gathering, speeding dissemination of data and siring major news agencies that are still extant. Telegrams soon shaped the presentation of news, abbreviating and homogenizing it. The establishment of news agencies accelerated these outcomes. Charles Havas in France and his disciples, P.J. Reuter in Britain and Bernard Wolff in Germany, started the benchmark services in Europe, while owners of New York dailies forged the Associated Press. Committed to sharing the task of news collection, these affiliations initiated a global information network that was relatively quick and cheap, albeit one that further standardized news. The agencies also were the first transnational link among journalists, foreshadowing their cooperative endeavors and comradeship in the next century. Like telegraphy, the later and even faster telephone and photography were serendipitous for the newspaper. Journalists,

Introduction

nevertheless, were perennially fascinated by technology. For instance, from *The Times*' introduction of the steam press in late 1814 London, there was ongoing pressure everywhere to improve typesetting and printing. Constant upgrades contributed to efficiency of a process that eventually produced enormous numbers of pages. As economies of scale permitted reduction of costs, the press was more accessible to more people. This circumstance and print journalism's monopoly of the information-transfer business that evolved in the nineteenth century were pivotal prerequisites for the mass media that arose before the First World War.

Directly connected to technology was advertising. Most of the nations studied in this book accepted it as a prime source of revenue, one that paid for the latest machines and the ongoing expenses. Both those countries that relied on advertising in budgeting and those that did not were aware of its implications. Placement, wording and art were obvious concerns, but the extent to which capitalism could taint journalism was a constant worry.

The interaction between business and journalism was most apparent in the late century when the mass press was born except in Germany. Successfully initiated by the French, the mass press was the dominant one by 1914. Whether it was the child of incipient democracy or widespread literacy rates, this press represented journalism as business. Previous definitions of the press — as a forum, an instrument of education and acculturation, or a medium of propaganda by or against government — dissipated once owners realized that the potential for profit was greater if gazettes were politically neutral, or even politically oblivious, rather than partisan. News rather than opinion was a priority, cold facts rather than heated critiques. Winning a mass audience meant responding to popular penchants beyond politics. As prices dropped, content and layout labeled "new journalism" changed to suit buyers with a variety of predilections. Staccato but accurate news, mindless but entertaining trivia, rousing stories about causes real or invented were its chief traits, but sensationalism, however defined, was the mantra that reconfigured every page of papers in larger urban areas. Marketing the press increasingly fell to moguls so committed to selling that they were willing to indulge the lowest personal tastes or to spin the widest public crusades, domestic and international. By 1914 these tactics weakened respect for but not addiction to journalism.

In addition to these commonalities, there were narrower overlaps. For example, the British borrowed the interview and the big headline from the United States. Both countries wrestled with the issue of war correspondence in a free society at war. The Canadians likewise copied American formats and the Australians, British. The Germans drew inspiration from the French in 1830 and 1848, and both, together with the British, utilized money deposited in advance as a safeguard against libel.

While the newspaper has a paramount position in every essay, each one also highlights periodicals. Again, there are similarities among the countries. The Germans copied Britain's *Penny Magazine*. Canada's labor periodicals were the offspring of Americans who crossed the border actually or ideologically, whereas Australia's were somewhat more home-bred. The Americans, the British and the Germans all circulated specialized periodicals, such as those intended for women.

Just as journals had kindred features, so, too, did journalists exhibit certain characteristics. Until the eve of the twentieth century many of those involved in the occupation came to it from other employment. Without specialized training for the field, they tended to apprentice in one way or another. In Australia and Canada virgin colonies, and in the United States the frontier, offered opportunities to launch papers. In Britain and Germany local gazettes and then news agencies had jobs available. In France journalists shuttled back and forth between political and press engagements. Only latterly did journalists try to organize, though their associations lacked real strength even in 1914. Editors of top serials were routinely stars everywhere, and publishers were occasional ones, notably in the United States. In Australia and Canada, local dynasties fueled newspapers as the press barons eventually would in Britain.

These patterns of interconnectivity confirm that global journalism has a long and momentous history. Yet each country had its own discourse, its own flavor. What may seem like discordance is mainly the result of milieu, but discordance is, in any case, not a bad thing. It evidences that diversity did not reduce the influence of journalism, an influence that each chapter explores at length.

Rod Kirkpatrick's investigation of the Australian press explains how it flourished in an environment that was hardly congenial at the outset. He demonstrates that the chief mission of early journalists was to escape, or least to evade the limitations placed upon their activities by unsympathetic governors. The necessity to move equipment thousands of miles and to maintain it once arrived was also not conducive to publication. Although the newspaper first surfaced in convict settlements, it thrived in nascent colonies. Perhaps its biggest midcentury boost came from reporting from the gold fields.

Introduction

Papers provided data about the lodes but were often more crucial as conduits of knowledge about relatives gone off to find gold. This human interest strain is one that did not appear in all of Australia's press contemporaries. Another element of Australian journals that was unusual was the vibrancy of those in mining towns or for workers, both somewhat less temperate than the metro dailies and the smaller provincial weeklies, which Kirkpatrick spotlights with expertise.

The Canadian press, which David R. Spencer delineates, was similar to the Australian insofar as both commenced in an age when newspapers blossomed in separate colonies. Unlike Australia, the Canadian settlements in 1815 had populations that migrated from not only Britain but also France and the young United States, loyalists who arrived after 1783. The Canadian journals that arose in the nineteenth century reflected the medley of cultural backgrounds, but, akin to Australian gazettes, the North American all initially quarreled with government. Using publications to enter the debate about responsible government instantly politicized the eastern colonial press. After resolution of this issue, the nascent western settlements showcased local issues. While dissident sheets were extremely active, as Spencer explicates, the fundamental contour of Canadian journalism after 1865 was one that emulated the American. There was a steady stream of news and views from the United States. The exchange was not absolutely unilateral as the imaginative Canadian illustrated periodicals proved.

French journalism is unusual because at its core were some of the most powerful journalists in Europe. They acquired that power by abetting, if not engineering two revolutions, in 1830 and in 1848, which altered domestic politics and one might even say, European politics. The French revolutions were closely watched and led to similar unsuccessful attempts elsewhere, such as in the German states, that in turn affected the international press. Writers who jockeyed between being ministers and editors, who owned papers as easily as others owned houses, were distinct from their brother scribes in other countries. Still the French, too, struggled to survive when government severely leashed them and strived to maintain dignity and honesty when they were free. Outstanding writing and imaginative cartoons were the landmarks of Parisian papers, the heart of French journalism even before the Third Republic granted it the widest liberty of any of its peers. Almost at the same moment, the emergence of the world's cheapest newspaper expanded readership tremendously. The advantages of liberty and large audience, nevertheless, did not compensate for insufficient funding of a press that disdained advertising. The willingness

Introduction

to take bribes in the run-up to World War I poisoned public perceptions of French journalism.

The analysis of the German press by Ulf Jonas Bjork bares governmental interference akin to that in France but with a different outcome. In some ways the German press before 1871 was in the same situation as the journalism in early Australian and Canadian colonies, each under a separate governor. Yet, as Bjork details, the German states had some degree of uniformity because of the Diet of the German Confederation. As in France, there were extensive and multifaceted efforts before midcentury to censor journalists. Some practices imitated the French, but uniquely Teutonic rules were often more insidious. German policies after 1871 were complex, albeit unification made for greater coherence. The first and long-time chancellor of the German Empire, Otto von Bismarck, resorted to covert funding and finagling and an official press bureau to curb journalists. Because of his tactics, German newspapers did not resemble the party papers of France or the editorial columns in American and British gazettes. Since reporting news before and after 1850 was tentative at best, fiction served as a cloak for political commentary but soon attracted another audience. The difficulty of editorializing on politics likewise caused journalists to write more on culture than their compatriots elsewhere, which further differentiated the country from nations where a mass press was prospering.

British journalism, already with a track record in 1815, was much broader in scope and greater in number than any of its contemporaries. Newspapers during the nineteenth century encompassed everything from preeminent metro dailies to isolated rural weeklies, from organs of fierce partisanship to those of friendly advice, from the intellectual to the illustrated, from the gossiping to the gory. Periodicals included expensive annuals, authoritative quarterlies and magazines for every preference. That other countries appropriated British innovations and lifted British texts was a testimony to success, but the press did not grow unimpeded. Government issued regulations, later replicated in France and the German states, but official interference evaporated earlier than in those locales. Moreover, proprietors recognized from the start the importance of technology and advertising. By the high noon of Victorianism after 1851, the newspaper was the chief medium of public communication. "New Journalism" in the 1870s slowly infiltrated gazettes but did not undermine this rank. More significant were the *fin-de-siècle* modifications effectuated by Alfred Harmsworth and his fellow press barons. Given the range of the British press in the era, it is not surprising that

Introduction

journalists were an inchoate lot. Once perceived as disreputable, they won some accolades after war correspondence developed and eventually gained public respect.

Carol Sue Humphrey's discussion of the American press tracks shifts in its content, size and location throughout the nineteenth century. As in Britain, technology and advertising were critical, but the centerpiece of American journalism was its freedom from official intervention. Although the country had a hearty political press, the independence of penny papers addressed to workers eroded the ties between the authorities and journalists. The Civil War, as Humphrey notes, was another turning point in the style of newspaper reporting, and the so-called yellow press marked a third alteration. Responsible for these telling adjustments were owners and editors, such as James Gordon Bennett, Horace Greeley, Charles Dana, Joseph Pulitzer and William Randolph Hearst. Some of these giants were confreres of the British press barons, but they were also icons of a press in which personality rather than government or politics determined direction. While the newspaper dominated the journalistic arena in the United States, magazines were not marginal. Particularly influential were those directed to women and those open to muckrakers. Both underscored the might of this medium to broadcast community issues and to spur action to deal with them.

The breadth of this book should not conceal the fact that it barely exposes the links that exist in the press. Much work remains to be done. Constructs customarily applied, about historical time, space and especially theme, need reconsideration. For example, does the label Victorian connote real time in an international or even a European world of journalism in the nineteenth century? Did telegraphy globalize information sufficiently to make irrelevant for media studies the ordinary definition of space? Does journalism itself cut across intellectual lines in ways that do not fit neatly into the traditional categorizations of history? Rethinking habitual classifications and concepts is, we think, worth the effort in order to situate journalism as an active institution in and not as a passive chronicle of the past.

Australia
Shaking Off the Shackles to Earn the Badge of Independence

Rod Kirkpatrick

Issued by Authority and Subject to Prior Restraint

Newspapers emerged in Australia when England was mixing colonial expansion with convict transfer overseas as a solution for its overcrowded prisons. Stuart Macintyre described the first Australian colony, New South Wales, as "a product of maritime exploration, trade and penology." Pioneer Australian newspapers were issued "by authority" and suffered prior restraint. The governor had the final say on whether to publish. In 1815 Australia had only one newspaper, a weekly. Two others (both fortnightlies) had been initiated but had died quickly. The publication of all three papers had been authorized by the governors of the existing colonies, New South Wales and Van Diemen's Land (a sub-colony of New South Wales until 1825 and renamed Tasmania in 1856), and had been subject to censorship. This was a fact of life in varying degrees for the earliest newspapers in New South Wales (which incorporated Victoria until 1851 and Queensland until 1859), Van Diemen's Land and South Australia. In Western Australia, permission to publish had to be sought through the lodging of recognizances, affidavits designed to discourage outspokenness against the government. Except for government intrusion, the development of newspapers in the six colonies that eventually formed a federation in 1901 differed widely.

The lone newspaper existing in 1815 was the *Sydney Gazette and New South Wales Advertiser*, launched in 1803 by a "ticket-of-leave" convict, George Howe. This criminal, transported as were so many from English prisons and given a provisional pardon since his arrival in Sydney, had become only the second government printer in the colony a year before he began publishing the *Gazette*. The newspaper was printed on an obsolete press that had been brought to New South Wales in 1788 with the First Fleet (which included 736 convicts). Government type, government ink and government paper were used, and the content was reviewed by the governor. There was enough type to set up only one page at a time, so each page had to be printed and the type dismantled before the next page could be composed.

Howe was still publishing the *Gazette* in 1815, although he had suspended publication twice, for six weeks in 1807 because of a lack of paper and eight months in 1808–09 because of the gathering row that resulted in the overthrow of Governor William Bligh in the so-called Rum Rebellion of 26 January 1809. The never-ending difficulty of obtaining paper, in whatever size, shape or color, and the sharply increasing price he had to pay for it led Howe to reflect in the *Gazette* on a publication "conceived in doubt, brought forth in difficulty, and reared in many an altered shape." Howe was a one-man show. Writing about himself in the third person in 1819, he noted that "he bought the Paper at a very dear price, he distributed his type, he invented and obtained *new* matter, without any auxiliary assistance, he worked the Paper off at Press; and he afterwards carried it out, that is to say, delivered it to Sydney Subscribers." From 1811, under Governor Lachlan Macquarie, he received sixty pounds a year as government printer. When Howe died on 11 May 1821, his son Robert, then twenty-six, took over the newspaper and succeeded his father as government printer.

In the island colony of Van Diemen's Land, two gazette-style publications had been initiated by 1815, one in 1810 and the other in 1814. Both had appeared fortnightly, the first, the *Derwent Star and Van Diemen's Land Intelligencer*, appearing twelve times, and the second, the *Van Diemen's Land Gazette and General Advertiser*, nine times. Importantly, they laid the groundwork for the third publication, the *Hobart Town Gazette and Southern Reporter*, which began on 1 June 1816. The publisher, Andrew Bent, became known as the father of Australian journalism because of the campaigns he waged in his newspaper for freedom of the press and trial by civil jury.

The First "Free" Newspaper

In the early 1820s the two *Gazettes*, for Sydney and Hobart Town, continued to publish official government notices as well as news and advertisements, although the publishers had begun to sense a greater measure of freedom and exert a great degree of ownership. Robert Howe owned all the printing equipment and type because his father and he had replaced the outmoded originals. In Hobart Town, Bent struck trouble early with a new governor, Colonel George Arthur. Arthur wanted to assert his power and influence through the newspaper and insisted that the government owned the press and plant of the *Hobart Town Gazette*. Bent appealed to a higher authority, Major-General Thomas Brisbane, Governor-in-Chief of New South Wales, of which Van Diemen's Land was, in effect, a remote outpost. In September 1824 Brisbane ruled in Bent's favor. He ruled also that the "by authority" regime in newspapers should end, opening the way for two barristers to launch boldly the first newspaper in Australia without a governor's approval.

William Charles Wentworth and Robert Wardell started publishing the *Australian* in Sydney on 14 October 1824, and Governor Brisbane did not intervene. The next day, Robert Howe obtained the Governor's permission to publish his *Gazette* without any prior restraint. Brisbane ruled that Howe, and not the government, owned the copyright of the *Gazette*. For 150 pounds a year as Government Printer, Howe published all the Government Orders and Notices and supplied twenty-five copies of each issue of the *Gazette* to the government. "Published by Authority" appeared at the masthead until May 1826, for the Orders bound officials as soon as they were published in the *Gazette*. Confusing, but not surprising, there were readers who mistakenly thought that the inscription gave the stamp of authority to editorial content, according to historian R.B. Walker. The *Australian* exhibited the spirit of reform that Wentworth had noted during his visit to England. Wentworth, as a *Times* (London) subscriber, had observed the power of popular journalism to influence the great public issues of the day. Wardell, too, knew *The Times* well and had worked as a journalist on London's evening *Statesman* and Sunday *Constitution*. The *Australian* set out to be outspoken, independent and not at all respectful of authority. Confident, well-versed in the law and in touch with the latest political and intellectual currents of British and European life, Wentworth, Wardell and others like them soon transformed the terms of political debate in the colony.

Hall Draws on Long Tradition of English Dissent

Even more outspoken against the government was the *Monitor*, first published in Sydney on 19 May 1826. Its editor and part-proprietor was

Edward Smith Hall, a belligerent advocate of working men's rights. Ralph Darling, the New South Wales Governor, 1825–31, saw Hall as purveying a relentless, corroding journalism that deliberately courted martyrdom. Hall's early journalism drew on the long tradition of English dissent. It is probable that his paper took its name from the English *Monitor,* prosecuted at the height of the radical political activity in England in 1762–63 that was inspired by John Wilkes. The relentless policing of authority by the *Monitor* derived from the central Wilkite belief that government should be, at all times, accountable to the people at large. Drawing on the ideas and language of the radical press of Britain and the United States, including contemporary writings on American democracy, Hall attempted to inspire his readers to fight for "Liberal Principles and Free Institutions, Rational Liberty and Equal Justice." To bring the colonists to a proper sense of their rights, Hall quoted extensively from works on democracy and freedom by Benjamin Franklin and William Cobbett.

The *Monitor's* damning critique of the cruelties and inequalities of the penal era strongly influenced later writers and contributed to the condemnation of the entire convict system by Marcus Clarke and a whole succession of literary authors in Australia. Hall's journalism reached a more humble audience than his solidly liberal contemporaries at the *Australian.* His writing on politics was lively and engaging. The paper's columns were filled with the wants and sufferings of working people, whether convict or free. Hall sympathized with the plight of oppressed convicts at the secondary penal settlements and criticized the massacres of Aboriginal people on the pastoral frontiers. His firebrand editorials were meant to stimulate ordinary colonists to think for themselves and to pull down the gentlemanly few who ruled the colony.

Jail for Outspoken Editors

Both Hall in Sydney and Bent in Hobart were jailed a number of times for seditious libel, but their publications and their editorials continued. Bent was incarcerated when Arthur pursued him in the courts for penning editorials and publishing letters that had attacked the administration. Arthur decided he must have a government publication, so he installed James Ross and George Terry Howe (half-brother of Robert, of Sydney) as government printers and pirated the title, the *Hobart Town Gazette,* which had been Bent's for nine years. Bent was soon forced to publish his newspaper under another title, the *Colonial Times and Tasmanian Advertiser*. The feud was not over, for Bent's attacks had lost none of their sting. Governors Arthur in Hobart Town and Darling in Sydney went beyond the bounds allowed by British law — so Chief Justice Francis Forbes ruled in Sydney — as they pursued punitive measures against the colonial publishers who were presenting "a potent mix of virulent abuse of the penal administration, and reformist ideas," as Sandy Blair put it.

Arthur destroyed Bent's career, but Darling was less successful in his war against Hall. In an effort to silence Hall, still busily writing from prison, Darling passed through the Legislative Council in January 1830 a new Press law, based on one of the repressive Six Acts of 1819 Britain. Under the New South Wales statute it was mandatory for the court to impose a sentence of banishment on any person convicted of seditious libel for the second time. The *Australian* ran no editorials from 24 February to 7 April 1830, publishing instead a picture of a printing press chained by a military officer with the printer hanging by the neck from a metal spike. Hall mourned the death of the free press by printing a coffin with an appropriate epitaph in Latin in place of the paper's customary leading article. He resumed writing only on receiving news that Darling's act had been disallowed by the British Parliament, which had been in the process of repealing the very sections of the 1819 English statute relating to banishment. Darling refrained from further prosecutions, believing, perhaps mistakenly, that the British authorities would not support him. He was recalled to Britain in late 1831.

Sydney Herald *Outlasts Its Predecessors*

Only a few months before Darling's recall, a weekly newspaper began that would become known within twenty years as "Granny" because it had outlasted all its predecessors. By then it would be owned by a family that would retain control for only six weeks short of 150 years. The *Sydney Herald*, launched on 18 April 1831, was the fifth newspaper started in Sydney. It appeared daily from 1 October 1840 and changed its name to the *Sydney Morning Herald* on 1 August 1842. The title and the publication frequency have endured to this day. The founding proprietors were three recent immigrants in their twenties: Alfred Ward Stephens, an Englishman; Frederick Michael Stokes, a qualified printer; and William McGarvie, who since his arrival in 1828 had been in charge of a library and stationery warehouse belonging to the *Sydney Gazette*. Stephens and Stokes had worked for the *Gazette*, as clerk and bookkeeper, respectively. The name for the new paper came from McGarvie who had had some connection with the *Glasgow Herald*, but he sold his share in the *Sydney Herald* to Stephens and Stokes after the fifth number and opened his own stationery business.

The circulation of the paper rose to 750 in the first month, and 1,100 in the first year. By 1836 each issue of the *Herald* (by then semi-weekly) was selling 1,600 copies, considerably more than any competitor. Price and policy were the main reasons for the *Herald's* commercial success. At a cover price of sevenpence from the outset, it undersold the *Gazette* by a penny, and the *Monitor* and the *Australian* by more. The cover price dropped to sixpence when the *Herald* became semi-weekly on 17 May 1832, but rose to ninepence when it was enlarged on 3 March 1834. As a neophyte, the *Herald* was untainted by the partisan vehemence and overheated controversy that characterized the other papers. The *Herald* made it clear it did not admire the virulent attacks on Darling, and it refrained from attacking its competitors.

Herald *Takes Stranglehold*

Under the next governor, Sir Richard Bourke, a period of liberal government began in New South Wales. Bourke favored trial by jury, representative government and full civil rights for emancipists (paroled convicts); he believed that "without free institutions where the Press is wholly unrestricted no Government can go on." In the 1830s Sydney newspapers proliferated, diversified and competed strongly, resulting in a general lowering of prices. This period of expansion and vigorous competition ended in October 1840 when the *Sydney Herald* went to daily publication and took a stranglehold on the market, soon boasting a circulation of 3,000 per day. Concurrently, a financial depression started in the second half of 1840 and continued for three years, triggering insolvency, unemployment and irreversible changes in newspaper fortunes. At the end of 1840 the *Herald* absorbed the Reverend John Dunmore Lang's politico-religious paper, the *Colonist*; in 1841 the *Monitor* closed; and in 1842 the *Sydney Gazette* closed. The *Australian* struggled with heavy debt until the mortgagee James Macarthur, a political aspirant, bought it in 1843. The paper made a brief comeback in 1844 under new owners, Thomas Forster and E.H. Statham, who published it daily throughout the year, but they were short-staffed and wilted under the workload. The paper slipped into heavy debt again, reduced publication frequency to thrice and then twice weekly, and finally succumbed on 23 September 1848. The *Herald* reigned supreme.

Taking Political Sides

In Van Diemen's Land, the departure in 1836 of Governor George Arthur and the arrival of Governor John Franklin resulted in a brief lull in press criticism of officials before the newspapers regrouped as pro- or anti-government agents. The educational projects of the Franklins prompted academic discussion in the newspapers. Original items in verse or prose were encouraged, and articles from the British magazines, as well as imperial and international affairs, gained prominence. The Tasmanian weekly newspapers of the 1840s gave their readers value for money: they combined the features of a weekly review with those of a straight-out newspaper, recording political, legal, commercial and personal news, while leading articles still played a distinctive role. When Eardley-Wilmot replaced Franklin as Governor in 1843, the *Courier* and the *Advertiser* changed to the opposition side. The *True Colonist* ended in December 1844, after twelve years of publication, with the departure of Gilbert Robertson from the colony. Robert Lathrop Murray's *Review* became a government organ and vigorously defended the Governor against various accusations but criticized the British Cabinet. The *Colonial Times*, with its motto of "Open to all — influenced by none," echoed Murray's defense of the Governor. Murray closed the *Review* in 1845 after having written weekly editorial articles almost continuously for twenty years. He was among the most outstanding Australian editors of his day.

A Difficult and Tenuous Hereditary Line in Western Australia

In Western Australia, a colony based on a system of land grants, the Swan River settlement (now Perth and Fremantle) gave birth to a profusion of newspapers, the first within a year of its founding in 1829. At least six handwritten newspapers came and went between 1830 and 1833. To a large extent they contained only items of colonial news and information on legal transactions, such as purchases of property and changes in ownership of businesses. The first printed newspaper, the *Fremantle Observer, Perth Gazette and Western Australian Journal*, appeared on 25 April 1831. This newspaper set out to be a journal of record but was soon afflicted by dissension between the partners, one of whom, Charles Macfaull, launched in Perth on 5 January 1833 the *Perth Gazette and Western Australian Journal*. This is the paper to which the *West Australian*, Perth's only daily at the beginning of the twenty-first century, likes to trace its roots, but the hereditary line is complex and tenuous.

The *Gazette* was challenged from 6 October 1836 by the *Swan River Guardian*, edited by William Nairne Clark, a young, radical Scottish lawyer with definite views about how the colony should be administered. He delighted in taunting Macfaull, describing the *Gazette* as "being of sombre taste and singular dullness" and "the tool of a party [the Colonial Government] who considered it better to say nothing than tell the truth." The *Guardian* survived only sixteen months, defeated by the repression of a government that resorted to the well-established tactic of requiring newspaper proprietorships to lodge expensive recognizances against libel. A longer-lasting publication, the *Inquirer: A Western Australian Journal of Politics and Literature*, was launched on 5 August 1840 by Francis Lochée to present an independent stance. Lochée and Macfaull were immediately at one another's throats, as the files of the *Inquirer* indicate. Charles Macfaull died on 13 December 1846. His widow, Elizabeth, ran the *Perth Gazette* for twelve months before Arthur Shenton bought it. This transfer is where the first break in continuity from the original *Perth Gazette* of 1833 to the *West Australian* of 1879 occurs: Shenton changed the title on 1 January 1848, his first issue, to the *Perth Gazette and Independent Journal of Politics and News* and labelled it No. 1 to indicate the break with the past. He published an editorial that outlined his policy.

Strife and Quarrels in "Orderly" South Australia

South Australia was envisioned as a colony that would avoid the evils of the two methods of "planting European civilization in Australia" that had been tried: penal settlement and land-grant paradise. The so-called Wakefield system of colonization, upon which South Australia was founded, aimed at the orderly transplantation of a highly organized, ready-made civilization from the old world to the new. Despite the planning, "South Australian history in 1837 and 1838 is essentially a story of strife, and in all the quarrels of the day the press was deeply involved," to use George H. Pitt's description. The press had an important place in the planning process because everyone expected that many years would pass before the colonists would have a parliament. Meanwhile, their interests must be safeguarded against autocratic mismanagement and injustice. Fortunately, among those attracted by Edward Wakefield's ideas were Robert Thomas and George Stevenson, men determined to open a newspaper. Printer Thomas, a law stationer from Wales, and editor Stevenson, a former journalist who had become private secretary to

Governor John Hindmarsh, produced the first number of the *South Australian Gazette and Colonial Register* in London on 18 June 1836. The types, presses and paper were shipped with one batch of settlers. The second issue of the newspaper was supposed to appear on their arrival at the end of 1836. It did not materialize until 3 June 1837, partly because Thomas's printing apprentice died after becoming lost on Kangaroo Island and partly because much of the type and plant were carried on to Hobart Town by mistake.

The newspaper said it combined the *Gazette*, recording "official acts and orders of the Colonial Government," and the *Register*, "devoted to the elucidation of the principles of colonisation, to the record of the establishment and progress of the colony, and the general news of the place, and of the day, which is altogether non-official, and under independent control." This combination of roles did not change until there was a change of Governor in 1838. Editor Stevenson had declared that it would be "our strenuous endeavour to place ourselves beyond the accusation of inconsistency," but he was in an impossible situation, especially when Governor Hindmarsh and the Resident Commissioner, James Hurtle Fisher, disagreed on everything from where the capital city was to be sited to the salaries of officers. Stevenson's editorials unrelentingly presented the Governor's viewpoint. As Clerk of the Court, Justice of the Peace, Registrar of Shipping, Postmaster and Customs Officer, and, most importantly, Private Secretary to the Governor, Stevenson was able to exert great influence over Hindmarsh and was claimed to be the "unofficial governor of the colony," for he wrote Hindmarsh's dispatches and composed proclamations and Acts of Council. From his editorial chair Stevenson struck blow after blow at the Governor's opponents; the Governor's foes were his foes.

A Legal Problem Halts the First Paper in Victoria

In Victoria, or the Port Phillip District of New South Wales as it was until mid–1851, the whaling camps of Port Fairy and Portland Bay were the first permanent settlements, dating from the late 1820s. On 1 January 1838 Melbourne gave birth to a newspaper. The proprietor was John Pascoe Fawkner, the founder of the *Launceston Advertiser* in Van Diemen's Land nine years earlier. His belated first application to establish the *Port Phillip Advertiser* was refused because he had not lodged the customary affidavit in Sydney before publication. Thus, the *Advertiser* ceased after three months, having been issued in manuscript form for nine weeks and in printed form from 5

March. Thomas Strode and George Arden overcame such obstacles and launched the *Port Phillip Gazette* in printed form on 27 October 1838. They attested their document in Sydney before starting publication in Melbourne. Meanwhile, Fawkner completed the formalities properly for his second mainland paper, the *Port Phillip Patriot and Melbourne Advertiser*, out on 6 February 1839. Melbourne gained a third newspaper when George Cavenagh, a former editor of the *Sydney Gazette*, commenced the *Port Phillip Herald* on 3 January 1840. In late 1840 the *Gazette*, the *Patriot* and the *Herald* were semi-weeklies appearing on different days, giving Melbourne a newspaper six days a week. The *Patriot* became the first Port Phillip daily on 15 May 1845, four months before Fawkner sold it. The *Patriot* absorbed the *Standard and Port Phillip Gazetteer* on 1 October 1845 when it changed its sub-title slightly to *Morning Advertiser*. It changed its name more significantly to the *Melbourne Daily News and Port Phillip Patriot* on 9 October 1848. The *Port Phillip Herald* became a daily, as the *Melbourne Morning Herald*, on 1 January 1849, and the bemused *Argus* became a daily on 18 June 1849. The *Melbourne Daily News* (formerly the *Patriot*) was incorporated in the *Argus* from 1 January 1852. The *Herald* continued.

The Courier *Begins and Continues in Queensland*

In the Moreton Bay District of New South Wales — which became Queensland from 10 December 1859 — the only newspaper issued before 1850 was the *Moreton Bay Courier*, inaugurated on 20 June 1846 by editor Arthur Sidney Lyon and printer James Swan. It did not face prior restraint. This newspaper, after various changes of title, including the *Courier* and the *Brisbane Courier*, and an amalgamation with the *Daily Mail* in 1933, survives as the *Courier-Mail*, the sole daily in Brisbane in 2006.

Gold Changes the Face of Australian Society

In the 1850s the Australian colonies experienced massive change because of the gold discoveries near Bathurst in New South Wales (NSW) and near Ballarat and other towns in the newly separated colony of Victoria. The Port Phillip District of NSW became Victoria on 1 July 1851; and within a week the first gold discoveries were reported there, following the discoveries near Bathurst two months earlier. The resultant "rushes" in Victoria principally and in NSW changed the face of Australian society, accelerating migration from England and North America and hastening the development of rail and port facilities and the electric telegraph. Initially, the rushes to Ballarat in 1851–1852 adversely affected newspaper development. Newspapers ceased publication in centers such as Geelong, Warrnambool and Adelaide as thousands of their readers and advertisers — and, in some cases, members of their staff— joined the headlong scramble to the goldfields.

Soon there was a positive impact on the press as more goldfields opened, at Sandhurst, Mount Alexander, Beechworth, Ararat, Stawell and other places in central Victoria, and at Araluen, Kiandra, Lambing Flat, Forbes and Grenfell in NSW. Newspapers sprang up to meet the emerging needs for the expression of views, the telling of news and the advertising of goods and services. The papers also carried messages to and from home. For example, the Adelaide papers were full of notes from the diggers and to them, a sort of "lost and found" column of persons. Many could not read or write, so those who submitted messages hoped that those who *could* read would pass on the words. The population of Victoria outstripped NSW during the decade, as did the number of provincial newspapers established. NSW did not catch Victoria, in population and provincial press numbers, until the late 1880s.

The Argus *and the* Age *and a Policy Vacuum*

In Melbourne, the early *Argus* reflected the radical aspirations of the colonial period. William Kerr, founding proprietor and editor, and Edward Wilson, who replaced him as editor upon buying an interest in the paper, were responsible for this radicalism. The *Argus*, a daily since mid–1849, took full advantage of the opportunities afforded by the gold rushes, championing the rights of people to the lands of the colony and providing small advertisements cheaply to attract newly arriving immigrants. It provided late, full and reliable news from the diggings, without neglecting overseas news. In 1852 Lauchlan Mackinnon, a pastoralist, became a partner in the *Argus* with Wilson and took over the business side. The paper, despite its enormous increase in circulation and influence under Wilson, was near financial collapse. Persuading Wilson that he was charging twopence for a paper that cost almost three times more to produce, Mackinnon insisted on doubling the price and on increasing advertising charges by 25 percent. This ensured prosperity for the journal. Between 1852 and 1853 it doubled in size and overcame several rivals. Until 1854 it backed the miners wholeheartedly, but when they took matters into their own hands at Ballarat, the *Argus* turned from them. The change of direction was clear and sudden and came after Wilson had retired in favor of a more temperate editorship. The *Age*, launched six weeks before the first strike, was quick to fill the policy vacuum left by the *Argus*. Nevertheless, the *Argus* continued to flourish, though it was no longer quite so dominant. It upheld free trade, not tariffs and stuck with that line long after it was clear that protection, which the *Age* endorsed, had won.

The *Argus* introduced a weekly, the *Australasian*, in 1865 as a competitive response to the *Age's* weekly, the *Leader*, launched in 1856. Both were aimed at country readers. In the early 1860s government and unsympathetic commercial interests withdrew advertising from the *Age*, intending to kill it. Over eight years, David Syme, who ran the paper after 1860, slashed the cover price from sixpence to threepence (1860), threepence to twopence (1867), and twopence to one penny (1868). The circulation bounded ahead, aided by the growth of the railway network and demand for the *Age* in such provincial cities as Ballarat, Sandhurst and Castlemaine. The *Argus* cut its price from sixpence to threepence three days before the *Age* in February 1860 but did not follow the *Age* in further cuts until 1884 (twopence) and 1893 (one penny). The owners of the *Argus* believed the paper offered such quality that it was worth more than a penny. The anonymous writer of a brief history of the newspaper said in 1892 that "no other million of Her Majesty's subjects anywhere [outside of Melbourne] have planted amongst them a journal so ample in its range of news, so authoritative in its criticism of affairs, and so high in its literary standard as the *Argus*."

The *Age* had left the *Argus* a long way behind in the circulation race by the end of the 1860s and was selling more than the *Argus* and the *Herald* combined. But it could not print more than 4,000 four-page papers per hour, whereas it needed to print at least 10,000. To keep pace with the increasing circulation and to expand it, Syme imported in 1872 from Liverpool, England, a Victory rotary web-fed printing press that could service the demand for speed and volume. The *Age* committed itself to producing a double number — an eight-page issue — each Saturday and began publishing fiction, generally in the form of serialized stories. Sixty novels were serialized in the *Age* over the next twenty-eight years.

When the first eight-page issue appeared on 20 April 1872, Syme apologized: "Our newly imported machine for printing from a continuous web of paper — turning out *Ages* by the mile — is not yet in working order, so that a severe strain is put on the ordinary machines, such a quantity of working having never before been exacted from them, or from any of their kind in these colonies." Soon Syme ordered another Victory press for the *Leader*, but both machines had limitations because the manufacturers were still sorting out teething problems and Melbourne was so far from the Liverpool factory

John Lamont Dow and his son, David McKenzie Dow, working in the agricultural editor's room of the *Age* and the *Leader* office in Melbourne about the end of the nineteenth century.

that when orders for parts were not met efficiently, there were enormous delays in obtaining replacements. For three years the new presses posed "serious" mechanical difficulties, worsened by the "disgraceful" condition of the imported rolls of newsprint. Nonetheless, the *Age's* circulation grew from 2,000 in 1860, to 15,000 at the end of 1868, 26,000 in 1876, 35,000 in November 1878, 81,000 in 1889, 101,000 in 1892, and 120,000 in 1899. In 1894 the *Age* boasted that its circulation was four times greater than that of any other morning paper in Melbourne. In proportion to population, the *Age* became the largest circulating newspaper in the British Empire.

Syme Becomes a King-Maker

The *Age* ruled what was then the leading Australian colony for many years insofar as the paper had a large measure of control over Victoria's governments and sometimes even helped to select them. It also imposed upon the colony an economic policy that was later to become that of the Australian Commonwealth. All this was the work almost entirely of one man, David Syme, a Scot (1827–1908), who stands head and shoulders above other Australian owner-editors. The *Age* did not pass into the hands of the Syme family until 1856, when its influence was already evident, but not until four years later did David Syme take charge. The journal had seized the opportunity afforded by the gold rushes. While making it clear that its sympathy with the diggers "extended no further than the limit of constitutional agitation," the *Age* insisted that they had heavy grievances and supported the appointment of a Commission to investigate them. From then on, it was the popular paper, though the better-off classes did not approve of its general attitude.

The main point in the *Age's* policy under Syme was tariffs, which it preached day in day out, with the result that it was more than once boycotted. There were protectionists in Victoria before Syme, for with the working out of the alluvial gold deposits, the poor man's fields, jobs had to be found for thousands of displaced diggers. Opposition to the importation of articles that could be made in the colony and support for setting up and protecting local industries against overseas competition rose. A Tariff Reform League had been formed in 1859, but Syme, through the *Age*, organized and led the protectionist movement and provided it with a body of doctrine, including the demand for a living wage in a subsidized industry. Syme later claimed that his was the first voice and power that made protection the fiscal faith of Victoria. Not only was the *Age* well arranged and set out, but its leading articles were more commanding and vigorous than those of any contemporary Australian newspaper. Syme drove his paper through all opposition. By the seventies it was the dominant force in Victorian politics, and people had begun to speak of "King David."

Syme negotiated an unusual deal in November 1868. For 2,000 pounds he acquired the threepenny morning daily, the *Herald*, and its associated weekly journal, the *Illustrated Post*. He converted the *Herald* to a penny evening daily in January 1869 and employed Graham Berry, a parliamentarian and owner of the *Geelong Register*, as the editor. If Syme had intended to eliminate one of the morning competitors for the *Age*, he failed. A group of journalists and compositors, some of whom had been employed by the old morning *Herald*, created a cooperative and launched a new morning paper, the *Daily Telegraph*, on 8 February 1869. The *Telegraph* was always the straggler in the morning circulation race, with the *Age* in front and the *Argus* a clear second. The *Telegraph* business became a proprietary company in 1883, but it closed, insolvent, on 30 April 1892. Although Syme owned the *Herald* for about three years, he was never closely involved in its day-to-day management. Attempts were made in the first half of the 1870s to establish a firm foothold in the Melbourne evening market, but none of the newcomers — the *Express, Evening Tribune, City News, Echo* and *Evening Post*— provided enduring competition for the *Herald*.

Parkes and Bennett Provide Opposition for Fairfax

The *Sydney Morning Herald* was alive to the new opportunities of the fifties. By paying higher wages during the gold rushes, it managed to retain the bulk of its staff, and it sent correspondents to the Victoria diggings as well as to those of its own colony. Its advertisements and its circulation grew enormously. By 1854 it had doubled its size. To provide more space for news, it widened its columns and printed its advertisements in smaller type. It began to attach great importance to leading articles. By 1850 the *Herald* was the only Sydney paper appearing more than once a week. But Henry Parkes, later to be the Premier of NSW and a father of federation, soon changed that. He started the *Empire*, with the backing of various men of property and business wealth, on 28 December 1850, as a weekly and issued it daily three weeks later. Parkes was an ivory turner by trade, a poet by mistake, a businessman by misfortune, and a writer, orator and politician by talent. It was not until 1854 that the *Empire* first made a small profit, and even then Parkes did not manage to make it a solidly dependable business. He lost possession of it in August 1858 after being declared insolvent, and Samuel Bennett, who had been a printer and overseer in the *Herald* office, revived it in May 1859.

In the first issue of the restored *Empire*, Bennett stated that the paper would uphold "radical" principles and be the organ of the liberal party; it would serve both the business community and the family reader. The *Empire* shared none of the dread of the *Herald* about the onset of democracy. Readers of the *Empire* were probably lower on the social scale than those of the *Herald*. Between the fall of the first *Empire* and the rise of the second, the liberal cause was upheld by a small and undistinguished evening daily, the twopenny *Sydney Evening Mail*. First published on 7 February 1859, it was apparently held by several proprietors, but by May was owned solely by Edward Greville, a Sydney press and news agent. The last known issue appeared on 18 May 1859, only five days before Bennett's *Empire* began.

After eight years of running the *Empire*, Bennett saw an opening for an evening daily and launched the *Evening News* on 29 July 1867. He made sure his evening paper was not a rehash of the morning papers. In the introductory editorial, Bennett took some subtle swipes at the *Sydney Morning Herald*, declaring the *News* would not "ransack the *Encyclopaedia Britannica* for material" so that when Sydney's water supply was threatened, he would not bore his readers with a discussion on Roman aqueducts. Instead, the *News* would speak in the language of ordinary people and present facts and discussion in a calm and impartial manner. "We do not enter the field as gladiators," Bennett said. This first penny paper in New South Wales printed 2,000 copies of the first issue, but by December 1867 its circulation was 8,000. There were no regular sections on special topics, such as music, art or gardening. The lightest matter was the "filler" clipped from other papers — low in topicality, high in human interest. But the *Evening News* aimed primarily to inform rather than entertain. Its late telegraphic items updated what had appeared in the morning papers, attracting those who had read the *Herald*.

From 1 January 1868 the *Empire* became a penny daily, but Bennett failed to alter radically its contents. Except for a serial story, the penny *Empire* was a scaled-down version of its former self. The *Evening News* outshone the *Empire*, so, when the *Empire's* compositors gave notice of a strike, Bennett suddenly closed the paper on 9 February 1875 and incorporated it in the *Evening News*. After his death on 3 June 1878, Alfred Bennett ruled the family company in what were remembered as "exciting, bewildering days" until disposing of his interest in 1895. The management was taken over by Frank and Christopher Bennett, on behalf of the founder's trustees. There followed the benevolent regime of Christopher Bennett.

At the *Herald*, John Fairfax had installed a six-cylinder Hoe rotary press by mid-1860. From July he used it to publish a weekly, the *Sydney Mail*. With a cover price of threepence, the *Mail* was a cheap, condensed version of the preceding six issues of the *Herald*. Its target audience was country people who received mail deliveries only once or twice a week and were eager to avoid the task, and expense, of reading bulk issues of the *Herald*. But it was also snapped up by Sydney workingmen who could ill afford a quarterly subscription to the *Herald* or *Empire* (five or six times as expensive as the *Mail*). Sales of the *Mail* reached 5,000 within six months and 10,000 in four and a half years. The early *Mail* was highly informative rather than entertaining, but it changed over time. By 1869 its sixteen demy pages included agricultural, pastoral, mining and sporting sections, as well as general news. Competition in

January 1871 from Bennett's *Australian Town & Country Journal*, caused the *Mail* to modernize, adopting the smaller page size of its rival and introducing small illustrations, and to issue a monthly supplement, a large lithograph of a colonial townscape or landscape. From May 1871 the *Mail*'s price dropped from sixpence to fourpence, undercutting the *Town & Country Journal* by twopence.

An Independent Overseas News Service

From October 1858 Sydney was linked by telegraph to Adelaide, while in the northern hemisphere the telegraph ran from London to Alexandria, and by 1870 to Galle, at the southern tip of Ceylon (now Sri Lanka). Steamships and the Suez Canal had shortened the average London-Australia run to about 45 days, but for urgent news this time could be further reduced, perhaps even halved, by the telegraph. A faster service was soon available once the Eastern Extension Telegraph Company laid a submarine cable from Alexandria to Darwin by way of Madras, Penang, Singapore and Java. Lauchlan Mackinnon, the dominant member of the *Argus* partnership, was convinced that the cable news service needed to be independent. In 1870 he tried unsuccessfully to form a press association embracing all colonial newspapers, one which would receive news telegrams direct from London and end the reliance on Reuters for foreign news. By 1872 when the link with Britain was established, he had succeeded in achieving a partnership among the Melbourne *Argus*, *Sydney Morning Herald* and the *South Australian Register*. The partnership, known as Australian Associated Press (AAP), received Reuters exclusively and sold it to other Australian papers. AAP arranged to get the news in London, to make its own selection and transmit only those items to Australia. The cable rate was initially ten shillings per word; until this was reduced, AAP's daily file rarely exceeded fifty words. As the cable rate cheapened, from 1878 (6s. 5d.) to 1891 (1s. 10d.), so the wordage increased until by the early years of the twentieth century the average daily file was about 700 words. Overseas cabling was enhanced by the laying of a second cable to Darwin in 1880 and of a line to Broome in north-western Western Australia in 1889.

Daily Telegraph *a Serious* Herald *Rival*

In Sydney, another serious competitor of the *Herald* emerged on 1 July 1879. The new *Daily Telegraph* sold for one penny, half the price of the

Herald but also, at four pages, less than half the size. The paper, launched by a partnership, struggled during its first three or four years. Its projector and founding editor, J.M. Lynch, quit in March 1882. The new manager, Watkin Wynne, reconstructed the shareholding and senior staff of the company, building the editorial platform on which the *Daily Telegraph*'s success rested. He installed as editor Frederick Ward, a former Wesleyan minister who had edited the *Echo*, 1879–84, for the Fairfax family. A strong editorial support team included news editor L.J. Brient, who had been an editorial writer at the *Herald*, and associate editor Henry Gullet, who was lured from the editorship of the highly regarded Melbourne weekly, the *Australasian*. J.R. Carey was named chairman of the board and served in that role until 1921.

Imbued with "the spirit of the new journalism springing up" outside Australia, the *Daily Telegraph* management decided to discard the old approach to news and replace it with "something bright, light and entertaining." The *Telegraph* believed that people wanted "something that takes little trouble to master." Old-style journalism with its heavy, ponderous "slabs" of columns upon columns was thrown to the winds. Long reports, excerpted with interesting portions highlighted, were liberally cross-headed and plentifully sub-headed. Brightly-written paragraphs were scattered throughout the paper. Circulation jumped, advertising revenue swelled, and within a year the mechanical department needed bigger premises. The *Telegraph* scooped the world press on the German annexation of North New Guinea. In 1887, after a 25 percent rise in circulation, the paper was able to pay its first modest dividend (5 percent). It was soon regularly paying dividends of 10 to 15 percent, and its circulation overtook the *Herald* at the end of the 1880s. No actual figures can be located before 1891 when an "independent" audit reported an average circulation of 35,092. The *Telegraph* published a weekly, the *Tribune and News of the Week*, from October 1882, but closed it in June 1889 after its advertising level stuck at around 16 percent.

The Sydney evening market became the scene of constantly changing competition from the mid–1880s. In 1884 the *Evening News* claimed a circulation more than double its nearest competitor, and in 1888 a circulation four times that of any other daily. W.H.L. Bailey started the *Sunday Times* on 15 November 1885, the first Sunday paper to surface for many years, and the evening *Globe*, the next day. By early 1886 the *Globe* claimed to be the largest evening paper in Australia, measured in column inches, and to have more than fifty agents in Sydney and as many again in the country. It supported the eight-hour day and was rather hostile to squatters. Like the *Evening News*, it supplied a good deal of entertainment in serial stories and miscellaneous fillers. Perhaps it was too much like the *Evening News,* for it ceased publication in June 1887. Within six months of the *Globe*'s demise, the *Australian Star* began, with W.H. Traill as editor and with many workers as shareholders. The *Star* supported the protectionist cause, whereas the other four Sydney dailies supported free trade. By the end of the 1880s, a pattern of two morning dailies and three evening dailies existed in Sydney. Except for the twopenny *Herald,* each of the dailies sold for one penny. The *Echo* disappeared in 1893 when the *Herald* reduced its price to one penny (26 June 1893), and the *Australian Star* was remodelled and re-launched as the *Sun* in 1910. But for these changes, the daily press of Sydney was the same in 1914 as it had been at the end of 1887. Heavy capital costs, the failure of the *Daily Post* in 1895, and the monopolistic practices of the cable combine deterred the establishment of new papers.

The first Australian-born editor of the *Herald* was T.W. Heney, who succeeded William Curnow in 1903. Heney, the son of a compositor, joined the *Herald* in 1878 and was associate editor from 1898. By 1914 the *Herald* was producing 120 pages a week. Regarded as the voice of conservatism, it was nearly always critical of trade unions and the labour movement. Its usual tactic was to concede the right to strike and then to demonstrate how a current strike was not justified. Yet the *Herald* had a calm style, gravity, a reasoned approach and admirable news coverage. It tried hard to avoid sectarianism, which was then a powerful undercurrent in colonial society. In one way, the *Herald* abandoned the conservative commitment to old political forms and sponsored a radical change: federation of the colonies. The paper early on had published John West's articles on federation and republished them in 1867. But both times the colonies were more intent on enjoying their newfound independence under responsible government than in surrendering part of it to a federal authority. When a convention finally drafted a scheme in 1883 and the Federal Council, without NSW participation, first met in 1886, the *Herald* opposed the plan. Three years later the journal's response was more favorable, and by 1891 it highly commended the constitution bill and urged its readers not to vote for free-traders opposed to federation. To promote a "Yes" vote in the referendum of 1898, it published 160,000 copies of a special federation issue (25 May 1898). For the second referendum a year later, it printed 273,000 copies, or about one for every elector in the colony. The *Herald* also published many articles by colonial leaders who supported federation. The *Daily Telegraph,* considered to wield great political influence, strongly advocated a "No" vote, so the *Herald* was delighted when the people voted "Yes" and 25,000 thronged the streets near the *Herald* office to watch the poll figures go up.

Tasmania on the Cusp of Change

In the 1850s Van Diemen's Land was on the cusp of change as were its newspapers. Transportation of convicts to this island colony off the southern tip of the Australian mainland ceased, and in 1856 Tasmania received a constitution. In the 1850s Tasmania gave rise to ten newspapers that survived from a few months to a few years, even though some swallowed others in desperate attempts to extend life. But Tasmania at that time also spawned one newspaper that outlasted — and outswallowed — them all: the *Hobarton Mercury*, soon simply the *Mercury*. Even its birth, on 5 July 1854, was marked by the swallowing, or incorporation, of an earlier title, the *Hobarton Guardian*, established on 15 May 1847 as the weekly *Guardian or True Friend of Tasmania*. Its founder, John Moore, changed the title to the *Hobarton Guardian* with the fourteenth number when it became a semi-weekly.

One of the more colorful and short-lived titles of the period was the *Irish Exile and Freedom's Advocate*, an eight-page weekly, published from 26 January 1850 to 12 April 1851 and printed by the *Guardian*. Proprietor Patrick O'Donohue denied that the paper had been started by, or would be the organ of, the "State prisoners," or Irish rebels. Soon to be a "Probationer Prisoner of the Crown," O'Donohue declared he would be responsible for "every syllable" in the *Irish Exile*, whose aims were to "tear away the mask which cloaks Irish misrule and to mourn over the misfortunes which hang round our loved land" and to fight for Irish exiles in this new land.

A wealthy pastoralist, Auber George Jones, financed a former convict, John Davies, to buy the *Hobarton Guardian* in 1853 and re-launch it as the *Hobarton Mercury* in 1854. The *Guardian*, a supporter of Roman Catholic interests, was snuffed out because Davies reckoned that its "cause has now passed away, and with it all dissention [sic], strife and schism — the necessity, therefore, of an advocate no longer exists." What was needed instead, Davies declared, was an agent to obliterate past quarrels and grievances. When the *Mercury* was two months old, Davies became the sole proprietor; when it was five months old, he made it a tri-weekly; and when it was ten months old, it faced competition from the *Tasmanian Daily News*. When the *Mercury* incorporated the oldest Tasmanian (and Australian) title, the *Colonial Times and*

Tasmanian, on 24 August 1857, the *Mercury* talked, prophetically, of other takeovers. And so it came to pass: the *Mercury*, a daily on 1 January 1858 (calling itself the *Hobart Town Daily Mercury*), absorbed on 1 June 1858 the *Tasmanian Weekly News* and on 1 June 1859 the *Daily Courier*. On 2 July 1860 the *Hobart Town Daily Mercury*, confident in its status, became simply the *Mercury*. Reflecting on the previous six years, the paper remarked upon the ease of its passage so far: "We have won the race in a canter — if not by merely walking over the course."

Between the 1860s and 1880s, the *Mercury* had virtually no opposition. The main rivals were the *Tasmanian Times*, 1867–1870 (which absorbed two other papers, the *Evening Mail* and the *Weekly News*, in January 1870), and the *Tasmanian Tribune*, 1872–79. John Davies, who was prone to settling disputes with his fists, died unexpectedly at the age of fifty-eight in 1872, eight months after relinquishing control of the paper to two sons, John George (later Sir George) and Charles Ellis. The Davies dynasty at the *Mercury* continued until 1986.

South Australia, 1850–1914

In South Australia the *Register* was one of the few Adelaide papers to survive the effects of the Victoria gold rushes, which sucked most of the workforce out of its neighbor. The *Register* printed a "Diggers' edition" and sent weekly mails to the goldfields. From 1 January 1850 it was a daily (though an experiment with the format in 1844–45 had lasted only seven weeks). By 1890 it had doubled its number of pages and adopted modern broadsheet size. The *Adelaide Times*, established on 2 October 1848, also appeared daily in 1850, from 1 April. The *Register* and the *Times* shortly issued weekly editions of news from their dailies, for distribution to country readers. In an 1852 effort to entice money back into the Colony, the South Australian Government authorized the offer of a higher price for gold in Adelaide than in Melbourne. By the end of 1852, there was a marked improvement in the Colony's economy, but several newspapers had ceased publication. The *Adelaide Times* lasted by becoming a weekly before reverting to a daily in 1855, only to expire in May 1858. Its place was soon taken by a new morning daily, the *South Australian Advertiser*, which first appeared on 12 July 1858 and still flourishes today (as the *Advertiser*).

In the 1860s Adelaide gained three daily afternoon newspapers, the *Telegraph*, the *Adelaide Express* and the *Evening Journal*— two being offshoots of the morning newspapers — and the country press began solidly with six provincial titles, the *Northern Star*, Kapunda (1860), the *Border Watch*, Mount Gambier (1861), the *Bunyip*, Gawler (1863), the *Kapunda Herald* (1864), the *Wallaroo Times and Mining Journal* (1865), and the *Southern Argus*, Port Elliott (1866; it moved to Strathalbyn in 1868). In addition, religious papers also appeared and, in the period 1860–79, many weekly journals of a satirical and critical nature commenced. Several carried lithographic caricatures of prominent people, especially politicians. During the final two decades of the nineteenth century there was a proliferation of newspapers and periodicals in Adelaide catering to the commercial and entertainment interests. A daily newspaper supporting the political Labor party sprouted in 1910 from a weekly — it was to last for fourteen years. Adelaide's first major independent weekend paper, the *Mail*, was established in 1912 in three editions: the *Sporting Mail*, out on Thursday; the *Saturday Mail*; and the *Mail*, out by Saturday midnight.

In what was then known as the Northern Territory of South Australia, the earliest newspaper was the *Moonta Herald*, published seven times on board the ship that brought South Australian Surveyor-General George Goyder and his team of surveyors and workers to Darwin (then Palmerston) in 1868–69. The first machine-printed newspaper in Darwin was the *Northern Territory Times and Government Gazette*, originating in November 1873 in the back room of a government office. The new Government Resident, George Byng Scott, started the machine that printed the first copy. The editor was Richard Wells, formerly a journalist on the *South Australian Register*. The *Times* survived until 1932. From 1883 until 1890, a rival newspaper, the *North Australian*, was published in Darwin by George Mayhew and Charles Kirkland. The two papers presented markedly different versions of events and different viewpoints. In 1890 Mayhew and Kirkland bought the *Times* and amalgamated the two titles from 6 June under the *Times* banner.

Queensland, 1850–1914

In Queensland, newspaper developments occurred rapidly in the years immediately before and after Separation from New South Wales in 1859. The *Moreton Bay Courier* had competition after 19 July 1850 from the *Moreton Bay Free Press*, which appeared semi-weekly for two years. The *Courier* was not a semi-weekly until January 1858 and a tri-weekly only four days before Separation. The *Free Press*, in a spirit of celebration, became the *Queensland Free*

Press from 30 August 1859 but expired three months later, less than three weeks after Separation. New competition arrived on 31 March 1860 with the *Queensland Guardian*, weekly at first, then semi-weekly from the beginning of 1861, tri-weekly from 26 March 1862 and daily from 4 April 1863. It stopped on 27 June 1868, absorbed by the *Brisbane Courier*. The *Moreton Bay Courier* itself, a daily from 14 May 1861 as the *Courier*, became the *Brisbane Courier* on 11 April 1864.

Brisbane had a number of other moderately successful dailies, 1850–1914. The *Telegraph* commenced as a penny evening daily on 1 October 1872 and survived until 1988. The *Evening Observer* began in June 1870 as the semi-weekly *Ipswich Observer* before the proprietor shifted the paper to Brisbane in January 1880, six months after changing it to a daily. Bought three years later by the *Brisbane Courier*, which planned to close it, the *Observer* continued when the books showed it was performing unexpectedly well. Charles Hardie Buzacott, as managing director of the Brisbane Newspaper Co. Pty Ltd, made the purchase and then paid for a grand five-story newspaper building to house the morning and evening dailies and the highly successful illustrated weekly, the *Queenslander*. Buzacott was managing director from 1883 to 1894 when the company underwent a restructure. He resigned but returned to the Brisbane daily newspaper scene in 1903 as the managing director of the new company behind the *Daily Mail*, which disdained being "the mere organ of any party, sect or clique." It competed strongly in the morning market against the *Courier* until the two papers amalgamated in 1933 to become the *Courier-Mail*.

Western Australia, 1850–1914

A newspaper that lived only twelve months had a big impact on the shape of the Western Australian press in the second half of the nineteenth century. Edward Willson Landor (1811–1878), barrister, author and former commissioner of the Court of Requests in Perth, Guildford and Fremantle, launched the weekly *West Australian Times* on 1 October 1863. At the end of the *Times*' first year of publication, *Perth Gazette* owner Arthur Shenton bought the newspaper from Landor and merged the two papers on 7 October 1864 as the *Perth Gazette and West Australian Times*. Landor's farewell editorial complained of the lack of a big enough niche market for the special publication that the *Times* had aspired to be. The new paper, starting from Vol. 1, No. 1, presented a brief policy statement that did not say much more than that it would "view public matters in one light only — as affecting the welfare of all."

When Shenton died on 16 March 1871, aged fifty-five, his death was blamed to a large extent on his having been jailed for two months and fined 100 pounds in a contempt-of-court case. Shenton had used forthright language in the *Gazette* to protest the conviction of a young solicitor, S.H. Parker, for malpractice. The editor of the *Inquirer*, who had been lodged in the same cell as Shenton, said he was able to observe the very hurtful physical and mental effect that the incarceration had had on Shenton. Shenton's widow, Mercy, ran the *Perth Gazette and W.A. Times* for three years until a group of Perth businessmen bought it. They made the paper a semi-weekly and changed its title from 3 July 1874 to simply the *Western Australian Times*. Breaking continuity again, the owners started at Vol. 1, No. 1 and declared: "We trust also that the title we assume will be received as the badge of independence ... Our political motto is therefore 'Measures, not men'." They published an extensive policy statement, unnecessary had the paper wished to convey continuity of title and ideals. However, the new management wanted to discontinue that "which has ceased to be appropriate" and to align themselves with the ideals of *The Times* of London to make their title "a badge of independence."

Charles Harper (1842–1912) acquired the *Western Australian Times* for 1,100 pounds in 1879. Harper, enriched by his pearling ventures in the north of the Colony, supplied the money, and his associate, Sir Thomas Cockburn-Campbell, the editorial brains until 1887. Under the new regime, the paper entered a period of lively progress. The links with the *Perth Gazette* of 1833, now so tenuous and frayed, must surely be regarded as having been severed when the new proprietors renamed the paper the *West Australian* on 18 November 1879 and began the folio numbers again as Vol. 1, No. 1. They said they wanted to make their journal something great, something national, something like the important newspapers of the eastern colonies. The *West Australian* increased its size in 1880, appeared thrice instead of twice weekly from 18 October 1883, and became a daily on 1 January 1885. It was not the first daily in Western Australia. That honor belonged to the *Express*, which George Barrow launched at Fremantle on 3 January 1870. It ceased publication on 13 May, resumed with a different ownership and a "New Series" folio on 1 July, but died on 28 January 1871. The *Express* title was resurrected in Perth twice — in 1872 for a semi-weekly publication and again in 1905. Another to beat the *West Australian* to daily issue was the *Daily News*, which started on 26 July 1882 and endured more than a century.

At the *West Australian*, Cockburn-Campbell's predecessor as editor, 1874–79, was William Henry Hillock. He had campaigned strenuously for responsible government, causing serious concern among conservative colonists who were content with London's rule. Though he was regarded as one of the old-guard elite of the colony, Cockburn-Campbell was not opposed to self-government. But he feared it might arrive before the colony was developed enough to stand on its own feet. As editor he therefore aimed at stemming public agitation for the reform, arguing that self-government for a mere 28,000 people in such a huge area was premature. He was proven right when responsible government was granted in 1890 on far better terms than the British government would have allowed in the early days of the reform movement. In its final stages he was one of its most ardent advocates. In 1887 John Winthrop Hackett became editor of the *West Australian*, serving in that role until 1916 and as sole owner from 1913. Hackett was slow to settle into the editorship. His paper displayed racial intolerance in attacks on the Rev. John Gribble who exposed the exploitation of Aborigines in the pastoral and pearling industries. Its image likewise suffered when Hackett sided with Governor Frederick Napier Broome in the fracas between governor and officials that led to the suspension of Chief Justice Alexander Campbell Onslow. Worse, some irresponsible editorials by Hackett resulted in conviction of the paper's proprietors for defamation.

The Dailies from the 1880s

The main changes in the daily-newspaper scene in the Australian capitals between the mid–1880s and 1914 were undramatic. In Sydney occurred the births in 1891 of the *Daily Commercial News and Shipping Gazette* and in 1910 of the *Sun* (a bold remake of the former *Australian Star*); in Melbourne, the closure in 1892 of the *Daily Telegraph*; in Brisbane, the launches in 1903 of the *Daily Mail* and in 1912 of the Labor paper, the *Daily Standard*; in Adelaide, no shifts; in Perth, the closure in 1909 of the *Morning Herald*; and in Hobart, the start in 1908 of the *Daily Post* and the closure in 1911 of the *Tasmanian News*. In 1914 Sydney had two morning dailies and three evening dailies; Melbourne, three morning and one evening; Brisbane, four morning and one evening; Adelaide, two morning and two evening; Perth, one morning and one evening; and Hobart, two morning.

Provincial Press Began Slowly

The provincial press of Australia had very little presence in the first half of the nineteenth century. The earliest local newspapers were printed in Van

Diemen's Land in the 1820s and 1830s, followed by the irregular *Port Lincoln Herald* in South Australia in 1839–40, and the regular mainland provincial publication, the *Geelong Advertiser*, Victoria, in 1840 (still published today). By the beginning of 1850 thirty newspaper titles had come off the hand-operated presses in Australian provincial towns: eleven in Van Diemen's Land, nine in the emerging colony of Victoria, seven in the Middle District of New South Wales that still included Moreton Bay and three in South Australia, two of which were German-language newspapers published for the town of Tanunda in the Barossa Valley. Their fortunes varied widely: almost half of these titles did not survive until 1850, but three of the twelve that did are still in operation today. In New South Wales, for example, four titles were published in 1850, and four had already failed. The colony's first two provincial newspapers were in Maitland, one lasting only six months, the other continuing today. The *Hunter River Gazette* first surfaced on 11 December 1841, but its proprietor, Thomas Strode, who had been the mechanical superintendent at the *Sydney Herald* for several years and joint founder with George Arden of the *Port Phillip Gazette* in 1838, discontinued it after twenty-nine issues on 25 June 1842. Shortly after, in January 1843, the first number of the *Maitland Mercury* appeared.

After this fairly slow start, however, the provincial press went through a period of rapid expansion from the 1850s to the 1890s. The number of country papers increased thirty fold. By the end of 1887, there were 406 Australian provincial papers and by 1891, 475 or one newspaper for every 4,300 country-dwellers. In the 1850s expansion was prompted initially by the gold rushes, especially in Victoria and NSW. In Victoria there had been only four provincial newspapers in print before 1 January 1850, but new papers mushroomed in the 1850s as immigrants headed for the mining fields: three new titles in 1850, three in 1851, two in 1852, three in 1853, four in 1854 and — with the introduction and spread of the electric telegraph — fifteen in 1855, sixteen in 1856, seven in 1857, thirteen in 1858 and six in 1859. Just as it had become the dominant colony from industrial and population perspectives, so Victoria dominated the Australian provincial press scene.

Provincial newspapers could appear daily, tri-weekly, semi-weekly or weekly. Some opened as dailies: the *Daily Times* (Geelong, 1858), the *Daily News* (Braidwood, 1859), the *Newcastle Morning Herald and Miners' Advocate* (1876), the *Barrier Miner* (Broken Hill, 1888) and the *National Advocate* (Bathurst, 1889). Most increased the frequency of their publication, from weekly to semi-weekly to tri-weekly to daily as their towns grew. In Victoria, eleven provincial titles became dailies in the 1850s: three at Geelong, three at Ballarat, three at Sandhurst (Bendigo) and two at Beechworth. The *Geelong Advertiser* (established 1840) was the first provincial daily in Australia, from 13 November 1849, and the *Ballarat Times* (1854) and the *Courier of the Mines and Bendigo Daily Mail* (1855) both became dailies on 1 January 1856. Victoria had seven country dailies in print by 1 January 1860, nine in 1870, thirteen in 1880, fourteen in 1890 and twelve in 1900. The process was much more gradual in NSW; in 1880 only one provincial title was a daily, the *Newcastle Morning Herald*. In 1881 there were four more and eleven more before 1890. Some of these were short-lived, for only seven dailies were published at the beginning of 1890, including three in Bathurst and two in Broken Hill. In Queensland, the 1880s also marked the first significant period of daily publication, with the main activity being in the gold-mining town of Charters Towers and its port, Townsville, where three or four dailies operated in both centers for much of the decade. Queensland gained its first provincial daily in January 1873 and the second in 1875. Both were published in Rockhampton, the first having been established in 1861 and the second in 1863.

Australian provincial newspapers drew from the British experience where, from about 1726 onwards, the locals fell into two broad groups: (1) the papers which flung themselves wholeheartedly into the political fray; and (2) those which avoided the outspoken political essay and strove to steer a middle course between the two parties. Among the latter in NSW were such papers as the *Armidale Telegraph* (established 1865) and the *Grafton Argus* (1874), which declared that they were sworn to no political master. But they were the exception. Country newspapers in the nineteenth century were based "as much on differences in editorial policies as on commercial competition." As G.H. Mott, editor of Victoria's *Chiltern Standard*, noted in 1860: "Party feeling usually runs pretty high in small communities, and if it so happens that any considerable section of such a community are disappointed with the result of an election, or are dissatisfied with the management of the local press, the first thing done is to start a newspaper to represent their particular views." After the gold discoveries, rival newspapers were established in many towns to represent the contending interests in the land controversy: the squatters, who had gained ownership of land by occupying the land or "squatting" on it, and the free selectors who had applied through government channels. For example, the *Free Selector*, with editorials written in the first person singular by Hanley Bennett, was introduced in Tamworth at the end of 1874 and in southern NSW the *Yass Free Holders' and Free Selectors' Advocate* was issued monthly from November 1875. The *Albury Banner and Wodonga Express*, a weekly bordertown newspaper for ninety years from 1860, became known as "The Cocky's Bible" because George Adams, who bought it in 1862, advocated the cause of free selectors so forcefully.

The Bulletin

A distinctive development in the Australian press began on 31 January 1880 when two journalists, John Haynes and John Feltham Archibald, started a weekly paper, the *Bulletin*, which others soon dubbed "the Bushman's Bible." It carried an eclectic mix of news, cutting and sometimes humorous comment, social jottings and literary bits and pieces. Intended to be a clever and humorous weekly with a Catholic flavor, an unlikely and perilous combination, the significance of the *Bulletin* is not that it was started but that it survived. The two proprietors had limited capital, "just enough to buy a little type and a lot of credit," furnished by bachelor Archibald recently returned to Sydney from a spell in Queensland, and modest goals, to earn for themselves "bread and butter" and "to please the people around us." As a model for the paper, Haynes chose the *San Francisco News Letter and Commercial Advertiser*, founded in 1856. Archibald's prototype was the *Stockwhip*, which had flared briefly in the mid-1870s in Sydney. His strong preference for a title was the *Lone Hand*. The *Bulletin* quickly expanded a solid initial readership: in its first year, it sold around 4,000 copies an issue in February, 10,000 in June, and 16,000 in October. Its size jumped from eight to twelve and then sixteen pages.

The *Bulletin*, although sympathetic to Labor, always remained independent of formal attachment to any party. Managed by a London Scot, illustrated by an American, sub-edited by a Glaswegian, edited by a Victorian who rechristened himself "Jules Francois" and pretended that he had been born in France, the *Bulletin* expressed a vociferous Australian nationalism, Anglophobe and republican. It was also blatantly racist, which was not unusual for the time. In 1893 it favored "Australia for the Australians.— The cheap Chinaman, the cheap Nigger, and the cheap European pauper to be absolutely excluded." The *Bulletin* would become preeminent in the field of humor and the political cartoon. It started with careful line drawings but later developed its own style. Platemakers, etchers and artists were imported from England and the United States to give the *Bulletin* an unrivalled artistic and technical team. An Australian, Norman Lindsay, joined the staff in 1901 and became a significant artistic contributor while making a name for himself more widely as an artist.

Journalists Organize

Journalists began to organize from the early 1880s, but the Australian Journalists' Association (AJA) was not formed until December 1910 in Melbourne. A New South Wales branch was established the following year. The first strike by Australian journalists began on 19 January 1912 at the Perth *Daily News*. The stoppage was not authorized by the federal body, which vainly tried to prevent it. Yet it lasted for five days, and the journalists returned to work, having won all five points in their dispute. After they finished work, the proprietor, Arthur Lovekin, cleared the reporters' room and provided his journalists with a banquet to celebrate their victory. The AJA did not solve the industrial problems, but it did provide a focus for those eager to improve the status of journalists.

Labor Papers

Newspapers interpreting the world from the workingman's perspective sprang up across Australia in the 1880s and 1890s. One of the first was the *Boomerang*, launched in Brisbane in 1887 by William Lane. Other significant early newspapers supporting the cause of labour were the *Worker* (Brisbane, established 1890), the *Westralian Worker* (Perth, 1890), the *Australian Worker* (Sydney, 1891), and the *Labor Call* (Melbourne, 1906). Joining them were gazettes in provincial centers, such as Charters Towers and Cairns, Queensland, and Grenfell and Grafton, NSW. The *Boomerang*, which presented a point of view characteristic of the 1890s and the emerging struggle for workers' rights, and the Queensland *Worker*, which Lane founded in 1887 and 1890 respectively, were the main organs through which he "educated" workers and helped to create the modern Australian labour movement. The *Boomerang* declared itself "loyal to Australia" and added that, though it had no enmity for Britain, "if Australian interests ever came into collision with foreign interests, we are for Australia, whether the foreigner be Britain, Germany or Japan." The most notable contributor to Lane's papers, from a literary point of view, was the poet and author, Henry Lawson. His "Freedom on the wallaby," first published in the *Worker*, seemed a call to militancy during the maritime and shearing strikes of the early 1890s because of its famous conclusion:

> We'll make the tyrants feel the sting
> O' those that they would throttle;
> They needn't say the fault is ours
> If blood should stain the wattle!

Though by no means brilliant, and no better got up than other labour papers of its day, the *Boomerang* was conducted and written with vigor and enthusiasm. It contained a number of sketches and sections intended to appeal to varying tastes as well as short stories and a serial that were always Australian. A much more literary publication was the *Australian Worker*, which started in 1891 as the *Hummer* in Wagga Wagga, New South Wales, in 1891. The journal, soon rechristened the *Worker*, shifted to Sydney in 1893. It absorbed the *Australian Workman* in 1897 and became the *Australian Worker* in 1913. The talent of some of its contributors and staff members lifted it above the ruck of just about all other labour papers. Some of the smaller capitals had labour dailies before Sydney. Melbourne had one, the *People's Daily*, 1903–04, but it soon failed. Adelaide had one from 7 March 1910 when the sixteen-year-old *Weekly Herald* became the *Daily Herald*, and Brisbane had one from 10 December 1912 with the launch of the *Daily Standard*. *Direct Action*, a radical paper representing the Industrial Workers of the World in Australia, appeared in Sydney in January 1914 and was famous during World War I for whipping up opposition to two plebiscites on the question of conscription. Both plebiscites were defeated.

Conclusion

In the century under review, the Australian press mirrored the growth of the society it served. The gold-rush period of the 1850s was undoubtedly the biggest growth trigger for the Australian colonies, especially Victoria, New South Wales and Western Australia, and gold, in turn, hastened the expansion of the newspaper industry enormously as it accelerated the development of railways, port facilities and the electric telegraph. The early decades were difficult times for the newspaper as owner-editors sorted out working relationships with governors and tested the boundaries of dissent. Once power had passed from governors to parliaments that became increasingly democratic, editors enjoyed more scope to criticize and faced less risk of being jailed if they overstepped the mark. From the 1870s, newspapers serving Sydney and Melbourne, in particular, began to take advantage of bigger, mechanized presses as they sought ways to meet circulation demands that exceeded the capacity of the smaller presses. In Melbourne, the *Argus* aimed constantly for quality, and the *Age*, under David Syme, wielded power and influence. In the second half of the nineteenth century, evening dailies, Sunday papers, illustrated weeklies and weeklies designed for the country reader began to emerge. In 1815 Australia had one weekly newspaper; in 1914 Australia's state capitals boasted twenty-two daily newspapers, demonstrating the growth of a nation whose white population grew from the seeds of a penal colony.

Bibliography

Brodsky, Isador. *The Sydney Press Gang*. Sydney: Old Sydney, 1974.
Bunbury, W. "Newspapers and Literature in Western Australia, 1829–1859." *Westerly*, No. 1 (March 1878): 65–83.
Carey, Susan. "The Prolific Press: Newspapers in South Australia, 1836–1890." B.A. (Hons.) thesis, School of Social Sciences, Flint University of South Australia, October 1978.
Curthoys, Ann, and Julianne Schultz, eds. *Journalism: Print, Politics and Popular Culture*. Brisbane: University of Queensland, 1999.
Gilson, Miriam, and Jerzy Zubrzycki. *The Foreign-language Press in Australia*. Canberra: Australian National University, 1967.
Goff, Victoria. "Convicts and Clerics: Their Roles in the Infancy of the Press in Sydney, 1803–1840." *Media History* 4 (1998): 101–20.
Greenop, Frank S. *History of Magazine Publishing in Australia*. Sydney: K.G. Murray, 1947.
Kirkpatrick, Rod. *Country Conscience: A History of the New South Wales Provincial Press, 1841–1995*. Canberra: Infinite Harvest, 2000.
_____. *Sworn to No Master: A History of the Provincial Press in Queensland to 1930*. Toowoomba, Qld: Darling Downs Institute, 1984.
Lloyd, Clem. *Profession: Journalist: A History of the Australian Journalists' Association*. Sydney: Hale & Iremonger, 1985.
Macintyre, Stuart. *A Concise History of Australia*. London: Cambridge University, 1999.
Manion, James. *Paper Power in North Queensland: A History of Journalism in Townsville and Charters Towers*. Townsville: North Queensland Newspaper Company, 1982.
Mayer, Henry. *The Press in Australia*. Melbourne: Lansdowne, 1964.
Miller, E. Morris. *Pressmen and Governors*. Sydney: Angus & Robertson, 1952.
Pitt, George H. *The Press in South Australia, 1835–1850*. Adelaide: Wakefield, 1946.
Ratcliff, Patricia Fitzgerald. *The Usefulness of John West: Dissent and Difference in the Australian Colonies*. Launceston, Tasmania: Albernian, 2003.
Robb, Gwenda. *George Howe: Australia's First Publisher*. Melbourne: Australian Scholarly, 2003.
Souter, Gavin. *Company of Heralds*. Melbourne: Melbourne University, 1981.
Walker, R.B. *The Newspaper Press in New South Wales, 1803–1920*. Sydney: Sydney University, 1976.
Woodberry, Joan. *Andrew Bent and the Freedom of the Press in Van Diemen's Land*. Hobart: Fullers Bookshop, 1972.

Canada's Victorian Press
Influences from Home and Abroad
David R. Spencer

Historical Background

Canada's Victorian press was a genuine melting pot of influences both from home and abroad. On the surface at least one might think that the English-language journalism that matured in the mid-nineteenth century would be connected directly to the press in the motherland, namely Great Britain, and that the French-language press would be the stepchild of practices in France. In part, these suppositions are accurate. Canada's English language press certainly demonstrated some British influences, but in the main, it was very much a creature of North American practices. As for the French, they had been cut off from Europe since the fall of Quebec in 1759. Thus, as the Victorian age progressed, both the English-language Canadian press and the American, especially in the years after the War of 1812–14, influenced the French. The main difference between the English and French presses in Canada had little to do with style or content but with language.

Prior to the nineteenth century, the press in both parts of what was to become Canada was if not limited, not yet developed. The first newspaper to appear north of the thirteen colonies was the *Halifax Gazette* in 1752. Its founder was Bartholomew Greene, a military man from Massachusetts who died before the first edition hit the streets of the Nova Scotia capital. The business went to John Bushell who eventually lost control of the *Gazette* due to mismanagement probably exacerbated by his over-consumption of alcohol. The newspaper survived. Despite numerous configurations, it did not become a Canadian journal in fact until the American Revolution and in law until Canada's Articles of Confederation were enacted in 1867. The *Gazette* is the ancestor of the current *Halifax Chronicle-Herald*.

Halifax in the eighteenth century was part of the larger British Empire, which included the American colonies. The imperial enemy at that point came from the French possessions along the St. Lawrence and from Northern New Brunswick. With the conquest of Quebec in 1759, the British occupiers were astounded to discover that the only press in French Canada was restricted to printing religious tracts.

In the years between the fall of Quebec and the War of 1812–1814, no fewer than twenty papers in English and French sprang up in Canada. They were not newspapers in the sense we understand them today. Their pages were filled with religious discussion and debate and a variety of scientific and literary material culled from newspapers overseas. Religion played a particularly strong role in both the hearts and minds of immigrants from the thirteen colonies and of French communities in Canada. The contents of local journals consisted mainly of advertising for land sales, shipping news and similar ventures. True news exchange remained very much an oral experience, one which took place following church services, at county fairs and at any number of regularly scheduled festivals. This form of communication was due in part to the fact that literacy remained the preserve of the upper classes. However, a press for the lower would shortly emerge, thanks primarily to the efforts of William Lyon Mackenzie.

William Lyon Mackenzie and the Beginnings

Mackenzie, a fiery Scottish rebel, would become Canada's most important early journalist as well as the first mayor of Toronto and the grandfather of the country's longest-serving Prime Minister, William Lyon Mackenzie King. Mackenzie had no problem attracting attention. He would be removed from his seat in the Upper Canada House of Assembly on several occasions for unacceptable behavior, burned in effigy more than once, and victimized by angry mobs that resented his reformist and perhaps republican tendencies. The young Mackenzie willingly clothed himself in the mantle of rebellion espoused by English political activist William Cobbett and adopted the political philosophy of Andrew Jackson, whose hatred of banks and paper currency only provided more inspiration for the restless Canadian.

In 1824 Mackenzie established his first newspaper, *The Colonial Advocate*, at Queenston on the Niagara River across the gorge from Lewiston, New

York. But the real action in Upper Canadian politics was taking place across Lake Ontario in the provincial capital of York, now Toronto. It was there that Mackenzie would make political decisions that nearly cost him his life. He was determined that his newspaper would be the voice of both reason and rebellion, seeing no conflict between the two. Once he moved to York, his influence spread and, much to his regret, was the topic of conversation in the colony's halls of power.

In the early nineteenth century, the British North American colonies were all in the east. The franchise in Upper and Lower Canada, Nova Scotia and New Brunswick was almost universal among male property holders, yet none of these dependencies could be described as a democracy. The executive was a governor appointed by the British Crown. The legislature was bicameral. The upper house, known as the Legislative Council, consisted of men appointed by the governor on the advice of local officials. The lower chamber, the House of Assembly, was elected by most males. However, both the upper chamber and the governor had the constitutional power to veto any initiative of the lower chamber, which they did with impunity. In Upper Canada, some of these so-called local officials formed what came to be known as the Family Compact. Their leader was the Anglican Bishop of Upper Canada, John Strachan, the father of Trinity College, which became the cornerstone for the University of Toronto. At any given time, the membership in the Family Compact, a kind of all-powerful, feudal dynasty, did not number more than eight. In Lower Canada, the equivalent to the Family Compact was the Chateau Clique. The name may have differed but not the approach to politics and attitude. Mackenzie made it his life's mission to reduce the Family Compact membership to zero.

Mackenzie lived dangerously. He attended Strachan's sermons, then not only reported but commented on them in his journal. Blood began to boil in official circles. In June 1826, while Mackenzie was hiding out to avoid arrest for failure to pay his bills, a group of young supporters of the colonial establishment paid his print shop and newspaper office a visit. Mackenzie fled. When he thought it safe to return to York, he found his establishment in shambles. Not one to be deterred, he reopened the paper, again targeting all members of the Family Compact and anyone deemed to be their fans. The so-called Type Riot, which was actually reasonably orderly, impacted negatively on the Family Compact and its reputation for being able to keep the peace. Mackenzie had opened the floodgates that would eventually lead to constitutional reform in all four British colonies, not just Upper Canada.

In the years prior to 1837, Mackenzie drifted in and out of the newspaper business. Rightly or wrongly, the journalist was accused of being the catalyst who inspired the rebellions of 1837–1838 in both the Canadas. By all standards, these were little more than organized disobedience and the word "organized" must be taken lightly at that. In Upper Canada, a motley crew of dissidents armed with side arms, knives, shovels and anything that resembled a weapon decided to march on the capital and overthrow the government. They were no match for the troops in the local garrison, and the uprising was put down as quickly as it had begun. When the prisoners were rounded up, Mackenzie was nowhere to be found. He had made a mad dash for the American border. New York State gave him protection until he was pardoned, and he eventually returned to Toronto to take up life in politics.

Upper Canada was not the only jurisdiction that displayed unhappiness with its government. Lower Canada too broke out in a rebellion that was more of a shooting war than events in Upper Canada. British troops were called on to break up insurgent groups in the Richelieu Valley south of Montreal and St. Eustache north of Montreal. Unlike the Upper Canadians, Lower Canadians fought pitched battles with the soldiers but were also suppressed. Like Mackenzie, the leader of the Lower Canadians, a Montreal lawyer named Louis-Joseph Papineau, fled to a safer environment. Nonetheless, journalists remained in the government's cross hairs. Etienne Parent, the owner/editor of *Le Canadien*, a French-language publication in Montreal, went to jail briefly in 1838 because he was suspected of having supported Papineau. Parent's only crime was advocating the protection of French Canadian rights by a British colonial regime that was, for the most part, English-speaking, Protestant and the guardian of the canons of common law. If Mackenzie and Parent contributed only to the birth of a strong advocacy press in Canada, one which remains to this day, they made an extremely valuable contribution. Interestingly, when the Spanish Civil War occurred in the late 1930s, Canadian volunteers who fought for the republican government named their company the Mackenzie-Papineau brigade.

The rebellions of 1837–1838 alarmed the British government, which sent John Lambton, Lord Durham, to investigate and report on the situation in the Canadas. His observations led to the end of the Family Company and the Chateau Clique, the merger of the two colonies, and the onset of real democracy in the colonies. As a result, political parties began to emerge, and as they did, great and open debates on the future of the country took place. Simultaneously, the newly formed political parties, the Liberal-Conservatives led by Sir John A. Macdonald, later Canada's first Prime Minister, and the Reform Party, under the direction of George Brown, looked to journalism to advance the cause of partisan politics. Thus, the political press appeared, one that would eventually form the backbone of a commercial, daily press in the closing decades of the century.

The Founders: John Henry Walker and George Brown

The 1840s would prove to be critical in the emergence of a Canadian journalism. As in many other social arenas, persons of Scottish and Irish heritage would prove to be the movers and shakers. Canada's first major daily, the *Toronto Globe*, the child of George Brown, commenced publishing in 1844. It continues to thrive today as the Toronto-based but national-oriented *Globe and Mail*. In 1849 John Henry Walker, a young immigrant from Antrim County in what is now Northern Ireland, launched Canada's first satirical and comic magazine. Discussed below, its heritage could not be in doubt because Walker christened his journal *Punch in Canada*. However, unlike the *Toronto Globe*, it was short-lived, dying after three years.

George Brown, a Scotsman, first went to North America in order to assist his father Peter, the publisher of a Free Kirk Presbyterian religious journal in New York City. The Church of Scotland was smarting over theological battles between conservatives and reputed liberals. Recruits for the Church's causes were considered essential for its religious survival, and North America, with its many Scottish enclaves, was considered prime territory to find activists. While in New York, the Browns regularly traveled north to Toronto to keep in touch with the Scottish community there. Eventually, the Browns decided that Toronto needed a Free Kirk journal. George was assigned the task of establishing one. Consequently, in 1843, he moved to Toronto where he founded *The Banner*. A year later, after devoting some of *The Banner's* pages to secular news, he started a four-page weekly that he crowned *The Globe*. By 1853 the newspaper was publishing daily and claiming it was the first journal to do so successfully. The claim would prove to be an exaggeration.

Brown was very much the product of the political climate in Great Britain from which he had emigrated. In many respects, he was the Canadian version of a Victorian liberal, a characterization equivalent to a modern neo-conservative. He was in every respect a product of the version of liberalism, both social and economic, that was espoused by the Manchester school of academics and industrialists. Brown was convinced that everyone had a right to practice the sacred tenet of individualism without fear of interference by others. He was also intrigued by the concept of survival of the fittest that would later emerge in the works of Charles Darwin and Herbert Spencer. Hence, his newsroom was his fiefdom, and he ran it ruthlessly. Needless to say, Brown's world view was not popular with his employees, especially those who believed in collective action to resolve difficulties and differences. Brown's rigidity eventually led to collisions with the Printers' Union in 1853 and again in 1872, events which forced the Canadian government to legalize trades unions.

The world of George Brown, at least in terms of the evolution of the press, was a deeply divided one. These divisions were reflected in the emerging press before the Canadian Confederation of 1867. Like their peers in the United States and Great Britain, Canadian political parties heavily emphasized getting their messages to the faithful and converting others. Partisans perceived the press as the best vehicle to deliver their message.

The stakes were high. In many respects, the Canada of pre–Confederation days was a colony deeply divided between two conflicting and seemingly irreconcilable camps separated by differences in religion, language and culture. Durham's demand in 1839 for responsible government had led to an ill-fated merger of Upper and Lower Canada into a single legislative union in which the two provinces acquired new labels: Upper Canada was Canada West (now Ontario) and Lower, Canada East (now Quebec). On one side of the new chamber sat French-speaking Roman Catholics, largely collectivist in attitude, and on the other, English-language Protestants, whose political perspectives were divided between those espoused by George Brown and by Sir John A. Macdonald. *The Globe* was Brown's forum, and the *Toronto Mail* and *Toronto Empire* were the pillars of Macdonald's party.

Insofar as he wished to suppress Canadian Toryism, Lord Durham was a failure. As a result of his recommendations, the more authoritarian aspects of the Tory collectivist, elitist philosophy disappeared. Nevertheless, Tories retained an unshakeable belief that an elite had a right to rule and a duty to take care of those who could not take care of themselves. Although adherents would never admit it, Canadian Toryism in the 1840s and 1850s was a more inclusive and more democratic form of serfdom. Out of the ashes of the Family Compact and the Chateau Clique Macdonald had formed the Liberal-Conservative Party, a coalition of anti–Brown liberals and dedicated Tories learning to deal with the uncertainty of electoral politics.

Across the parliamentary floor from the alcoholic Macdonald sat George

Brown and his Reform Party members. He coveted the role of political innovator, which had led him to seek political office. While Macdonald successfully forged a working alliance with Quebec Tories led by Sir Georges Etienne Cartier, Brown fumbled along with a cluster of economic liberals, many of whom went far beyond the ideas of Adam Smith. Brown placed great faith in the freedom of individuals to create wealth and remain free from any and all collectivist ideals. Given this position, there was no way that he would share with Macdonald a common vision for the newly emerging country. In fact, as time passed, the political differences between two of the founders of the Canadian federation deepened into personal bitterness, an alienation which lasted until Brown was murdered by a disgruntled employee of *The Globe* in 1880.

The date was 25 March 1880. The owner was working in his office located on a staircase just below the editorial rooms. Hearing a noise, he looked up and saw one George Bennett. Brown did not know Bennett, but Bennett certainly knew of Brown. Bennett reached into his pocket and showed the journalist a piece of paper which contained notes indicating that Bennett had been employed by *The Globe* for a five-year period. He demanded that Brown sign the paper in order to confirm its contents. What Brown did not know about Bennett was significant. The intruder had been dismissed from *The Globe* for various offences including drunkenness on the job, neglect of duties and wife beating. Brown also did not know that Bennett was out on bail for failing to provide support for his estranged wife or, more important, that Bennett had concealed a loaded revolver under his jacket.

Brown had little patience for most things and that included appeasing Bennett. He instructed the former employee to obtain the proper signatures from the foreman of the department that had previously hired him. Bennett told Brown that the foreman had already refused to sign. So Brown told Bennett to seek out *The Globe's* treasurer who, he assured Bennett, would be more co-operative. Then Bennett lost his patience and charged Brown's desk screaming "sign it, sign it!" Brown was furious, but in his rage he noticed that Bennett had produced the revolver. Brown jumped his assailant, and the gun discharged. Three members of the editorial staff who were also working late heard the shot and ran to their owner's aid. Both the police and a physician were called. Bennett was arrested yet one more time, and Brown was treated for what was considered a minor flesh wound.

Whether the treating physician was incompetent or underestimated the gravity of Brown's injury is still a point of debate today. Four days after the shooting, Brown was in pain from an ever-spreading infection in the wound. Nonetheless, he insisted on remaining active in spite of the situation because his beloved Reform (Liberal) party was once again sitting in opposition to a Macdonald government. Macdonald had been returned to power in 1878 after a five-year hiatus caused by a scandal. Brown had recently developed an editorial agenda designed to make what he considered a brief Tory tenure as uncomfortable as possible. Brown was mistaken. The next Liberal government would not take office until 1896.

As the editor's health declined, a host of doctors was called in, but the infection proved stubborn. After falling into an irreversible coma, George Brown died on 9 May 1880, a few months before his killer. Brown's brother, Gordon, took the reins at *The Globe* and eventually sold the journal to the Toronto-based Jaffray family. Although the Browns practiced a strict form of Presbyterianism, their prudery was no match for the new owners who proceeded to ban advertising of spirits, tobacco, cheap clothing and female girdles. It would be nearly three quarters of a century before *The Globe*, having merged with *The Mail*, would in 1936 regain its place as Canada's leading newspaper and its truly first national one in the English language.

Brown's *Globe* and the *Toronto Mail* and the *Toronto Empire* were not unique in reflecting pre–Confederation political divisions in the country. Akin to newspapers in Britain, Canadian journals took sides between Reform and Liberal-Conservative constituencies in the wake of the 1830s rebellions in Upper and Lower Canada. The Tories set out to destroy any newspaper that would not toe the party line. They had a large group from which to choose because anti–Tory gazettes were not hard to find. Following William Lyon Mackenzie's lead, newspapers promoting a more liberal version of society sprang up in most of the country's larger cities.

Creation of the Dailies: A Period of Growth

In London, Ontario, William Sutherland, a young journalist, was driven from a journalistic career. He had founded *The Canadian Free Press* in 1849 primarily as a liberal newspaper supporting responsible government. The news of this "heresy" did not take long to reach the meeting places of the local Tory establishment. Young thugs invaded Sutherland's newsroom and demolished not only his press but also the furniture and the equipment needed to get the editions to readers. Sutherland recouped and put out a newspaper until 1851 when, exhausted by ongoing threats and overwork, he sold the journal to

Josiah Blackburn, a local Tory who immediately turned it into an organ for Macdonald's Liberal-Conservative coalition.

When George Brown arrived in Toronto in 1844, the city did not have one daily newspaper. Dailies had been tried in both Toronto and Montreal, but all had been unsuccessful. The most common formats were weeklies, semi-weeklies or tri-weeklies. In spite of his innovative spirit, Brown was not the first Canadian to publish a daily. When he decided to do so in 1853, dailies had already been tried in Kingston, Ontario, and in St. John, New Brunswick. With the rise of the daily, the influences that drove the creative and news-gathering energies of major city newspapers started to come not from Britain, but from south of the forty-ninth parallel, the United States.

Shortly after Benjamin Day in 1833 introduced the penny daily *New York Sun*, the Saint John, New Brunswick, *News* followed suit. According to Canadian press historian Douglas Fetherling, the *News* was the first penny newspaper in the British Empire. But it was not only the penny press that Canadians pirated from across the border. Most of New York's editors, flamboyant and conservative, set the tone for the Canadian press. Models ranged from the rascally James Gordon Bennett of the *New York Herald*, to the more conservative Horace Greeley of the *New York Tribune* and the editorial team that produced the *New York Times*.

Canadian journalism during the 1840s was growing in another way as its technical ability to produce larger and more impressive issues showed. When Samuel F.B. Morse demonstrated the effectiveness of his electric mode of communication in 1844, the newspaper would be the greatest beneficiary. No longer were editors confined to disseminating information only on those events within delivery range. The telegraph offered faster and broader news coverage, which propelled perpetual demands for timely and interesting stories.

In 1848 six New York newspapers joined together to form the Associated Press. It would not take long for other American dailies to benefit from this union. And it did not take long for Canadian newspapers to realize the benefits of collaboration in news-gathering. In 1859 twenty-one Canadian newspapers followed the lead of their New York cousins and established a similar consortium, the Canadian Press. Throughout the nineteenth century, the Associated Press and Canadian Press cooperated with each other in the delivery of world and North American news. However, the alliance was not as smooth as some may have wished. Rival services sprang up in Western Canada. And Canadian newspapers using the cooperative complained that edited abstracts of longer stories were often the only versions available from the Associated Press' New York offices. In addition, one of the major outcomes was that Canadian newspaper readers were being fed information produced and edited in a foreign country. To many Canadians, this smacked of colonialism.

When the first reliable transatlantic cable opened in 1858, it provided Canadians with yet another window on the world. British as well as American news could be reproduced in Canadian newspapers and would shape journalists and readers. In many ways, Canadians had no choice but to retrieve their news from two of the important nations in the world. Economy of scale dictated then as today. Britain's influence as a net exporter of news still exists through agencies such as Reuters and the BBC while the United States seems to be a global force in communications.

Journalism and Pictures

As Brown and his competitors fought for reader's political allegiance, another form of journalism was taking hold in Montreal. John Henry Walker certainly did not receive the prominence in history bestowed on George Brown, partly because Walker's journalistic career was short. Still, it was also significant because his role in the emergence of illustrated journalism cannot be underestimated. Born in 1831, the young Walker was removed to Canada when his father, an Irish physician, took an appointment in Montreal. The younger Walker maintained a studio in what is now the older part of downtown Montreal. There is no direct evidence that he read any English or Irish newspapers, but it is clear that he was familiar with *Punch*, the humor magazine first published in London in July 1841. Within two years, *Punch* was full of engravings and sketches of a decidedly political nature.

Walker was determined to bring the humor and sarcasm of the British publication to Canadian audiences. Although the British *Punch* was the first magazine devoted to sketched humor, it was following a tradition of illustrated satire that had surfaced almost a century before. In 1756 a young military officer named George Townshend teamed up with an artist and engraver in London to produce a series of political drawings that were posted throughout the city on lamp posts and vacant walls, in taverns and eating establishments. In some ways, it was an early version of graffiti. The next year marked the birth of James Gillray, one of Britain's most popular political caricaturists and a beacon for *Punch* artists.

As the clouds of war began to gather over France and Britain in the mid–1700s, Townshend found himself in a military uniform and on his way to Canada. His commander was James Wolfe whom Townshend passionately disliked. During those inevitable quiet periods that occur in any war, Townshend used his time to draw exceptionally unflattering images of his commander. Wolfe apparently had a mania for clean latrines, a mania which Townshend felt dominated his commander's thinking and posed a threat to the troops. After Wolfe died in the heat of battle, even his soul was not spared in Townshend's drawings.

Townshend may have been influenced by the art of William Hogarth who many argue was the father of political commentary in illustration. Regardless of whether or not the assertion in true, it is well known that the eccentric soldier returned to Britain where he continued his politically inspired drawing. His illustrations not only caught the attention of a willing and ready public but also of pamphleteers. Their work became the basis of a journalistic culture that surfaced as Britain relaxed its restrictive press laws. So, it seems, illustrated journalism traveled from Britain to Canada and back to Britain in a very short period of time. It was a genre of journalism that beckoned John Henry Walker.

Walker was only eighteen when *Punch in Canada* first appeared in Montreal. One of the catalysts for publication was a movement, organized by a number of prominent Montreal businessmen, to advocate annexing Britain's Canadian colonies to the United States. For Walker, a Protestant, Tory Ulsterman, this cause was unacceptable. Proponents of annexation, which was relatively popular in elite circles in Montreal, became a target for his numerous sketches. But they were far from alone. Living in a Montreal that had a large and dominant English-speaking population, Walker was insensitive to the prejudices to which many French-speaking, Roman Catholics were subjected. Like many Tories of the day, he firmly believed that French Catholics were an inferior race of people in need of a cultural uplifting that he and his fellow British were only too willing to provide. Walker's approach to French-English relations in Canada thus bordered on a racism that would not be tolerated in modern society.

Punch in Canada, publishing in both Montreal and Toronto, died in 1851. Walker then offered his services as a free-lance cartoonist to other publications. He took a listing in the Montreal City Directory in which he described himself as a wood carver and engraver. A popular artist whose work took him to various Montreal locales, which he sketched, Walker also produced cartoons that regularly appeared in late 1860s magazines, such as *Grinchuckle* and *Diogenes*. In the early 1880s, when smallpox threatened the cultural and economic life of the city, Walker was commissioned to draw for a pro-vaccination journal called *L'Ami Du Peuple* (Friend of the People). There is little doubt that Walker's contributions influenced a generation of journalists who used both image and word to create a form of journalism that makes the very foundations of the state objects of piercing analysis, comic relief and sometimes even derision. He died in Montreal in 1899.

A number of magazines took their cue from Walker. Among them were *The Jester, The Wasp, Stadacona, The Gridiron, The Free Lance, The Bee, The Dagger* and *Paul Pry*. All had fairly difficult runs. Walker's most successful descendants would be the periodicals of the Desbarats. This family developed several illustrated journals, some published in both Canada and the United States, and some, in both of Canada's official languages. In 1865 the first evidence of a Desbarats involved in illustrated journalism comes in a comic offering, *The Sprite*. Appearing on a military base in Quebec City, the serial listed a member of the family as the production printer.

The Desbarats probably also designed the *Canadian Illustrated News*, whose lineage is indisputable. This sheet, born in December 1869, was the Canadian version of *Frank Leslie's Illustrated Newspaper*, later known as *Frank Leslie's Illustrated Weekly*. Leslie was none other than Henry Carter, an expatriate Englishman who brought a wealth of experience to North America when he immigrated to New York in 1848. By the mid–1850s his illustrated publications were instrumental in establishing visual journalism in North America. There is a striking resemblance between the illustrated press of Canada and that of the United States, of Britain and of continental Europe.

Although the bulk of the *Canadian Illustrated News* could hardly be considered core journalism, the Desbarats family gradually encouraged both illustrated and written political commentary in the 11x17 inch broadsheet and its French-language equivalent, *L'Opinion Publique*. In this respect, the political drawings had a decidedly continental French flavor. They were usually printed on the front cover with written opinions on the second page. The remainder of the weekly consisted of black-and-white engravings normally devoted to travel, economic development in other parts of the country, or fluff articles on matters of the heart. The journal's most notable illustrator in its early years was Edward Jump who, in spite of his name, was born and brought up in France where he would have witnessed the growing influence of cartooning being driven by a French enthusiasm for the work of James Gillray.

Jump's early years in North America were spent in San Francisco where it is thought he made a living by designing labels for whisky bottles. In 1868 he found himself in Washington sharing a rooming house with Mark Twain. After marrying a French opera star, Jump moved to Montreal in 1871 and took up sketching for the Desbarats. His tenure in Montreal was short, ending in 1873 when he moved again, this time to New York, and gained employment from Frank Leslie. When Jump published a series of cartoons depicting Canadian politicians as classical figures, the world of political cartooning declared open season on elected officials, a position from which retreat was soon impossible.

Desbarats journals regularly featured the state of Canadian politics following the enactment of the Articles of Confederation in 1867. However, encouraged by the success of their Montreal ventures, the family went to New York in 1873 and established the *New York Daily Graphic*, a newspaper in which they claimed to have published the first halftone photograph in journalism history.

Taking a Stand

In the 1870s the campaign of the American *Harper's Weekly* against New York political boss W.M. "Boss" Tweed was reaching its climax. As the Harper brothers had discovered, publishing political cartoons, especially those as sarcastic as the work of Thomas Nast, sold magazines. Until 1873 Canada had no serious scandals to feed this sort of journalism, and when one developed, journalists did little to exploit it. Indeed, when the news leaked that Canadian Prime Minister Macdonald was involved in some serious influence peddling while awarding contracts to build the national railway, the Desbarats publications did not undertake an investigation or even comment with any gusto. Rather, it was John Wilson Bengough, who, following the revelations of Macdonald's misdeeds, founded in 1873 a comic weekly called *Grip*.

The magazine, named after the raven in Charles Dickens' *Barnaby Rudge*, reflected the influence of Thomas Nast. Bengough was an ardent admirer of both Dickens and the American comic master. Benough's lifelong love of anything Dickensian even led him to write a play based on the author's works, a play that mercifully never saw the stage. His awe of Nast led him to contact the *Harper's* cartoonist while still an aspiring artist in the small town of Whitby, Ontario, just east of Toronto. Nast encouraged the young Bengough who, perhaps more than any other Canadian journalist of the time, devoted himself to perfecting the art of illustrated commentary. Benough was not the artist that Nast was; nonetheless, there are some similarities in their drawings.

The illustrated press remained important in Canadian journalism in the 1880s but continued to draw its inspiration from the United States, Britain and continental Europe until the closing decade of the nineteenth century. As the newer dailies surfaced after 1867, more and more illustrations began to appear in their pages. In 1888 the *Montreal Star* hired its first full-time artist, Henri Julien, who had made his reputation sketching for the *Canadian Illustrated News/L'Opinion Publique as* well as New York's *Century Magazine*, among others. However, when illustrations and eventually photography became mainstays in the dailies, the illustrated press lost its most marketable commodity.

By the end of the Victorian age, the genre was virtually extinct with one notable exception. Political cartoons moved from the pages of the weekly

FENCING IT AROUND.

Uncle Sam:—"I reckun, neighbor, you needn't mind fixin' that fence for a spell yet. Your cows never trouble my farm."
Cousin John:—"That's so. But you see the trouble all comes from the other side, and I guess I'm going to stop it."

Fencing in Uncle Sam, *Jester* **magazine, Montreal, 27 September 1878.**

CANADA'S HINT TO THE NEW PRESIDENT.

Hoping for tariff relief, *Grip* magazine, Toronto, 18 November 1876. Both illustrations (page 55 and above) illustrate views regarding a tariff dispute between Canada and the United States.

illustrated press to the editorial pages of dailies, and the Desbarats family left illustrated journalism in 1888. *Grip* declined with the death of Sir John A. Macdonald in 1891, and by 1893 it ceased publication. Bengough thereafter drew for the American journal *The Public*. To supplement his income from journalism, he went on worldwide lecture tours with a sketch pad and a box full of chalk. He died at his easel in 1923.

The Victorian age was marked by vast improvements in journalism technologies. Faster and more efficient presses multiplied in newspaper establishments in both North America and Europe. The telegraph was making journalism an international business and urban dailies, due to extensive railway construction, were spreading their wings well beyond the cities where they were born. Telegraphy also gave rise to the voices of dissidents, persons and groups who felt that the commercial directions taken by the dailies effectively shut out their concerns. As a consequence, a new press, one which questioned the bases of Victorian society, saw the light of day. The new papers would share a market with the dailies until the economies of the early twentieth century consigned them to the same fate as that of their brothers and sisters in the illustrated press.

The Unionists and the Journalists: A Dissident Perspective

The connection between external influences and the rise of dissident journalism is easy to track. When the Philadelphia-based Knights of Labor decided to organize Canadian workers in 1869, the Knights brought with them their determination to educate the masses in the proper, namely working class, way of thinking. To accomplish this goal, the Knights used a weekly and occasionally a monthly newspaper dedicated to the union movement. They had good examples from which to copy. Labor journals had started in Britain quite early. For example, in 1819 a wool sorter named John Wade had commenced publishing a sheet called *The Gorgon*. Likewise, American unionists had been setting type as early as 1828, the date when the *Mechanics' Free Press* appeared on the streets of Philadelphia.

The cause of teaching workers as a prelude to alleviating their grievances got off to a rather rough start in Canada. Shortly after the Knights crossed the border, a savage North American depression came close to destroying the organization itself. Hence, it was not until the early 1880s that the Knights were able to establish their first Canadian newspapers. In the next two decades, Knights' newspapers opened in Toronto, Hamilton, Victoria,

Montreal and London, Canada's largest industrial centers. The gazettes operated under various names, such as *The Palladium of Labor*, *The Labor Union*, *The Wage Earner*, *The Echo*, *Le Trait d'Union*, *The Industrial News* and *The Industrial Banner*, among others. With the exception of the London, Ontario, monthly *The Industrial Banner*, which published for three consecutive decades, the majority of these journals teetered on the brink of extinction for most of their lives. In Montreal, the union published two newspapers, the English-language *Echo* and the French-language *Trait d'Union*. Although the American Knights began to decline in the early 1890s, the order remained a force in French Canada well into the twentieth century.

To declare that the Knights' newspapers had any clear ideological direction would be inaccurate. On one day they would demand the end of industrial capitalism. On another, they would demand the reform of industrial capitalism so that its immense profits could trickle down to workers. Nevertheless, the Canadian journals were consistent in one respect. They delivered the same message that the Knights disseminated from their headquarters in the United States. Local news was sparse, and the columnists who wrote front-page commentaries did not vary from the party line on too many occasions. That would remain the task of other nonconformists in Victorian Canada.

The newspapers started by the Knights of Labor were only a small contingent in a much larger anti-establishment press. Other trades unions regularly began publishing newspapers, but these were seldom successful. Many were patterned on American trades unions' journals. Like the publications of the Knights, most Canadian union newspapers carried little local news beyond announcing the arrival in town of union dignitaries and publishing advertisements for various pamphlets and local train and/or ship timetables. But union papers did carry significant selections from labor journals of the United States and Great Britain. Thanks to this practice, the international focus of the Canadian Victorian labor press was most visible.

One of the major contributors to the Canadian labor press, although it is doubtful that he knew it, was Julius Augustus Wayland, publisher of the Girard, Kansas, socialist newspaper *The Appeal to Reason*. It is virtually impossible to find a Victorian Canadian labor or socialist journal that did not publish excerpts from his writings. And while Canadian labor editors were helping themselves to the world according to Wayland, they also cribbed texts of more influential writers, such as Eugene Debs and Fred Warren.

Canadian labor journalists did not restrict their abuse of copyright to American sources alone. *Merrie England*, the book-length condemnation of capitalism by British socialist Robert Blatchford, was serialized in a number of papers. The commentary of Robert Ingersoll was particularly popular. So was the Christian Socialist document *Between Caesar and Jesus*. A number of other works of the Christian Socialist movements in both Britain and the United States also appeared regularly in Canadian labor journals.

Recipes for social reform were not the exclusive purview of unionists. The works of Karl Marx and P.J. Proudhon were regularly copied by other papers that addressed a working class but semi-literate audience after 1870 when elementary school education became compulsory. Monetary and agrarian reformers, single taxers, anarchists and prohibitionists all surfaced in the press. Noticeable in this development is that most critiques of Victorian social behavior were imported from thinkers beyond Canada's borders. Only one major ideology was home grown, a peculiar form of Canadian social democracy some of whose ideas can be traced to the English Fabians, notably Beatrice and Sidney Webb. The ideology also borrowed from preachers of the social gospel. The result, a unique blend of doctrinaire Christianity, fire-breathing prohibitionism and collectivist fervor, still enjoys some support in Canadian politics today.

Of the non-union dissident press, the agrarian reform movement's publications were the most important. They could be found on the reading tables of most farmhouses in the country. Although the majority of these publications did not appear until the depression years of the 1930s, they had their roots in Victorian Canada. Indeed, Saskatchewan's *Grain Grower's Guide* became the textbook for farmers to learn about Canadian socialism.

A London, Ontario, journal, *The Canada Farmer's Sun*, began publishing in 1892 and continued well into the twentieth century. Advocating various agricultural reforms, it derived much of its inspiration and much of its badly-needed capital from the American agricultural reform group, The Patrons of Industry. In the mid–1890s the journal actually toyed with the idea of setting up a co-operative in the Province of Ontario. The movement failed, but in 1895 the journal launched a socialist supplement called *The Brotherhood Era*. The newspaper was also a key player in an alliance of farmers and unionists that formed in 1893 to back agricultural reform candidates in the provincial election of that year. The final results scared the ruling elites when the coalition came within 3 percent of forming a government.

Both the farm reform movement and trades unionists supported the agenda of the various temperance movements in the country in the late 1890s. In fact, taking their cue from Frances Willard and other American opponents of alcohol, Canadian prohibitionists felt that cohesion in the movement could be best achieved by publishing a journal. *The Templar* began in Hamilton, Ontario. Its editor, George Wrigley, was a former labor journalist and convinced social democrat. His tenure was brief because the paper lasted only a few short years, but by 1899 he was back editing labor and socialist publications.

While this evolution occurred in Eastern Canada, journalism in Western Canada grew more slowly in the years before the 1867 Confederation. Although the main population bases in the country were in what are now Ontario and Quebec, there were significant settlements in the Atlantic provinces as well. Alternatively, the western territories from the Ontario border to the Pacific Ocean were one vast hunting ground thinly populated by several different, often hostile indigenous tribes.

Canada and the American Threat

In 1670 Charles II had granted a charter to the new Hudson's Bay Company. The Company, which still operates a number of department stores in Canada today, was commissioned to undertake business in the fur trade and other productive activities over a vast and basically unpopulated region. In a word, the territory soon amounted to a huge cash crop for beaver pelts destined for Europe. But as Canadian communications theorist Harold Innis has pointed out, by 1867 the scarcity of the beaver led to a big increase in the cost of the commodity and, as a result, an ever-shrinking market.

The fur trade, by its very nature, discouraged any form of immigration to the west with a view to settlement. When it became apparent that the fur trade was reaching the end of its profitability, about the mid-point of the century, the open lands of the west, in what was to become Canada and what was later a target for annexation by the United States, were on the agenda of both governments. The Americans approached Great Britain in the mid–1860s asking what price the Crown would accept to sell the regions known as The North West Territories and Rupert's Land. In Ottawa, the incoming Prime Minister, our old friend Sir John A. Macdonald, learned of Americans' interest in the area and moved to block them from having it. He was well aware of the fact that development in the mid-western and western regions of the neighbor to the south was advancing quickly. For example, in 1858 about thirty thousand American miners had set up camp in the new territory of British Columbia. In that same year, the Minnesota Territory, just south of

Canadian settlements near what is now Winnipeg, received permission for statehood. Canadian historian Donald Creighton has observed that commerce between settlements in British Columbia and San Francisco exceeded that within the rest of Canada. And near the end of its tenure as custodian of the western lands, the Hudson's Bay Company began to supply its needs from warehouses in Minneapolis and St. Paul, courtesy of a rail line that connected its bases in what is now Manitoba to the United States.

Eventually, the Macdonald government offered a total of 300,000 pounds, a considerable sum in those days, to acquire the territorial rights held by the Hudson's Bay Company. Out of this territory the government carved what was to become the Province of Manitoba in 1870. That same year, the British Columbia settlement joined the Canadian confederation as did the tiny Atlantic Prince Edward's Island. Macdonald promised to link the new nation by sponsoring the building of a national rail system with one branch, the Canadian Pacific joining Montreal and Vancouver, and the other, the Intercolonial bringing transportation to the Maritime Provinces. The railroad would have a tremendous impact on the press, not only in delivery but in content.

The decline of the fur trade coincided with the discovery of gold along the Pacific Coast from the American border to the Canadian territories just south of the tree line. Unlike the fur trade, gold mining encouraged settlement, albeit a limited form. In 1846 competing claims of the British and the Americans to territorial rights had largely been settled by the Oregon Treaty. Until gold came into the picture, there was no real incentive to build towns and villages. But once the dream of riches captured people's imaginations, miners streamed northward. The result was that an infrastructure in which a journal could prosper started to take shape in the west. George Brown's *The Globe* in particular took an interest in reporting the news from the west, and it was he who laid the groundwork for what was to follow, when journalism finally arrived.

Journalism Goes West

Ironically, when newspapers came to British Columbia, Canada's westernmost region, one with a scattered and tiny population base, journalists brought with them three different and very diverse interests. Needless to say, emigrants from the central provinces founded newspapers that looked like and behaved like those with which the settlers were familiar. Because of their modest markets, these journals tended to be somewhat smaller than their eastern counterparts. It was the potential growth of the area that attracted four young Americans, two journalists, H.C. Williston and Columbus Bartlett, and two printers, Abel Whiton and James W. Towne, who opened the *Victoria Gazette and Anglo-America* for business on 25 June 1858. From its initial run twice a week, the journal went to printing five days a week.

Later that year, on 11 September, a new newspaper surfaced in British Columbia designed to serve the French language colonies popping up in the province and to rival the dominance of the *Victoria Gazette*. *Le Courrier de la Nouvelle Calédonie, journal politique et littéraire, organ des populations Françaises dans les possessions Anglaises*, was the brainchild of Monsignor Modeste Demers, the Roman Catholic bishop of Vancouver Island. The newspaper's editor, Paul de Garro, was one of the district's more colorful characters, a man who claimed that he was an exiled French count. Alas, the French-speaking settlements did not greet the journal with any warmth, so within a few issues, it ceased publication.

As if the area lacked enough colorful characters, Amor de Cosmos, a career anti–American, created the next newspaper to emerge. His real name was William Alexander Smith, but he had earlier decided to adopt a more identifiable handle. The combination of the Latin-French and Greek name could be loosely translated as *Lover of the World*. His newspaper, the *British Colonist*, founded on 11 December 1858, continues to publish today in Victoria as the *Times-Colonist*. Smith, or de Cosmos, left his mark both on British Columbia journalism and British Columbia politics. He used his work as a journalist to enter political life and became the province's second premier. In many ways, his approach to journalism differed little from the politically-bound editors who launched and labored for the largely partisan party press in the Eastern regions about 1850.

Both British Columbia and Manitoba entered the Canadian Confederation in 1870, which, combined with the gold fever, lured numbers of land-strapped farmers in the central provinces to go west. But journalism did not come to Manitoba as quickly as it did to British Columbia. In the early years, the province had only one newspaper. The *Nor'Wester*, based in the Red River settlement of 10,000 persons (now Winnipeg, Manitoba), came into existence in 1859. The settlement was so isolated that the nearest community with which the citizens communicated and traded was St. Paul, Minnesota. Despite the presence of a large French-speaking community in the town of

St. Boniface and in the province's southern counties, French-language journalism was an even later arrival in the province.

The *Nor'Wester* lived a precarious life. When Métis leader and member of the federal parliament Louis Riel led the first of his two western-based rebellions, the newspaper became a target. The Métis were the offspring of interracial marriages, mainly between French-speaking trappers and aboriginal women. After seizing power in Manitoba, Riel closed the newspaper. It rose again and struggled on until 1872 when a mob of political rivals destroyed it, thus discouraging the number of pretenders who wanted to set up gazettes to compete with the *Nor'Wester*. However, Manitoba was not to be denied its press. Within months, two men, William Fisher Luxton and John A. Kenny, founded the *Manitoba Free Press* on 9 November 1872. Later it would be the home base for one of the country's most durable and influential journalists, John W. Dafoe. It continues to publish today as the *Winnipeg Free Press* and is one of the few major dailies not owned by Can West Global Communications.

At this time, what were to become the Provinces of Saskatchewan and Alberta were still known as the North West Territories and Rupert's Land. It was not until 1905 that two provinces and two large northern territories were carved out of the old Hudson's Bay districts. Well before that date, although settlements were sparse and populations thin, there was a steady trickle of immigrants into them, former British military men and central Canadians looking for a better life. This migration was gaining the notice of aspiring journalists. In 1878 Patrick Laurie founded the *Saskatchewan Herald* in the town of North Battleford. Not long after this newspaper commenced, more journals emerged, in Prince Albert and the soon-to-be provincial capital, Regina. Opened in 1883, the *Regina Leader* is today publishing as the *Regina Leader Post*.

Next door in Alberta, the growth of journalistic activity took a similar turn. In 1880 the newly-formed *Edmonton Bulletin* saw the light of day. A second newspaper came in 1882 at Fort McLeod. The following year, one of the country's most venerable journals, the *Calgary Herald* began. It eventually became one of the linchpin newspapers in the modern Southam chain, now itself owned largely by Can West Global Communications.

Farther to the north, when the gold rush hit the Yukon territories, journalists were willing and able to serve the information needs of the many would-be miners who were thronging to the area in search of fame and fortune. In 1897–1898 two newspapers, the *Yukon Midnight Sun* and the

Dawson Nugget, attempted to develop constituencies in the region. The *Klondike Miner* and the *Whitehorse Star* soon followed.

The majority of those who established newspapers in the Canada west of the Ontario-Manitoba border came from elsewhere, in the main from central Canada but in some cases from the United States. These people naturally brought with them a concept of journalism as it was practiced at the time. Their purview ranged from editorial policy to design and layout practices but did not overlook the business of subscription rates. In other words, the journalism that sprang up in the west was the result of external sources, of prior experiences of the people who went there for a variety of reasons. This habit of echoing outside journalistic trends continued. Thus, when a new, politically desensitized press blossomed in central Canada thanks to the introduction of the large-circulation dailies funded by advertisers, the west did not wait long to copy this model.

The World of the Victorian Daily

At the beginning of its great depression in the early 1870s, Canada had slightly fewer than fifty daily newspapers. Two decades later, it had twice that number, and Montreal was the leading newspaper town in the country. In 1872 the city boasted of four English-language journals and three French. During the next thirty years, twenty-three more papers popped up in Montreal to co-exist with the original seven. Ultimately, the market rationalized itself, and twenty-five newspapers, including four of the originals, passed into history. Nevertheless, the final three decades of the nineteenth century witnessed the birth of the modern newspaper. Canadian media historians Douglas Fetherling and Paul Rutherford both contend that this birth began with the severing of journalism's direct ties to the nation's political parties and with the increasing reliance on advertising as a source of stable funding.

As in the United States and to a lesser degree in Europe, the Canadian newspaper of the late nineteenth century lived in a journalistic world that was a competitive marketplace. Yet, as Fetherling has accurately observed, the press in these years reached its Victorian zenith. By 1870 Canadian journalism had started to break the ties that bound it to Canada's political elite. Newspapers slowly shifted their attention from supporting partisan politics to attracting readers. Publishers and their staffs tried to lure those who could afford to buy not only a daily but also the products and services advertised therein. However, the formal divorce from the political party system did not lead to a strong sense of editorial independence. Although cash no longer flowed into the coffers of the newspapers from politicians, an editor often remained loyal to the powerbrokers whom he preferred. Indeed, editorials clearly testify that the country and its editors remained divided between Liberal (Reform) and Liberal-Conservative supporters.

As John Nerone and Kevin Barnhurst have noted in their study of design evolution in American newspapers, the move to the eye-friendly journal was well underway by 1870. The same direction is discernible on the Canadian scene. As well, news itself was changing, partly due to Edwin Stanton, Abraham Lincoln's Secretary of War. Thanks to his solid insistence on publishing only those facts which one could verify, both Canadian and American newspapers turned to entertaining as well as informing their audiences. In many cases, it was difficult to determine where fact ended and entertainment began. When the yellow press, a curse to some, surfaced in New York in the late 1890s, the Canadian equivalent, although not so brassy, quickly blossomed in major Canadian centers.

The newspaper that began to dominate the world of information at the turn of the twentieth century could easily be mistaken for most editions of a modern journal. The earlier one had similar characteristics, including publishing in color. The pre–1914 Canadian newspaper, like its counterpart in the United States, still highlighted news, especially on its front page. However, inside the paper, editorial commentary was more clearly delineated as a blend of opinion and fact. Readers were made to understand that the same was true of the numerous columns in the off-editorial sections that ran adjacent to letters to the editor. Also increasing as supplements to the news were extensive sports coverage, lengthy features and pages devoted to advertisements of all sorts, from products and services to personal concerns. By this time, the only way to distinguish most Canadian and American journals in terms of content and style was by the masthead. Other than that, they looked very much the same.

One of the most popular developments in Canadian journalism was the brazen effort to duplicate the American Sunday edition. Because of market size the Canadian Sunday papers were never as big or as extensive as their sire, but the journalistic rationale for their existence paralleled the American, namely to sell papers. The Canadian press regularly commissioned work from American newspapers, such as the wildly popular Sunday color comics, and then added local material. Financial data, travel sections, women's news, farm news and gossip columns were among the sections in most Canadian gazettes, whether in English or in French.

Like the United States, Canadian journalism depended on strong-minded entrepreneurs with deep pockets. Primarily these people functioned in both the major cities, Toronto and Montreal. While urban proprietors tended to hire urbane journalists, this tendency should not be misread to suggest that smaller centers had no press leaders. However, those who set the late–Victorian journalistic agenda were certainly metropolitan in nature.

The strongest pro–American editor was E.E. Sheppard of the *Toronto News*. Sheppard was known for his foul mouth and strong anti-religious attitude. He was the son of a fundamentalist clergyman in Southwestern Ontario who, the editor recalled, had exposed the boy to religious tracts on an almost daily basis. As an adult, Sheppard bragged to friends that he had been so inundated so early with religion that he could quit going to church and still get into heaven. Sheppard could have given both William Randolph Hearst and Joseph Pulitzer a lesson in scandalous reporting. The *Toronto News* carried a column called Peek-A-Boo that pilloried prominent Canadians figures by means of a toxic mix of fact and fiction. His own great specialty was writing provocative and pointed editorials on causes in which he unwaveringly believed. The rascally editor also left Canadians with another legacy, *Saturday Night*. Sheppard intended it as a forum for social gossip. Later, the magazine evolved into a periodical home for intellectuals and artists. To many Canadian writers, the new version remains a venue to place one's work, although now it is distributed primarily electronically with limited paper circulation.

Some editors, drawing from Sheppard, focused more on the concept of news as entertainment, but the men who directed the press in the newsrooms in Montreal and Toronto were innovators. Although there were a number of prominent editors in the two cities, four of them stand out. Hugh Graham of the *Montreal Star*, Trefflé Berthiaume of Montreal's *La Presse* and John Ross Robertson of the *Toronto Telegram* were contemporaries in the 1880s. Near the end of the century joining them in stature was Joseph Atkinson of the *Toronto Star*. Atkinson earned the epithet "Holy Joe" because of his fanatical hatred of anything alcoholic.

Hugh Graham's journal was what modern analysts would call a causal institution. Graham had come to the conclusion, as had Pulitzer in New York, that the survival of a newspaper depended on an expanding jurisdiction. In Graham's case, that meant reaching the largest mass in the country, namely the working class. Following a precedent set in New York, Graham's paper created a fresh air fund to move city children into the country for a part of their summer recess from school. Emulating Montreal, the *Toronto Star* later initiated a fresh air fund in Toronto. Graham also supported Montreal's campaign to vaccinate unwilling citizens when the community was hit with two major smallpox outbreaks in the 1880s. He called his involvement in civic affairs the people's journalism. Although his efforts to secure a wide constituency were successful for decades, the *Montreal Star* succumbed to competition from the city's morning newspaper, the *Gazette*, in the early 1970s.

Across the great divide in Victorian Montreal, namely Rue St. Laurent if you were French or St. Lawrence Avenue if you were English, was the lair of one Trefflé Berthiaume. Like his compatriots in the United States, Berthiaume was well aware that late Victorian journalism was a business, one that needed to pay attention to new technologies. Thus, in 1894, *La Presse* installed Linotype machines in its newsroom. In 1897 the paper began printing its regular supplements in color and in 1900 started publishing photographs. Berthiaume had joined the newspaper as a successful printer. In 1889, its owner, a politician named Adolphe Chapleau, gave the paper to Berthiaume on the promise that it would support the federal Conservative party whose co-leader was the French Canadian, Georges Etienne Cartier. Berthiaume agreed, and the journal prospered under his leadership. It is still the voice of French Canada in Quebec.

In Toronto the most prominent press figure after the death of George Brown was John Ross Robertson. Like Graham, Robertson adopted the American style of editorial writing—short, pointed, colorful. His newspaper, the *Evening Telegram*, focused primarily on local news. The limited coverage it gave to international affairs was brief and to the point, and many editions carried no international news at all. Robertson, like Graham and Berthiaume, prided himself on his ability to spotlight civic affairs. As a result, the *Evening Telegram* was the organ for people with a cause to promote. Robertson also pictured himself as the appointed savior of the taxpayer. His campaigns to reveal how public money was spent never stopped. Although the *Evening Telegram* fell victim in 1973 to the preference for morning journalism, Robertson's legacy continues. A school in the city of Toronto and the hockey cup awarded annually to the champion in Canadian major junior hockey both bear his name.

Crime, Corruption and Sensationalism

The murder trial of Reginald Birchall in Woodstock, Ontario, in 1890 typifies the direction that the Canadian press would take in the years before

World War I. Birchall, posing as an English aristocrat, was involved in a scheme to defraud wealthy Britons. He had lured one F.C. Benwell to Woodstock where he promised to show the man some land that Benwell believed he had purchased. The two were seen going into the woods near the small village of Princeton, but only one, Birchall, was seen to return. Shortly thereafter, Benwell's body was discovered frozen in a small pond. Needless to say, Birchall was instantly suspected, arrested and charged with Benwell's murder.

Birchall's trial was held in a converted theatre due to the massive interest in the case. It was soon the focal point for newspapers, wire services and magazines. Interest in the trial was wide, particularly in England since both the central characters were British. Local curiosity was so extensive that spectators, including many journalists, swarmed into the courthouse to watch the trial. When they complained that all they could see of the defendant was the top of his head, the judge ordered Birchall's chair in the prisoner's box raised so that all could view the defendant. His fate was sealed when a detective with an interest in forensic science walked the Great Western Railway line backward from Princeton to Niagara Falls and located the murder weapon. Witnesses put Birchall on a train going to the Falls after he had emerged from the forest. The detective was able to show the jury that the gun used to murder Benwell belonged to Birchall, and scientific evidence accumulated by comparing bullets from the gun and those in Benwell's body proved that they came from the same weapon. These details generated plenty of stories.

Equally productive of news was Birchall's behavior. In spite of the fact that his life was in the balance, he played the role of a wrongly accused defendant to the hilt. He socialized with his guards in the Woodstock jail, ordered food from local restaurants, and spent his spare time reading the Bible. All of these shenanigans the press dutifully recorded at length. As with all spectacular cases, journalists did not ignore him after his conviction and before his execution. Birchall, during his wait for the hangman, accommodated them admirably. He commissioned a carpenter to fashion a casket of rosewood with a silk lining and a tailor to design an elegant burial suit. Birchall also consented to an experimental form of hanging in which the accused would be pulled up quickly as opposed to dropped. The method merely caused him to die from atypical strangulation. After the execution, this story ended, but the public taste for lurid columns persisted. Murder and its aftermath, the press quickly realized, was at least as important to sell newspapers to a mass audience as was a gospel of civic service.

Final Thoughts

During the nineteenth century, there were a number of significant developments that occurred concurrently with the rise of Victorian dailies, developments that made these journals more international in outlook. The first was the expansion worldwide of the telegraph system. As noted above, this expansion spawned the Canadian Press, a wire service in 1859. By 1914 it had agreements with British, American and French language services. The result was that Canadian newspapers were little different from their counterparts anywhere else in the industrial world, a collection of local stories supplemented by international news prioritized by agencies.

Another development of significance was a shift in business. Although the adoption of the Sunday supplement had helped to increase circulation in the country's major urban areas, newspaper financing came more and more from advertisers, the largest of whom were department stores. In turn, the newspaper encouraged the growth of the advertising agency. Not surprisingly, the first Canadian one opened in Montreal before the turn of the century in 1889. In a city that boasted twenty-three newspapers at one point, choosing the appropriate journal for one's needs seemed a daunting task. A.E. McKim, the owner of the pioneer agency, was ready to assist clients in identifying the gazette that best suited their goals. To do so, he verified circulation figures and checked the editorial perspective of each newspaper that his agency listed, lest a Liberal advertiser place anything in a Conservative newspaper. His system worked, and newspapers became inextricably linked to advertising in Canada as they would be in the United States and Great Britain.

Newspaper content and design likewise reflected shifts that were similar to ones elsewhere. The trend toward more spectacular news, more sports pages, more opinion editorials with more signatures, more feature columnists, and more readers' correspondence were not exclusive to Canada. Equally, modifications in design, while significant, were similar to those of American and British gazettes. Type variation improved, headlines became bigger and bolder, and visuals, especially photography, expanded. These commonalities clearly indicate that the paper of the masses was precisely that, a journal whose style knew no geographic boundaries.

Finally, the growth of the mass press was international not only in character but in ownership. Canadian journalism, as much as American and British, was increasingly in the hands of press barons. Their competition touched off the circulation wars prevalent in the three countries in the decade before World War I. In Toronto, John Ross Robertson, E.E. Sheppard and George and Gordon Brown were the major players. In London, Ontario, the wars pitted the Blackburn family against the Cameron interests. In Montreal, the *Star* under the leadership of Hugh Graham dominated the English-language market, while the French was in the grip of *La Presse* and its owner/editor, Trefflé Berthiaume. In all respects, however, unless one knew where a newspaper was published, it was difficult to distinguish among American, British and Canadian journals at the time. News-gathering had become global, something which would increase immensely when war broke out in Europe in 1914. Yet, to this day, the heritage of its own nineteenth-century journalism remains partly intact in Canada.

Bibliography

Barnhurst, Kevin, and John Nerone. *The Form of News: A History*. New York and London: Guilford, 2001.
Bengough, J.W. *A Caricature History of Canadian Politics*. Toronto: Grip, 1886.
Canadian Press, The. *A History of Canadian Journalism, Volume 1*. Toronto: Canadian Press Association, 1908.
Creighton, Donald. *The Story of Canada*. London: Faber and Faber, 1959.
Desbarats, Peter, and Terry Mosher. *The Hecklers*. Toronto: McClelland and Stewart, 1979.
Fetherling, Douglas. *The Rise of the Canadian Newspaper*. Toronto: Oxford University, 1990.
Hardt, Hanno, and Bonnie Brennen, eds. *Newsworkers: Toward a History of the Rank and File*. Minneapolis–St. Paul: University of Minnesota, 1995.
Innis, Harold. *The Bias of Communication*. Toronto: University of Toronto, 1951.
Kesterton, W.H. *A History of Journalism in Canada*. Toronto: McClelland and Stewart, 1967.
Rutherford, Paul. *A Victorian Authority*. Toronto: University of Toronto, 1982.
Sotiron, Minko. *From Politics to Profit*. Montreal and Kingston: McGill-Queen's University, 1997.

Traitorous Collaboration
The Press in France, 1815–1914
Ross F. Collins

Introduction

Successive French governments during the nineteenth century treated journalists as potential traitors for good reason: they were. In 1830 and 1848 the revolutions that toppled the monarchies were hatched in newspaper offices. A subsequent coup d'état, revolution and civil war all had histories tied to the press. The establishment of the first stable republic in France, in 1881, brought journalists and politicians together in parliament and in the offices of Paris dailies.

The tight bond between French journalism and political power shaped a nineteenth-century progression of governments unlike that of any other western nation. France moved from conservative monarchy to liberal republic through a ratchet of revolt. The world saw one of its greatest powers change governments four times violently between 1815 and 1881, plus a hideous civil war in 1871. These shifts do not include Napoleon Bonaparte's coup at the dawn of the century and his second effort that ended at Waterloo.

Political preoccupation seethed through the century. French society searched for stability but found none in a succession of kings and dictators. Its debates flowed through its journalism, and the power and legitimacy of successive governments flowed from its journalists. History of this journalism is a tug-of-war story between control and freedom.

This circumstance helps to explain the peculiarities of French journalism, in many ways different from that of other countries. Unlike newspapers in England and the United States, the French seldom took the lead in developing modern press techniques but did make two innovations. The world's first news agency, Havas, was established in 1832 in Paris. It became the model for Reuters in Britain and Wolff in Germany, and eventually the Associated Press in the United States. And France by the end of the century also could boast the world's highest circulation daily, *Le Petit Parisien,* 1.5 million.

These occurrences were exceptions. Technology generally came from the Anglo-Saxon countries, and some concepts specifically from the United States. Business principles of industrial journalism, that is, newspapers as consumer goods produced cheaply, appeared early in France, though not as early as in the United States. The "new journalism" of short, neutral, fact-based reporting washed into the Paris industrial dailies by the 1880s, but the initiative again was American.

Some of the century's greatest changes in the idea of what news ought to be barely touched France. Paris newspapers, as the penny press of other western capitals, reached more and more readers from the popular classes by 1900. Yet French readers cared less about "brutal facts," as Paris critics called the American model. Style was important — quality of opinion, literary finesse, art and theatre critique — as was the value of the independent writer who signed his name when other countries' journalists stayed anonymous. In fact, the literary priority of French dailies was obvious in the decades-long popularity of the serialized novel offered every day on the "ground floor" of the front page. Fiction in French newspapers remained a feature through World War I.

Also peculiar to the press in France were its domination by Paris dailies and its perennially low advertising revenue. No western country in the nineteenth century was so focused on its capital. All political power emanated from Paris to the provinces. Revolutions, when they were necessary, came from Paris. The rest of the country could but acquiesce. All events that could make news came from Paris. Provincial papers drew most of their content from Paris, except for local want ads, because editors found not much else worth printing. In fact, the man (almost never a woman at this period) who wanted to make it in journalism and politics would have to "go up" to Paris. The term was "go up," or, alas, possibly "come down" from Paris.

If Paris had all the big opportunities in politics and journalism, the capital did not dominate advertising. French publishers, like those in England and the United States during the first third of the nineteenth century, hit upon the idea of advertising as a way to pay for a newspaper, instead of relying on expensive subscriptions. But unlike the expanding American daily press, in France the businesses most expected to advertise tended not to do so. Advertising grew slowly, pathetically so when compared with that of England and the United States, for a variety of reasons. The result by the end of the century was a press dynamic in its vitality, fragile in its profitability. This consequence opened the door to the one thing that people in France remember today of the press during this period, its "abominable venality."

The Stage: France by 1815

The Bourbon monarchy restored in 1815 already had good reason to view newspapers with fear and loathing. The press in France had mutated from its docility of pre-Revolutionary days. Before 1789 the king allowed newspapers, but only as a way to announce the government's decrees. Tight crown control kept newspapers from actually discussing those decrees.

The French Revolution altered the role of journalism as dramatically as it put an end to the monarchy. As the cap of censorship came off, newspapers appeared like spring dandelions, a flowering of published opinion unknown in conservative Europe. Most of the revolution's major figures were journalists, whose journalism played a central role in the greatest revolt since the American Revolution that so inspired Paris. Newspapers became the public forum of debate and declaration.

Unlike the revolution which formed the United States, France's revolt turned into the bloody Terror, in which the monarch lost his head along with 18,000 other people. The press played a major role in the anarchy, so it would have to be re-conquered. This Napoleon Bonaparte understood as few other leaders would realize because Napoleon Bonaparte was a journalist. But he was not precisely a journalist as defined in modern terms. Napoleon did write newspaper articles from time to time. He even started newspapers. His *Bulletin de la Grande Armée* celebrated his military victories and contributed to his legend. He loved reading newspapers. But he was no friend of the free press. Rather, Napoleon was the architect of the comprehensive system of press control that formed the basis for three quarters of a century of French press law. Saying "If I left the bridle off the press, I would not last three months in power," the emperor went to great lengths to insure that the newspapers gave him absolute loyalty and unwavering servility.

This intimidation-based system controlling a hobbled, expensive, tiny circulation set of Paris newspapers faced the new constitutional monarchy in 1815. The Battle of Waterloo ended Napoleon's reign but nurtured a Napoleonic legend that would haunt the press nearly four decades later.

1815–1830: The Press of the Restoration

A country exhausted by revolution and war yearned for the supposedly peaceful age before 1789. The old Bourbon dynasty returned in the person of Louis XVIII, in exile since 1791. This Restoration government seemed like the *ancien regime*, but it was not quite so. In 1815 royal power was limited by a charter that included an elected parliament. Those doing the electing, males above thirty who paid relatively high taxes, were likely to support a conservative monarchy, but they represented only one percent of possible voters, about 100,000 out of a country of 30 million.

This group, however, read the newspapers. And from this group came the parliament that met 5 July 1815 to consider the monarchy's plan for the press. *Le Journal des Débats*, born in 1789, campaigned for a totally free press. Not a chance. The monarchy pulled out nearly every reason it could think of to harness French journalism. Even some in a conservative parliament questioned such severity. Benjamin Constant, author and journalist, warned that, with tight control, the government in effect would be responsible for everything appearing in the newspapers, exaggerating the importance of the press in society. But no arguments could move a monarchy that had seen the danger of a free press during the century just ended. Restoration press law set up three kinds of newspaper restraints, financial, administrative and legal. Most of these restrictions remained part of the government's anti-journalism arsenal until 1881.

Financial controls made it harder for a newspaper to publish by forcing owners and editors to draw on large financial reserves. French law interpreted this in three ways.

1. Postal fees. Newspapers had to use the government-owned postal service for subscriptions. Since in 1815 no newspaper was sold on the street, postal fees could be manipulated at government whim to punish the press.

2. The tax stamp. Borrowing from Napoleonic France, which had pirated this policy from Britain, the stamp required publishers to pay a tax on every issue printed. An ink stamp on page one proved compliance. The tax could be raised or lowered capriciously to curb recalcitrant editors by exacting heavy financial burdens. It also discouraged street sales, as no publisher dared risk costly unsold newspapers. Constraining publication also assured authorities that stray newspapers would not become easily accessible: it is hard to read the news if you can't find it. The authorities worried too that legal street sales would encourage "criers," news agents who prompted

sales by screaming "Extra! Extra!" to attract attention. Such a tactic might disrupt placid public opinion and rouse sentiments troubling to the government.

3. The caution system. Dating from 1819, the system obligated publishers to deposit a sum of money with the government to assure pleasing behavior. The deposit was held until the newspaper quit publishing. Violations resulted in fines drawn from the deposit. An offending newspaper would immediately have to replace the money, thereby costing its publisher double the amount. Repeated government raids on a newspaper's caution account could eliminate a publisher with even the deepest pockets.

Administrative controls bullied journalists by censorship or threat.

1. Censorship. The Restoration government relied on a team of censors, appearing as part of each newspaper's staff, "to assure perfect conformity with the demands of the law, public interest, and respect for the sovereign." Not subject to this rule were newspapers of religious authorities, in foreign languages, of judicial and parliamentary minutes, and exclusively on literature and theatre. Journalists detested the censor, and the job disappeared in 1828. Two years after, an attempt to return to the blue pencils brought the government down.

2. Warnings, the system of *avertissement*. A warning following publication of an offensive item effectively made newspapers self-censors. The efficiency of this control was not appreciated, however, until the Second Empire in the 1850s.

3. Permission to publish. The crown also relied on one of the oldest methods of press restriction, the license. Journalists intending to start a newspaper were required to state their intention to the French interior ministry. The office would investigate a publisher's background, and if acceptable, issue permission. Permission could be revoked at any time, and publishers were required to reapply at regular intervals. The system extended to independent printers, who could be put out of business for producing offensive newspapers, and even bookstores for selling them.

Legal controls relied on laws spelling out actions called press offenses. These might include any statements, such as commenting negatively about the king or the Catholic state religion, that the government did not like. The 1815 law described "seditious writing," that is, articles "tending to alarm citizens concerning authority or to disturb their loyalty." This ambiguous press offense existed in one form or another throughout most of the century. Publishers, editors and journalists tried and found guilty faced fines, prison or both. The most significant debates concerning this law centered on court jurisdiction: trial by jury (the "English system") or trial by magistrate. Liberal governments during the century favored the first because juries were often lenient to journalists. Magistrates, as professional judges, could be counted on to hand down harsher sentences.

During the Restoration, some fifteen laws and other official rules refined press controls These followed extensive parliamentary and press debates, as journalism was so important in French politics. Press controls eventually failed. But their application over decades probably more than anything else set the character of French journalism in its political, literary and economic role at the center of society.

At the outset of the Restoration French dailies faced harsh restrictions. The stamp tax was set at 1.5 centimes a copy for Paris dailies, initially for a legitimate reason, to pay reparations to countries that had absorbed the expenses of defeating Napoleon. The tax so pleased authorities that in 1818 it was made permanent. Successive royal governments raised it until the total reached nearly 6 centimes per issue. Circulations dropped as prices rose, assuring that only wealthy, and therefore conservative, "notables" had easy access to news.

Some publishers tried to skirt the law, as it applied only to periodicals. Constant and François-Réné de Chateaubriand were among many who tried producing "semi-periodicals" without fixed dates. One issue might be dated Friday. The next might be dated the previous Tuesday. Titles might change to elude authorities. *Le Constitutionnel*, one of the era's most important liberal dailies, changed names several times.

Le Constitutionnel's circulation, at only 3,000 in 1816, and only 23,000 by 1831, might seem small. Other important Paris dailies printed even fewer papers: *Le Journal des Débats*, 12,600 and *Quotidienne*, 6,500. The numbers are misleading. In an era when newspapers were rare and expensive, newspapers had no need for headlines or pictures to attract an audience. Each issue was read cover to cover by many people who subscribed to reading salons or clubs, or read in cafés, all of which the police kept under careful surveillance. In Paris and other major cities, purveyors offered people interested in the news a chance to see the day's papers by subscribing to a reading room at a

Opposite: *Journal des débats*, **22 August 1817. Its conservative approach and restrained content established it as one of France's most important dailies early in the nineteenth century. Note the tax stamp in the upper right corner.**

VENDREDI 22 AOUT 1817.

JOURNAL DES DÉBATS
POLITIQUES ET LITTÉRAIRES.

NOUVELLES ÉTRANGÈRES.
ALLEMAGNE.
Berlin (Prusse), 12 août.

D'après un ordre du Roi, adressé au ministre de la guerre, les régimens de *landwehr* recevront une autre dénomination, et seront réunis aux régimens d'infanterie de ligne cantonnés dans leur arrondissement. Les régimens de landwehr seront, à l'avenir, divisés d'après les dépôtations de régime, et porteront le nom du chef lieu de la province, et non celui de la province comme auparavant : ils recevront les numéros qu'ils doivent porter, lorsque deux d'entr'eux seront mis ensemble en campagne. Ainsi, par exemple, les deux régimens de landwehr qui ont été adjoints jusqu'à présent au premier régiment d'infanterie de ligne de la Prusse orientale, et ont porté le nom de premier et deuxième régiment de landwehr de cette province, porteront à l'avenir le nom de premier et deuxième régiment de landwehr de Gumbinen, et auront ensemble le numéro premier aussitôt qu'ils se trouveront en même temps à la guerre. Il y aura en tout trente-quatre numéros, chaque numéro comprenant deux régimens actuels de la landwehr.

Wisbade (Principauté de Nassau), 15 août.

Voici la décision qui a été rendue le 9 de ce mois par le synode général, convoqué pour la réunion des Églises luthérienne et réformée dans la principauté de Nassau.

1°. Les communions réunies auront le nom d'*Église évangélique chrétienne*.

2°. La surveillance générale sur tout le clergé se partagera entre les deux surintendans, d'après une ligne géographique, et sera ensuite réunie dans la personne de celui des deux qui survivra à l'autre.

3°. Les districts d'inspection seront, etc.

4°. Dans les lieux où les deux confessions sont mêlées, les biens respectifs des deux églises formeront une seule et même caisse, et resteront à l'église pour les frais du culte.

5°. Le bien central des deux églises sera réuni en un seul fonds, et servira à faire face au paiement des bourses et aux frais d'organisation du séminaire de Herborn pour les candidats en théologie.

6°. Dans les endroits où il y aura deux pasteurs de différente confession, ils y resteront provisoirement et distribueront la communion ensemble au même autel.

7°. On adopte provisoirement la liturgie palatine. Dans la distribution de la communion, on se servira régulièrement d'une grande hostie faite exprès pour cet usage, et l'on rompra en plusieurs parties. Ce mode sera suivi par tous les communians, qui seront confirmés à l'avenir. Les personnes plus âgées auxquelles il ne conviendrait pas, pourront recevoir la communion à leur manière accoutumée; mais en particulier, et après avoir exposé leurs raisons à leur pasteur.

Cette décision générale a été envoyée au duc régnant, et nous attendons incessamment sa sanction.

PAYS-BAS-UNIS.
Aix-la-Chapelle, 14 août.

Hier, à dix heures du matin, S. A. R. le prince héréditaire de Prusse, accompagné du président de la régence, se rendit à la salle d'audience de la Cour d'assises, où il assista, depuis le commencement jusqu'à la fin, à une séance de trois heures, qui a dû lui donner une idée de la forme de procédure usitée jusqu'à présent, et qui, dit-on, sera conservée. La cause qui se plaidait était relative au crime d'infanticide; mais la personne qui en étoit accusée a été acquittée d'après la déclaration du jury.

GRANDE-BRETAGNE.
Londres, 17 août.

Les personnes qui croient à un Congrès à Carlsbad disent que les négociations commenceront sous peu; que M. Lamb traitera au nom de l'Angleterre, le comte Capo-d'Istria pour la Russie, le prince de Hardenberg pour la Prusse, le prince de Metternich pour l'Autriche, et le comte de Caraman pour la France. M. de Krusemark, ministre de Prusse à la cour de Vienne, remplaceroit M. le prince de Hardenberg, dans le cas où ce dernier ministre suivroit le Roi de Prusse dans les provinces du Rhin.
(*The Times.*)

Un journal du matin a imprimé hier une lettre d'un de ses correspondans à Paris qui entre dans de grands détails sur les négociations entre la Russie et l'Espagne, et sur le prétendu congrès de Carlsbad, où il prétend que M. Lamb assiste pour l'Angleterre. Nous croyons pouvoir assurer que M. Lamb n'a pas été nommé en cette qualité, et nous regardons les nouvelles parisiennes comme la répétition de celles qu'un a fait courir dans quelques journaux de Londres. (*The Courier.*)

Des lettres de la Havane disent que, pendant la première semaine de juin, on a importé dans ce port six mille six cents esclaves nègres. (*The Weekly Intelligence.*)

FRANCE.
PARIS, 21 août.

FÊTE DE LA SAINT-LOUIS.
RÉJOUISSANCES PUBLIQUES.

Programme. — Le lundi 25 août 1817, jour de la Saint-Louis, dans l'après-midi, il sera fait, dans l'avenue des Champs-Elysées, des distributions gratuites de vin et de comestibles. Les chevalets, fontaines de vin et buffets, au nombre de quarante-huit, seront établis des deux côtés de l'avenue, depuis la place Louis XV jusqu'au lieu dit l'*Étoile*. Les fontaines de vin couleront à trois heures précises; la distribution des comestibles commencera aussi à la même heure.

Il sera établi, dans les deux carrés des Champs-Elysées, les jeux, spectacles, récréations et divertissemens publics, dont le détail suit; savoir:

Grand carré. — Huit orchestres de danse, d'harmonie et de chant; quatre mâts de cocagne, avec cinq doubles prix à chacun; deux théâtres de danseurs de corde, voltigeurs et sauteurs; un théâtre de vaudevilles, parades et scènes burlesques; exercices d'équitation, par les écuyers Franchoni et leur troupe (le cerf, le cheval gastronome, etc.) Feu d'artifice, etc.

Carré Marigny. — Quatre orchestres de danse, d'harmonie et de chant; un théâtre de danseurs et sauteurs de corde; un théâtre pour un faiseur de tours, un bateleur et un grimacier.

Des chanteurs placés sur les théâtres et sur les orchestres des deux carrés, chanteront et distribueront des couplets analogues à la circonstance.

Ces différens jeux, spectacles et divertissemens commenceront à deux heures, et dureront sans interruption jusqu'à onze heures du soir, après le départ du feu d'artifice.

Toute l'avenue des Champs-Elysées, les deux carrés et les quinconces seront illuminés.

Il y aura également illumination générale de l'Hôtel-de-Ville, des mairies, du Palais de Justice, des halles et marchés, des fontaines et châteaux-d'eau, et de tous les autres édifices publics de la ville de Paris.

La veille, dimanche 24, il y aura spectacle *gratis* à tous les théâtres.

Avant la messe, le Roi a reçu la visite de Mme la duchesse douairière d'Orléans. S. A. S. a ensuite fait sa cour à MONSIEUR, et à MADAME, duchesse d'Angoulême.

Après la messe, un camerier de S. S., sous le titre d'*Ablegas*, chargé d'apporter la barrette destinée à M. le cardinal grand-aumônier, a eu l'honneur de présenter ses lettres de créance à S. M., qui demain entendra la messe au bas de la chapelle, pour remettre la barrette à S. Em. avec les cérémonies accoutumées.

Le Roi est sorti à trois heures et demie, et a dirigé sa promenade sur Vincennes.

Ce soir, LL. AA. RR. Mgr le duc d'Angoulême et Mgr le duc de Berry sont arrivés de leur voyage de Compiègne.

— Samedi prochain, à midi, le Roi passera au Champ-de-Mars une revue générale des divers corps de la garde royale et des douze légions de la garde nationale de Paris.

— Il paroît que la plupart des nouvelles nominations aux archevêchés et évêchés, sont maintenant connues. En voici la liste, telle du moins qu'elle circule dans le public; c'est assez dire que nous n'en garantissons point la parfaite exactitude.

ARCHEVÊQUES.

Paris, S. Em. le cardinal de Talleyrand, grand-aumônier de France, ancien archevêque de Reims; M. l'abbé de Quélen, suffragant. — *Lyon*, M. de Bernis, ancien archevêque d'Albi. — *Sens*, M. de la Fare, ancien évêque de Nancy. — *Tours*, M. Duchilleau. — *Bourges*, M. de Latour. — *Auch*, M. de Chabot. — *Narbonne*, M. de Laporte. — *Toulouse*, M. de Boret. — *Arles*, M. Beausset, évêque actuel de Soissons. — *Strasbourg*, M. de Croy. — *Vienne*, M. Boulogne, évêque de Troyes. — *Besançon*, M. de Pressigny, ancien évêque de Saint-Malo. — *Aix*, M. de Beausset, ancien évêque de Vannes. — *Albi*, M. Brault. — *Reims*, M. de Coucy, ancien évêque de la Rochelle.

ÉVÊQUES.

Auxerre, M. Mannay. — *Blois*, M. l'abbé de Bombelles, premier aumônier de Mme la duchesse de Berry. (On dit qu'il passe à l'évêché d'Amiens, vacant par la mort récente de M. de Mandolx.) — *Castres*, M. de Thiolas. — *Chartres*, M. de Latil, évêque d'Amyclée, 1er aumônier de Monsieur. — *Orléans*, M. de Vareucourt. — *Langres*, S. Em. le cardinal de la Luzerne, ancien évêque de Langres. — *Châlons-sur*-

cost considerably less than the price of a newspaper subscription, 80 francs a year by the end of the Restoration. To put this number in perspective, the average Frenchman would have to work 421 hours to afford one year's subscription, payable in advance.

By 1830 1,350 reading rooms in France offered people who could read the opportunity to follow the Paris press. It was often necessary to make an appointment to see a favored newspaper; commonly 20–30 readers awaited each subscription. Besides clubs and cafés, dealers bought dailies from subscribers to resell the next day at a discount. Reading day-old dailies was not unusual in France when opinion and commentary counted more than modern event-driven journalism.

Reading a newspaper was a public event in France at this time as those frequenting cafés and reading rooms would discuss what they had read. Large cities such as Lyon even offered open-air reading kiosks. For the more than half the French who were illiterate until the free education law of 1833 created a generally educated public, other people read the news aloud. In an era before scientific surveys, ascertaining how newspapers influenced their readers is difficult. But considering how avidly journals were perused, their influence was apparently great indeed.

Excluded from these opportunities were women and children. The "family" newspaper of today did not exist, and politics was considered the purview of men. Women did not enter reading rooms or cafés, could not vote, and allegedly were not interested in politics. During the "July Monarchy" after 1830, periodicals for women and children developed. These two groups were not considered appropriate consumers of general-interest dailies until the dawn of the twentieth century.

Repeated debates in a parliament preoccupied with issues of the press led in 1819 to laws designed to reduce government power over journalism. The *lois de serre* removed the detested on-site censors. Government permission to publish was suspended. A newspaper publisher still had to declare his intent to publish, but officials could not deny him permission. In this less repressive atmosphere, newspapers proliferated, a familiar response throughout the century to any temporary lifting of restrictions. But along with fewer controls came one new and ominous idea, the caution deposit. The amount was set at 200,000 francs, enormous for the time. It became so costly to establish a newspaper that individuals could not hope to publish without support of a rich patron or without selling shares of stock.

The 1819 flourish of press freedom turned out to be brief, only a few months. Assassination of the duc de Berry, the king's nephew, provoked a nervous government to restore all the rules. Liberalism was blamed; "the dagger that killed the duc de Berry was a liberal idea," declared monarchist Chateaubriand. Press crimes (*délits*), that is, things a journalist could not say without fear of fine and imprisonment, included such vagaries as "bad faith."

Two years later the government calmed down and again lightened press controls, including censorship. Liberal governments became more tolerant of growing criticism from the left, even the anti-monarchy republican left. That was too much for Charles X, the conservative king who had replaced Louis XVIII in 1824. In August 1829 he brought in his old ultra-reactionary friend, Jules de Polignac, to counter this trend. The choice was a fatal error. Polignac targeted the press, the press targeted Polignac. The press won.

Revolution over Press Freedom

On 3 January 1830 a new daily appeared in Paris, *Le National*. Its founders were Armand Carrel from north France and Adolphe Thiers from south France. Both were squarely opposed to the Bourbon monarchy, now represented by the ultra-conservative Polignac government. Thiers, later to become one of the century's most important politicians, joined Carrel, one of the country's brilliant editors, and François Mignet to oppose the ultra-conservatives. On 26 July 1830 the government announced the resumption of the regulations of 1815, the censorship, the authorization requirement, the repressive list of press offenses. "A thick cloud put up by the newspapers obscures the truth and intercepts in several ways the light between the government and its people," declared a decree published in the government-controlled *Le Moniteur*. The press had become "an instrument of disorder and sedition."

Thiers and Carrel would prove that the government was right. Calling together journalists from sympathetic dailies around Paris, the directors of *Le National* declared that the authorities had issued illegal decrees to muzzle the press. Illegal decrees did not have to be obeyed. Forty-four Paris journalists representing twenty-two newspapers met in the *National* office to sign Thiers' declaration stating they would not obey the law. The next day the declaration was published in four newspapers, including *Le National* and *Le Temps*. The police raided the offices of *Le National* and *Le Temps*, arresting journalists and confiscating equipment. Parisians outraged at the affront against the press besieged the offices. In the ensuing riots students and workers left their posts to man the barricades in bloody clashes with authorities. The clashes became a revolution, and the journalists had taken the lead. Charles X fled to England, bringing the Bourbon monarchy to an end, and with it France's last nostalgic link to the *ancien régime*. But the country had still not had enough of kings.

Profiting from the Press

French journalists had wrestled with the ambiguous questions of profit since the days of Louis XIV. Newspapers before the Revolution separated respectable journalism from advertising. Advertising was acceptable for provincial newspapers but not for the important Paris journals that animated political opinion throughout the country. Paris merchants and other residents who wished to advertise could rely on gazettes devoted solely to small announcements, the shoppers of the day. Subscriptions, the only revenue source, covered the cost of the publication; advertisers paid nothing. At the turn of the nineteenth century, however, French publishers decided to borrow Britain's custom of charging advertisers. But only bookstores, as merchants of intellectual products, could advertise in the prestige press of Paris.

The separation of journalism from the supposed taint of advertising worked well as long as the high price for subscriptions guaranteed stable income. Because only the rich could afford these subscriptions, circulations were small, but expenses too were not high in the pre-industrial artisan press. Evidence indicates that strict government control of the press did not necessarily mean less profit. A successful newspaper, such as *Le Constitutionnel*, offered excellent returns to its investors despite numerous fines and press trials. Shares of stock issued by the newspaper at its 1817 founding, at 3,000 francs each, sold at 27,000 to 32,000 francs each ten years later. Of the newly emerging joint stock companies during this early period of modern capitalism in France, one-third published newspapers.

But profit became harder to squeeze out of subscription-based Paris journalism even before industrialization demanded expensive mechanization of newspaper offices. Complications sprang from publishers trying to comply with increasingly onerous government regulation. Increasing taxes, postal fees, caution deposits, fines and tax stamps squeezed solvency. To tighten control over private financial support for a newspaper, the government decreed that names of all stockholders or others with a financial stake in a newspaper must be made public, and so legally responsible, and that there could be no more than five stockholders. The caution deposit requirement stood at 200,000 francs. Newspapers were starting to cost even wealthy subscribers about as much as they were willing to pay.

The increases in these exactions forced many publishers to open their pages to expanded publicity. On 1 January 1828 the government raised postal fees for newspapers to two and one-half times the previous level. Only months before the stamp tax had reached an onerous 10 centimes per issue. Taxes and postal fees now totaled half the cost of publishing a newspaper. Such fees were less burdensome for conservative and monarchist newspapers, which enjoyed secret government subsidies. But they hit the liberal press hard, as intended. An obvious solution was to swallow pride and turn to the advertising that the Anglo-Saxon press had accepted decades before. The government actually encouraged Paris newspapers to add advertising, suggesting they could afford new taxes by emulating the British press in reserving space for "public utility." Although they never officially said so, ministers likely hoped this new publicity would also serve to diminish the newspapers' influence, since more advertising would leave less space for political polemic.

In 1825 *Le Constitutionnel* devoted 0.7 percent of its space to advertising, and *Le Journal des Débats,* 0 percent. In 1828 the newspapers announced that henceforth they would offer readers the public utility of advertising. Twenty years later advertising took between 17 and 18 percent of space in both newspapers. The era of a French press free of the perhaps insalubrious effects of mercantilist capitalism had come to an end. But French reader distrust of advertising lingered, leading to serious consequences decades later.

1830–48: The Press of the July Monarchy

The government of Charles X had tried to tame the press through a cascade of censorship and control. It failed. But the monarchy's collapse surprised even those who provoked it. Journalists had claimed in their July declaration that their revolt was only for their own ends. It was up to the rest of the French to determine "to what length they will go in their own resistance." They went all the way to revolution. Without today's statistical methods, determining how people responded to their newspapers in 1830 is uncertain. But one thing is clear about Paris that summer: people were willing to fight and die for a free press.

Succeeding governments did not learn that lesson, or perhaps could not bring themselves to permit open discussion of official policy. Conservative governments would try the same strategies again and again, laws and punishments designed to constrain this instrument of power, or to bend it to echo the voice of leaders. See-saw battles between press and authority continued to shape French political ideology for the rest of the century. The 1830 revolution also offers strong evidence that the deceptively small circulations of newspapers during this period belied their influence. Paris dailies together printed only 50,000 copies. What is more, probably half this circulation represented papers supporting the government. Yet journalists could mobilize a revolution. One principle of French journalism throughout the nineteenth century and into the twentieth was that high circulations were not necessary for significant clout.

News Was Pointless

During the first half of the century, journalists' impact can be tied to their unusual role in politically feverish France. Without true political parties until the early twentieth century, organized political power concentrated, by way of newspapers, in the hands of notables, those few men enfranchised. The *journaux d'opinion*, organs of commentary and debate, dominated journalism to mid-century because the notables made their political stands for parliamentary elections in this press. A newspaper favoring a particular slant, conservative, center, or liberal, would construct a platform associated with notables of that viewpoint. After candidates accepted this platform, newspapers attempted to persuade voters to endorse it. The tradition effectively meant that newspapers, not political parties, organized election campaigns.

The system in France helps to explain the long dominance of a press based on opinion and the seemingly obsessive preoccupation of successive governments to harness this commentary. Gathering news, defined as a simple compilation of the day's events, was for most Paris journalists a pointless effort. It could wield no power to sway governments or voters. It could not educate or influence the elite who read the papers. Moreover, Paris papers circulated slowly around the country. It took eighteen hours to reach the northern port city of Le Havre, eighty, the southern city of Toulouse, and even longer to reach smaller towns not well served by the post. Because railroads did not reduce that time until the 1850s, "news" would be old.

Repeated government attempts to control the press frequently exempted so-called "non-political newspapers." If a journal contained no politics, it did not have to pay the stamp tax or caution deposit or suffer surveillance and fines. Consequently, many editors started chronicles for literary criticism, theatre reviews or notes on Paris society. These periodicals interested an elite audience who had the money and time for high culture, particularly in Paris. The sophisticated reader valued writing as much for style and sparkle as for content. But this press thrived through the century on more than wit and literary criticism. Controversies over literary trends and social challenges inevitably spilled into politics. A non-political paper could include political commentary between the lines, often by relating a story from the past that was significant for the present. Metaphors, allusions, insinuations marbled their way through literary reviews, their authors writing carefully, precisely, stepping just up to the line, but not over it. Sometimes they tripped, and paid the fine. But the skillful writing in non-political newspapers in France created respect for the quality of the individual writer in a newspaper, a literary figure as opposed to an anonymous reporter of simple facts. Even today the French appreciate literary quality in newspapers, an ironic legacy of government attempts to control journalism.

The men who formed the provisional government of 1830 came from the politically powerful press of the era, and like so many French journalists, many of them joined the new government. Adolphe Thiers became interior minister and, in a succession of governmental roles, never looked back to the journalism that launched his career. The press had long been a springboard for politics. For the many provincial professors or lawyers who dreamed of a political career, the best entry was to become a journalist, at least part time.

But the journalists' provisional government faced a problem during the "Three glorious days" of July: it produced no obvious leader to form a new regime. To the disappointment of those who hoped to establish a republic, the revolution took a conservative turn. Louis Philippe was awarded the crown of the "July Monarchy," 1830–48. This choice was not a Bourbon, but a cousin from the Orleanist branch of the royal family, a branch reputedly more liberal. The "citizen king" established a constitutional monarchy. He brought back the revolutionary tricolor flag of blue, white and red. His government broadened the electorate, extending suffrage to all men over twenty-five who paid somewhat lower taxes than earlier voters. The pool of notables went from 100,000 to 250,000. Still barely more than 2 percent of potential voters, the newly enfranchised came from a more liberal bourgeois background that increasingly showed greater sympathy for democratic ideals.

At the outset, the provisional government of the journalists threw out all the restrictive press legislation. Again the result was a burgeoning of new titles, in Paris and the provinces. Amnesty was granted to journalists imprisoned or charged. Fees and taxes were reduced. Censorship was abolished. After the Polignac government's mistake of reconsidering censorship, no succeeding French government before World War I would dare reimpose it save for short periods under martial law. Outside the capital the press had been negligible, but in eighteen months twenty-six new titles appeared. Some of these would not outlast later government crackdowns. For the moment Louis Philippe faced other challenges. The former Bourbon monarchy came from the line of Louis XIV. The Orleanist king did not. Was he a legitimate king? The "legitimist" opposition said no, and their royalist press immediately began disseminating anti-government propaganda. The king was also squeezed from the left; it responded to the defeat of republicanism with invective of its own, some of it violent, much of it highly disrespectful of the crown. Moreover, the government faced a new journalistic threat that grew from infancy in 1829 to reach its golden age in the next few decades — the satirical caricature.

The Power of a Sketch

Small engravings had long been part of newspapers. But engravings took time, were expensive, and so they tended to be used over and over. The development of lithography made larger illustrations technically feasible but still difficult. Publishing a weekly illustrated newspaper required two armies, one of artists and a second of engravers, who still often worked in woodcuts. Studios were open twenty-four hours a day to keep up with the insatiable demand for engravings that show unmatched mastery of detail and technical execution. Only Paris had the resources to produce illustrated newspapers. The weekly *L'Illustration*, established in 1843, became famous along with *La Caricature* and *Le Charivari* for presenting brilliantly executed wood engravings and lithographs. Among their artists were André Gill and Honoré Daumier, still respected today. Their witty and irreverent takes on French society amused and sometimes shocked. The king and his minions were especially tempting targets.

This new force in France's political *presse d'opinion* finally was the last straw for Louis Philippe. When the king appeared drawn as a pear, the French

Opposite: Le Charivari, **14 October 1848. One of Paris' most famous satirical weeklies, this publication was particularly known for its fine engravings by well-known artists.**

Traitorous Collaboration (Collins)

SAMEDI 14 OCTOBRE 1848. DIX-SEPTIÈME ANNÉE.—N° 288.

LE CHARIVARI.

ASSEMBLÉE NATIONALE.
Séance du 13 octobre.

Aucun incident remarquable n'a signalé la séance d'aujourd'hui; il n'a même pas été prononcé de discours. Est-ce que l'éloquence parlementaire aurait donné sa démission.

La discussion n'était aujourd'hui qu'un prétexte pour ne rien écouter et pour entendre moins de choses encore.

Chaque fois qu'un orateur paraissait à la tribune, l'assemblée le regardait d'un air qui voulait dire :
— Eh bien , nous apportez-vous le nouveau ministère ? — Mais comme l'orateur proposait avec naïveté un amendement nouveau, l'assemblée honteuse d'avoir cédé à un premier mouvement, reprenait avec empressement le cours de ses occupations particulières.

Il a été décidé que le vice-président de la République ne pourrait être ni parent, ni allié du président jusqu'au sixième degré inclusivement, mesure prudente à laquelle il faut applaudir ; nous demanderons seulement à l'assemblée, en vertu de quel principe elle a refusé une allocation annuelle au vice-président.

Pourquoi a-t-on accordé une indemnité de 25 francs par jour aux représentans, si ce n'est pour rendre accessible à tout le monde la représentation nationale qui était autrefois le privilège des grands censitaires ? En réduisant le vice-président à ses propres ressources, vous vous mettez dans l'impossibilité d'élever à ce poste nouveau un homme qui n'aurait que la capacité nécessaire et pas de fortune. Il n'est donc rien de moins démocratique que ce vote de l'assemblée qui ne s'est guère piqué de logique en cette occasion.

Les représentans reçoivent une indemnité afin qu'aucune préoccupation matérielle ne vienne distraire une partie du temps qu'ils doivent au pays. Est-ce que ce n'est pas aussi des affaires du pays que s'occuperait le vice-président ? L'assemblée entend peut-être qu'il vive, comme les anciens prophètes, dans une caverne où un corbeau lui apporterai un petit pain chaque jour.

Vers quatre heures, l'assemblée, sur la demande du général Cavaignac, a décidé qu'elle nommerait une commission pour entendre un rapport du gouvernement relatif au maintien de l'état de siège. Aucune communication officielle n'est venue du reste confirmer les bruits qui courent au sujet d'une modification dans le cabinet.

Au moment où le général Cavaignac répondait à des interpellateurs qui lui demandaient les noms des nouveaux ministres, disait : « Il n'y a point d'autre gouvernement que celui que vous connaissez », on a vu M. Sénart faire un mouvement sur son banc où il a été retenu presque de force par son voisin. M. Sénart voulait simplement monter à la tribune et donner à l'assemblée communication de la lettre du général Cavaignac par laquelle il a appris, hier soir, qu'il avait cessé d'être ministre ce matin.

On s'est beaucoup occupé, depuis hier, des nouvelles arrivées de Vienne. La lutte sanglante dont la capitale de l'Autriche a été le théâtre a laissé la victoire aux démocrates. L'empereur a publié un manifeste parfaitement ridicule qui ne paraît pas de nature à exercer beaucoup d'action sur les événemens à venir. La révolution allemande sera, nous l'espérons, le signal de l'affranchissement de l'Italie.

BONNAL MORDU.

— Vous savez la nouvelle ?
— Dites.
— M. de Girardin vient de mordre l'ami Bonnal.
— Je ne suis étonné que d'une chose, c'est qu'il n'ait pas mordu l'ami Gilles. Il le mordra, soyez-en sûr. Mais que dit Bonnal de sa morsure ?
— Bonnal est très vexé, mais il pardonne. Il comprend et excuse les fureurs de son ami qu'il attribue aux injustices de l'opinion. C'est aux électeurs de Paris qu'il en veut d'avoir été mordu, c'est contre eux qu'il garde une dent ; du reste Girardin lui a envoyé son médecin, attention qui a touché Bonnal jusqu'aux larmes.
— Le pauvre diable ! Sachez pourtant bien une chose, c'est qu'avant peu vous entendrez dire qu'il a été mordu de nouveau ; il en sera ainsi tous les huit jours. Ce malheureux Bonnal traînera une vie malheureuse, de morsure en morsure, à moins qu'il ne prenne le parti de rompre avec Girardin, mais il n'en aura pas la force, parce que Girardin lui enverra chaque soir son médecin. Ceci vous prouve que l'on a toujours tort de s'inféoder à un homme. Maintenant voulez-vous savoir d'où vient la fureur de M. de Girardin ?
— Parlez.
— Elle vient de ce qu'il se sent à la fin de sa carrière, justement à l'âge où les hommes de quelque valeur sont dans le plein exercice de leur force, et si M. de Girardin est à bout, c'est qu'il a toujours été l'agent de sa personnalité égoïste et jamais l'homme d'une idée. Prenez-le à son début. Il songe d'abord à faire sa fortune ; il y songe à vingt ans, à l'âge où M. de Châteaubriand promenait ses rêves inspirés dans les solitudes du Nouveau-Monde, où Lamartine écrivait ses *Méditations*, au bruit harmonieux de la mer de Naples, où Byron rêvait l'affranchissement de la Grèce, à cet âge que cherchait M. de Girardin ? Il rêvait au moyen d'affranchir la chaussure de ses concitoyens de la crotte des rues ; il inventait le paracrotte !

Si vous l'avez oublié, quelques actionnaires s'en souviennent encore. Que resta-t-il de ce mouvement subit imprimé à l'industrie par M. de Girardin ? Rien que des souvenirs d'agiotage. La carrière de M. de Girardin, comme homme d'affaires, était terminée. Il était devenu, toute proportion gardée, aussi impossible que Law après la chûte des actions du Mississipi.

C'est alors qu'il se tourna vers la politique. Quelle idée retrouvait dans la *Presse* ? aucune. C'était le journal des intrigues parlementaires. La République surprit M. de Girardin au moment où il faisait une guerre à outrance au ministère et à la cour qui le jouaient depuis dix ans. Cette opposition violente, dans un temps où la France entière était dans l'opposition, lui avait valu une sorte de popularité qu'il eut un moment l'espoir d'exploiter avec la République. C'est alors qu'il répétait chaque matin : Confiance ! une idée nouvelle par jour ! c'est-à-dire : Encore un peu et je serai ministre ! Il voyait les hommes s'user rapidement, il avait eu 75 mille voix aux élections de la Seine, il croyait toucher à son but. Tout à coup l'insurrection de juin éclate ; un homme nouveau, le général Cavaignac, est porté aux affaires et M. de Girardin, qui se pose en victime du despotisme militaire, perd cinquante mille voix aux élections nouvelle.

Après cela on peut mordre Bonnal.

Il y a des gens qui ont la bonté de croire que M. de Girardin fait aujourd'hui la guerre à la République, dans l'intérêt d'une dynastie quelconque, c'est lui faire trop d'honneur. M. de Girardin pour arriver

The Rise of Western Journalism, 1815–1914

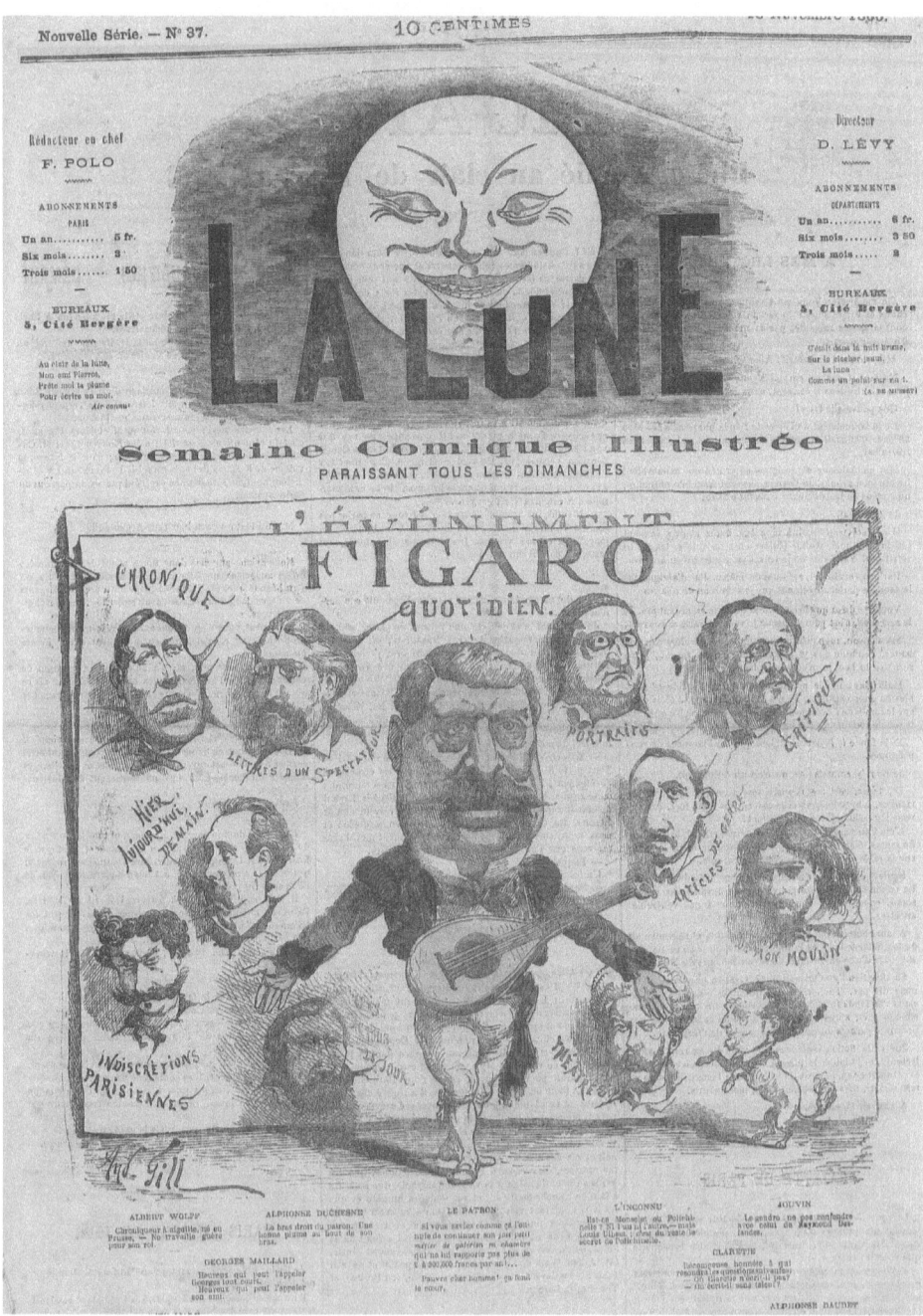

word for dope or dummy, the government cracked down in a return to harsh press control laws. In three years 150 prison sentences were handed down to the press, and thousands in fines. The pro-republican *Le Tribune* alone paid for its anti-government polemic with 114 trials and 150,000 francs in fines. An 1835 assassination attempt on Louis Philippe, blamed on press provocation, put a permanent end to the short free-press era of the July Monarchy.

Despite the strictures, the July Monarchy could not constrain the press from introducing some of the most important changes in its history. The 1830s in many western nations saw the first stirrings of true "mass media." In France the birth of journalism as industrial merchandise and the senescence of journalism as artisan handcraft are reflected in the stories of two entrepreneurs, Charles Havas and Emile de Girardin.

A News Bureau and Industrial Journalism

In 1832 Havas, then fifty and a failed banker, decided to restart his life by taking advantage of his gift for languages. He established a service translating the foreign press for French newspapers. In an era when opinion made news, and facts were irrelevant, no Paris daily kept close tabs on developments elsewhere. Basic information was not worth the cost of collecting to a press preoccupied with the critiques and commentary that formed its base of power. Havas filled this gap. He soon moved from merely translating press clippings to collecting his own foreign news. In 1835 he opened the world's first international news agency. It gathered news mailed by correspondents from important European capitals to Paris. Five years later Havas tried to speed the process by abandoning the post office for a team of carrier pigeons stationed in London and Brussels. It may seem quaint and almost laughable today to learn that news agencies employed pigeons, but before telegraphy and the telephone pigeons could be an editor's speedy feathered friend. Pigeons transmitted stock and sports news through the 1890s, when pneumatic tubes became standard. The last tube line was closed in Paris as late as 1984.

Havas was also a pioneer in his decision to offer news without commentary and to support whatever government was in power. He took on

Opposite: This illustration from *La Lune*, 18 November 1866, features the staff of the most important newspaper ever to appear in France, if judged by longevity—*Le Figaro*—established in 1854. The creator of this engraving, André Gill, was one of the nineteenth century's most important artists working in this medium.

associates who left so impressed that they began their own agencies, P.J. Reuter in London and Bernard Wolff in Berlin. The three agreed to divide the costly business of covering the world. The Associated Press (USA) joined the alliance in 1875.

The second entrepreneur, Girardin, is sometimes called the father of modern French journalism because he sired so much of what came to define the French press by the end of the century. But Girardin at heart was not a journalist. He was a businessman. That was the key to another French revolution, this one not political, but journalistic.

In 1836 Girardin jumped into the Paris world of journalism with an idea pioneering for its time. He planned to make the press like any other business whose primary purpose was to make money by selling a manufactured product. In this case the product happened to be a newspaper. Girardin proposed to turn journalism into a metaphorical daily bread loaf. First, he eliminated most of the commentary because, he argued, polemics and opinion skewed to support an ideology were old-fashioned. People did not want preaching but information and diversion. Second, he thought that most readers would not pay the price that political newspapers charged, 80 francs for a subscription, but they might buy at 40 francs.

Girardin planned to cover the half-price issues by relying on advertising. Although advertising had existed in the political press for nearly a decade, no one considered it a true substitute for subscription fees to pay for a newspaper. Girardin believed he could profit because a 40-franc reduction would triple circulation, allowing him to set higher advertising rates based on something new to France, the number of subscribers. Other newspapers were charging advertisers the same fee, no matter how large the circulation. The system favored small circulation political newspapers but poorly served advertisers.

Girardin was not finished with innovation. His cheaper daily, *La Presse*, appeared in 1836 with something new on the "ground floor," that is, bottom of the front page. The first installment of *La Vieille Fille* ("The Old Girl") by an author already famous, Honoré de Balzac, was the first novel serialized in a French newspaper. Girardin explained that this feature would introduce a larger audience to the joys of great literature, but it was as likely designed to entice a larger audience to purchase *La Presse*. Girardin's invention twinned two old formats of French journalism. The *feuilleton*, which really has no good English translation, began in French newspapers as a weekly chronicle on a particular theme, from theatre to science, to complement political opinion. Fiction or tall tales, offered as books or pamphlets, had been part of the fare of itinerant merchants throughout France since the *ancien regime*. Girardin's idea to combine the two became the rage of France. Serialized novels soon proved absolutely necessary to sell any newspaper. Even the sober old *Journal des Débats* succumbed to the frenzy. Every major French author of the century published them. In fact, Alexandre Dumas' *The Three Musketeers* (in *Le Siècle*, 1844) and *The Count of Monte Cristo* (in *Le Journal des Débats*, 1845), two of the world's enduring favorite stories, were originally serialized in French newspapers. Important novels are still dozing in the archives: in March 2005 a researcher discovered a previously unknown Dumas novel published in the pages of *Le Moniteur universel* of 1869. The prolific Balzac published thirty-three novels in thirteen different newspapers during the July Monarchy.

Critics detested what some called "industrial literature." They insisted that newsprint novels corrupted morals, turned people away from politics and towards passivity, and fed emotions instead of intellect. Readers loved the genre, which remained mostly a phenomenon of the French press. Serialized novels also made extra money for a newspaper which later compiled installments into a book, or sold rights to newspapers abroad, particularly in Germany. Successful authors wrote in a style that left audiences breathlessly waiting to see what would happen in the next installment, a technique still used in modern television dramas.

In sum, Girardin had the audacity to publish for profit, not edification. He gave people not what they should read, but what they wanted to read, and he made it cheap enough for more of them to read it. He did not create a true "penny press" in France — that would come later — but his kind of newspaper appealed to the growing middle class of craftsmen and shopkeepers. The end was in sight for the reading rooms, where journalism was a public activity, and for the old-style *journaux d'opinion*.

Duels and Economic Challenges

This new approach upset other editors who knew a threat when they saw one. Girardin faced howls of criticism from the old-line political "press of the notables" that accused him of pandering to low taste, of degrading the dignity of journalism, of unseemly interest in profit at the expense of thoughtful opinion and debate. The vituperation among journalists during this time frequently led to the challenge of a duel, and Girardin fought his share. In 1836, in the Vincennes woods east of Paris, he faced one of Paris' most important editors, Armand Carrel of *Le National*. Pistols. One shot each, fired at the same time. Girardin was wounded in the leg, an injury that troubled him the rest of his life. But 36-year-old Carrel, hit in the stomach, died two days later. The tragic outcome was no deterrent; journalistic dueling persisted throughout the century. Because the court system represented press repression, journalists preferred to settle their differences more directly. The duel likewise had an aura of honor based on the journalist's presumption that he was part of an elite aristocracy of the written word. A duel became a rite of passage for the new ink slinger. Most well-known writers fought a dozen or more. Some newspapers even established as an annex to the newsroom an armory and offered sword and pistol training to their recruits. Between 1885 and 1895, journalists fought 150 duels in Paris. But this code of honor through ritual violence lost its charm following the butchery of World War I.

Girardin pushed his critics into a new era, as many realized that they had to adopt mercantile methods or face ruin. One by one the political press reduced subscription costs, advertising fees, or both. They picked up serialized novels. The one thing they did not do was offer neutral, fact-based news. Paris seemed unready for this kind of content. Readers did not know what to make of the content in *La Presse*, a newspaper that didn't seem to stand for anything. While profit eluded Girardin, a competitor, Armand Dutacq, who established *Le Siècle* about the same time, sold more copies by adopting a clear central-left political slant that appealed to the tastes of the new bourgeoisie. *Le Siècle* reached more than 33,000 subscribers by 1840, while *La Presse* never pushed above 22,000.

But old-line political newspapers were big losers. *Le Constitutionnel*, once the country's most important daily, fell to a circulation of only 3,600 by 1844. It tried to turn around with a serialized novel, *Le Juif Errant*, by Eugène Sue, the era's most successful author of the new genre. That boosted circulation to 25,000, but *Le Constitutionnel* still found prosperity elusive. In that it joined the Paris press generally. Cheaper subscriptions raised circulations, which increased the burden of stamp and postal taxes. These taxes grew to total nearly two-thirds of expenses for a larger circulation daily such as *Le Siècle*. As long as the government kept that vise squeezing earnings, the French press could not flourish.

Girardin chose to launch a press revolution just as France fell into economic recession in the 1840s. Discontent in the newspapers reflected discontent in the streets despite ever harsher repression of the press. The republicans who had revolted in 1830 in hope of seeing democracy planted in Paris had been lying low, but secret republican societies surfaced in cafés or Masonic lodges. The word "socialism" first appeared; its think-tank was Paris.

"Opinion," observed Balzac in 1843, "is made in Paris, and it is made with ink and paper." Five years later, in February 1848, ink and paper would again become the critical factor that led another charge of students and workers to the barricades and an invasion of the parliamentary building. Leftist legislators wanting no repeat of the July Monarchy proclaimed a republic. When the National Guard would not support the crown, Louis-Philippe abdicated. His would be France's last monarchy, although that was not clear for another thirty years.

Again a provisional government was established from the newspaper offices. *Le National*, a key player in the 1830 revolution, this time was joined by a newer republican and pro-socialist daily, *La Réforme*. From their two offices would emerge the wobbly Second Republic. From their journalists would come the Republic's principal ministers.

One of the first moves by these new officials concerned the press. Many laws that bridled this "precious instrument of civilization and liberty" were again swept away. After the stamp tax and caution deposit were suspended, newspapers burst forth with the daffodils that spring. Three hundred new titles appeared in Paris within a few weeks of the February revolution, many sold by now-legal criers working the streets. Everyone had to run a newspaper, or so it seemed. Famous authors and intellectuals jumped in with the rest: Dumas, Pierre Proudhon, George Sand, Victor Hugo and Alphonse Lamartine were among the many literary and political figures who began newspapers. Lamartine actually became head of the provisional government, a rare historical example of a poet-politician. More freedom also came to the people with the declaration of universal male suffrage.

1848–1871: The Press of the Second Republic and Second Empire

Paris journalists once again had formed a new government, an action unthinkable for newspapers in the United States or Great Britain. In France it made sense. Political ideology and platforms emanated from these same Paris newspaper offices, and Paris politics dominated the country. But it seemed clear in 1848 that the men who ran the journals understood journalism first and political power second. They were not able to galvanize the rest of the country behind the government. The prestige of their press led the journalists to an intellectual arrogance that divided them from France beyond the metropolis. Paris, after all, had long determined the way of the land. The role of provincial France was to follow. It was that presumption that cost Paris a bloody civil war less than a quarter century later.

Effervescence thanks to broader liberty crystallized into extremist invective, particularly from the far left. Paris workers' riots of the 1848 "June days" threatened class war against the moderate republicans in power, playing into the hands of law-and-order conservatives. The socialist philosopher Pierre Proudhon ("property is theft") in particular sowed terror in bourgeois living rooms with his violently anti-capitalist workers' newspapers, *Le Représentant du Peuple, Le Peuple* and *Le Voix du Peuple*. General Godefroy Cavaignac, associated with the conservative republican *Le Nationale*, led the army that quelled the riots with bloodshed. After conservatives gained power in subsequent elections, the government hesitantly emulated the United States by creating a new position, "President of the Republic." Republican politicians feared that the position would invite a return to authoritarianism. In December 1848 Cavaignac was defeated in the election for president by a new man with an old name. Louis Napoleon Bonaparte, the famous general's nephew, became president. If there was one thing this second Napoleon hated, it was the press.

Even before Bonaparte's victory, the short period of press freedom finished in a new round of arrests and restoration of the caution deposit. At 24,000 francs this time, it was aimed directly at the far-left workers' gazettes. Papers faded as fast as they had bloomed. Among the protests, that of Félicité de Lamennais is most memorable. The publisher of *Le Peuple Constituant* cried, "You need money, a lot of money, to have the right to free speech. Silence to the poor." Girardin, by now the country's most famous newspaper publisher and a legislator since 1834, was jailed for nearly two weeks by Cavaignac during the June Days, mostly as retaliation for a long-standing press feud between the two journalist-politicians. Victor Hugo, the country's most celebrated author and a close associate of Girardin, made a strong protest in parliament. Even the British ambassador to France, Lord Normanby, declared himself appalled. Cavaignac paid for his fit of pique when *La Presse* supported his opponent during the presidential campaign. Louis Napoleon, the paper declared, was the only candidate who could reconcile the growing separation between the country's social classes in Paris and the provinces.

The accession of Louis Napoleon as president of the infant republic showed the conservative nature of provincial voters, a fairly accurate picture of public opinion now that universal male suffrage pulled influence away from the notables. They retained power, however, as the political face of conservative sentiment. As succeeding parliaments move further right, they twisted the vise on the press. Street sales of newspaper issues, possible in Paris since the 1848 revolution, were restricted, as was colportage, that is, distributing newspapers outside the postal system. The stamp tax returned. In an attempt to hold journalists accountable, a new law required all articles to be signed. The list of press offenses lengthened, and press trials mounted. Journalists found guilty could be sentenced to prison for one month to three years and fined 100 to 4,000 francs.

The government showed fairness in its treatment of all journalists, famous or obscure. Hugo's newspaper, *L'Evénement*, was suspended for a month in 1851. His son Charles was thrown into prison for writing against the death penalty. His brother François-Victor fared little better, forced behind the bleak walls of the medieval Conciergerie prison for nine months. In 1857 the government dragged Gustave Flaubert into court for serializing *Madame Bovary* in *La Revue de Paris*. The charge: immorality.

End of the Republic

Fetters on the press between 1848 and 1851 would prove to be just the beginning. Louis Napoleon's term as president was to finish in 1851, but he was not ready to leave. On 2 December 1851 he staged a *coup d'état*, and exactly a year later commenced the Second Empire. It seemed a logical step as the country had moved more and more toward conservative governments during the short-lived republic, but Napoleon quickly arrested journalists he feared would resist. Some called for a return to the barricades. This time Parisians hesitated, recalling the bloody repressions only three years before. Napoleon was able to argue that his coup was necessary to prevent a revolution of the extreme left. He also used that argument to justify consequent harassment of all republicans, extreme or moderate. One of his favorite targets was the republican press.

The Second Empire mirrored former regimes in its preoccupation with the press, but this time the dictator brooked no opposition whatsoever. In faithful homage to his uncle's formula, Napoleon III immediately closed nearly all the newspapers. None were left in the provinces except those published from government offices. In Paris, of sixty dailies, twenty-four were open, all supporters of the emperor. Many editors of republican tendency fled to Belgium or England. Hugo went initially to Belgium, eventually to the British island of Guernsey, where he critiqued "Napoleon the little" during the entire

Second Empire. The political "press of the notables" alone remained, and even these journalists took great care not to offend a government only too anxious to eliminate as many newspapers as it could get away with, those left useful only for propaganda.

Early in 1852 the emperor set up a comprehensive system of press control that certainly would have made his uncle proud. Paris dailies had shrunk to eleven, all of unquestioned loyalty. Republican journalism did not exist or published from abroad. The license system, requiring publishers to apply for permission, resumed. No reports could appear regarding legislative debates or court trials, particularly trials of newspapers, as these often served as an opportunity to criticize the government. Newspapers were required to print state communiqués, on page one, upper left. Tax and caution deposits increased except for the non-political press.

The government, perhaps fearing riots as in 1830, did not reestablish censorship. Instead, it relied on an innovation, the warning (*avertissement*) system. A newspaper disseminating material deemed offensive would be warned once without penalty. Upon a second warning, the newspaper would be suspended for two months. Upon a third it would be suppressed permanently. The system cleverly forced editors to self-censor. It worked so well that authoritarian Prussia and Russia borrowed the idea for their press repressions. These warnings poured down on editors like hail from a thunderstorm, hitting all sorts of supposed offenses, even turns of phrase. During 1852–53, ninety-three warnings were given. Republican politician Jules Favre concluded, "there is only one journalist, the emperor."

Such a full-scale attack on the press was ridiculously outdated. By the 1850s journalism in western countries had undergone tremendous changes, technological and philosophical. The United States had already adopted the penny press that addressed a new generation of urban workers, and Britain had shed most of its restrictive taxes. Public opinion emerged as a force in France no less than elsewhere, and its public space was the newspaper. While the official face of French journalism looked somber, republicanism continued to bubble in secret societies and workers' groups. The press of the late republic would not stay stoppered.

Le Petit Journal

The emperor wanted to call back time in his authoritarian state, but could not halt sweeping industrial and financial change. But economic stagnation is not always a consequence of dictatorship. Second Empire France coasted on Europe's wave of industrial prosperity that multiplied the numbers of a new class of bourgeoisie, entrepreneurs with money and business instincts. One possibility for investors looking for new venues to industrialize was the press. Girardin had demonstrated nearly twenty years before that a businessman's approach could sustain a newspaper tied to capitalism instead of politics. His techniques had become old-fashioned, however, or so concluded Moïse Millaud. The Paris press entrepreneur, born of a Jewish family from Bordeaux, acquired Girardin's stagnating *La Presse* in 1856. Millaud decided to abandon the venerable title and start over based on a formula that seemed to be working in the United States. His chance came after 1860 when the government decided to encourage capitalist journalism. Loosened press rules, a response to pressure from Paris business and finance people, spawned more newspapers. *Le Temps*, a new daily built on a platform of Alsatian industrials hostile to the empire's financial policies, appeared in 1861. Ancestor of today's *Le Monde*, it was to become the prestige journal of France, most complete, most concerned with foreign affairs, but certainly not with the highest circulation. Millaud launched that one on 1 February 1863: *Le Petit Journal*.

Millaud's goal was strictly business. No costly political polemic would trouble readers of *Le Petit Journal*. This meant Millaud could avoid paying for tax stamps and caution deposits and for expensive political journalists. His newspaper would concern itself strictly with material of interest to a growing population of literate workers who cared more about diversion than about ideology. It would appeal to them because it would be cheap, at 5 centimes the cheapest possible thing you could buy in France. That price was even less than Britain's penny press as the amount converted to a halfpenny. A year's subscription in Paris was only 24 francs. But most people would not subscribe to *Le Petit Journal*. They would buy it by the issue from the wide network of newsstands, especially those at rail stations operated by the Hachette monopoly, and from criers on the streets. Many people would want to sell it because, buying at a reduction, they would need to sell only 100 copies to make the equivalent of the minimum living wage.

Millaud realized as had Girardin that success would rest on large circulation, the economies of scale now possible with advances in printing technology. And the publisher hoped that a large circulation would bring in copious advertising. Girardin had found advertisers in France less than forthcoming, but Millaud planned to rely on the new department stores as a source. He also could reduce the cost of printing by putting more pages on a press at the same time. To do so, he compressed the size of the paper to half that of a regular newspaper. He called his journal *petit*, not only for its price, and for its target audience of workers and "petit bourgeoisie," but because it truly was petite.

If people were tired of long dry political debates, as Millaud surmised, what did the new paper propose to provide? A serialized novel, perhaps two, would surely guarantee success. Theatre productions, musical performances, art exhibits and other spectacles were multiplying in a Paris fast becoming the world's culture capital. A daily chronicle of these events was likely to lure readers. And offering a witty take on Paris society, the arts, science, morality and everyday events, written by someone who could become a sort of proto-media celebrity, might encourage reader loyalty. "Timothée Trimm," pen name of Léo Lespès, was nominated as first chronicler.

A new reading public attracted to a cheap paper would probably want to relax with the kind of shocking, sentimental, outrageous, lurid, but ever-entertaining tidbits they used to hear in the old days from the colporters roaming the countryside. Their news became what the French still call *faits divers*. It translates roughly into English as "news in brief," but that phrase neither really reflects the range of its meaning in French nor is it precisely the "sensationalism" that the Anglo-Saxon press honed to perfection by the close of the century. A *faits divers* section of a French *petit* newspaper could have had as a subhead, "amazing but true stories of life, love, death and tragedy." Most material came from police departments, and the more spectacular the crime, the more it would be played out in pointillist detail over many columns and many days. Murders were best if lots of gore was involved. Accidents would suffice, particularly spectacular fires. Professional *faits diversiers* and their editors tried to write in the style of serialized novels, promising suspense and intrigue. Hardly new to journalism, this approach had already formed a staple in Benjamin Day's *New York Sun* a quarter century before. But to French readers used to a journalism of political commentary and ideological debate, it was a dramatic change, one that soon became the rage of France. By October 1863 *Le Petit Journal* was selling more than 83,000 copies a day, far surpassing the old-style *Le Siècle*, and soon to spawn numerous *petit* imitators. Its biggest hit during the last days of Napoleon III followed a most unfortunate "crime of the century." On 20 September 1869 and subsequent days the bodies of an entire family of eight were found strangled, stabbed and beaten to death, hastily buried in a farmer's field. The execution by decapitation of Jean-Baptiste Troppmann, confessed serial killer, on 19 January 1870 was covered in gruesome detail that even today might make some readers queasy. France apparently loved to be sickened, because 500,000 bought *Le Petit Journal* that day.

Faits divers could but have a nefarious reputation among the more respectable journalists in Paris. Profit won over taste, as most newspapers quickly understood that adding a few *faits* was necessary to compete with the *petits*. Also clear was that most people would no longer pay 15 or 20 centimes for a newspaper when they could get one for 5 and that money, not politics, was beginning to drive French journalism. A publisher was less and less likely to get by issuing a newspaper that addressed an aristocratic elite, or one that only printed what an editor thought people ought to know. Newspapers had to satisfy popular wants. Like the French *baguette*, journalism was becoming a perishable consumer product to be manufactured and marketed.

As the Second Empire became more liberal, the press became more free. On 9 March 1868 the government dropped most of the draconian press constraints and lowered taxes. Relaxed laws germinated into another spring bloom of new titles, 140 in a few weeks. Many died shortly, but by 1870 in Paris every political shade once more had its newspaper. It was 1848 again — almost. Journalists still risked fines and imprisonment in the "journalists' prison," the converted convent of Sainte-Pélagrie in the Latin Quarter. The "liberal empire" after 1860 had hoped to gain support from the political left as it lost support from the right, but leftist journalists back in business offered no backing. Instead, journalism fueled the final collapse of Napoleon III that culminated in war against Prussia, a defeat in an embarrassing rout in which the emperor himself was taken prisoner, and another revolution.

On 4 September 1870 republicans were back in power. The force of the republican press had never been broken, only boxed, and its representatives joined a provisional government fraught with danger. With Paris under siege by the Prussians, the new government fled to Bordeaux. By the time the peace treaty was signed in March 1871, the old journalist Thiers had been named "chief of executive power," but by then he had become an old-fashioned moderate republican. Isolated Paris had been surviving for four months on cats, rats and animals from the zoo. The phoenix of socialism rose from the besieged capital, and its devotees took control of the city. On 18 March they formed the Commune, defended by the national guard. The conservative Thiers government met at Versailles, supported by Marshal Patrice MacMahon's recently defeated but still intact army, to challenge Paris. It would be civil war, short but dreadful.

Whether the press can be blamed for the excesses of the Commune or its loss and its savage punishment at the hands of the army is still in debate. The Communards suppressed dissenting newspapers and harassed, in one case murdered, opposing journalists. The more conservative newspapers, which had followed parliament to Versailles, depicted the Communards as failed journalists become vicious extremists. Perhaps this attitude spurred the fury of troops who in a frenzy executed at least 20,000 Communards — more deaths than during the infamous Terror of the French Revolution. J.B. Millière, editor of *La Commune*, was executed at the Pantheon crying "Vive l'humanité!" Two things were certain: Paris could no longer dominate French politics, and republicans could play as brutal a game of law and order as any monarchy. This pleased conservatives, some of whom thought Communard punishment should have been even more severe. The twenty-year suppression of the press under Louis Napoleon had ended in failure. But war and revolution supported conservative governments, which could only continue to do what they knew how to do. Again the press would be repressed.

1871–1914: The Press of the Third Republic

After suppression of the Commune, a conservative parliament moved back to Paris to plan the future. French state-of-siege legislation had already returned the press to the familiar regime of control and punishment — taxes, trials, harassment and suspensions — when Marshal MacMahon, a monarchist, became president of the provisional government in 1873. Parliament then considered possibilities to replace the Second Empire; monarchy seemed to be favored. Meanwhile, republicans promoted their alternative. Léon Gambetta, former interior minister who had organized resistance to the Prussian armies, stumped throughout the country with his message that monarchy and dictatorship had repeatedly failed to quell violence and instability. Only a republic could succeed in bringing France the freedom and peace it deserved.

The 1876 parliamentary election handed a big victory to the republicans. Legislator Alfred Naquet (*La Marseillaise*) proposed a bill to remove all restrictions from the press, a labyrinth of 325 articles and 43 laws. A commission created to examine the proposal issued its report on 15 May 1877. The report demanded modification of press law. The Chamber of Deputies approved the reforms, but not the more conservative Senate. The ensuing controversy over press freedom led directly to the "Crisis of 16 May." MacMahon dissolved parliament and ordered a new round of elections. Would the marshal lead a *coup d'état* as Louis Napoleon had in 1851? Control of France had reached a crossroads between the power of the notables and the power of the republicans.

There was no coup this time. But conservatives who dominated the government before the 1877 elections led one of the most vicious campaigns against republican journalists in French press history. Police intimidated, arrested and fined, using any pretext from morals charges to religious blasphemy. MacMahon's government poured 8 million francs into propaganda disseminated by the conservative press.

Study of press history repeatedly shows that consumers of the press do not read passively. They support newspapers that offer believable information from credible journalists and the kind of content they want to read. The elitist press of the notables by 1877 reached only a tiny French minority. Not only were these journals the voice of failure and repression, they could not adapt to the changing demands of modern journalism, chiefly reduction in price.

Triumph of the Journalists

MacMahon's gamble, that propaganda and press intimidation could recoup monarchy's power, lost, and it lost dramatically. The marshal submitted his resignation. The power of the notables disintegrated. The power of the journalists triumphed. It is easy to exaggerate the influence of the press on a country's government, but the fragile Third Republic clearly was more closely tied to journalism than any of its predecessors. All major republic leaders controlled their own newspapers. Every journalist associated with Gambetta's *La Petite Republique* became part of the government. Politics and journalism became a metaphoric revolving door, newspaper offices the green rooms of French political theatrics.

Parliament understood well that liberal politics had triumphed thanks to independent journalism. That should have been clear before, but after a century it was obvious that governments could not curtail the impact of a growing press. In fact, quite the opposite, as journalism under tight seal became a pressure cooker without a vent. If nothing worked to control the press, then perhaps nothing would work the best. That is, freedom.

A parliamentary committee under the prestigious Girardin revised French press law just after Jules Grévy (*L'Electeur*) succeeded MacMahon to become first president of the Third Republic. Committee members, looking for a model, examined press law in Britain and the United States. Should enemies of the republic, particularly monarchists still a threat, be allowed to criticize? Should extreme socialist militants be allowed to rant revolution? Antimonarchist parliamentarians argued that the monarchist press, at least, should be curbed as the monarchists had done the same to republican journalism for decades. But Georges Clemenceau (*La Justice, L'Aurore, L'Homme Libre*), the politician-journalist who through fifty years was closely tied to newspapers, helped to persuade the recalcitrant that there could be no exception to a free press. On 21 July 1881 one of the republic's most important single pieces of legislation passed parliament 444 votes to 4. On 29 July it became the most sweeping free press law in Europe. In the world it had no equal in any country except the United States. The taxes, the caution deposits, the licensing requirements, everything was swept away. Even posters, a significant means of mass communication in France, enjoyed more freedom. Remaining were a few rules on libel and calls to terrorism, and a requirement that newspapers deposit copies in the national library, but these regulations were rarely enforced. The law was slightly modified in 1882 to contain a burgeoning pornography industry and in 1892–93 to reduce anarchist tirades. Otherwise, the press in France was truly free.

Senator Eugène Pelletan (*Le Bien Public, La Tribune*), in presenting the law to parliament, declared that the duty of the republic was to guarantee to every voter a free press at a cheap price in order "to tie together the entire country as in a public place, a vast individual audience which attends our debates, hears our discourse, follows closely the acts of government and weights them with conscience." Clemenceau said a republic "lives from liberty. It could die from repression, as all the governments before it have, when they counted on a repressive system to protect them."

Republican leaders were more calculating than their inspiring words might suggest. French history had shown that newspapers and editors became more powerful when few other voices competed for their readers' attention. In encouraging as many voices as possible, the government counted on newspapers neutralizing each other's weight. In particular, extreme rightist and leftist voices would be lost in the forest of newsprint. Inexpensive newspapers would live by their capitalist wits. They could not afford to offend readers so would have to moderate their stands and support the status quo or face dwindling advertising and stockholder ire. As counter-intuitive as it may seem, for Third Republic politicians, a free press more than a repressed one assured public order. They gambled on this idea, which had never prevailed in France for more than a few months. The new republic faced plenty of powerful enemies. Their bet won.

Newspaper production exploded. By 1882 an intrepid Paris reader could choose from ninety dailies. Every possible interest was represented, politics, sports, fashion, finance, children, religion. Editors played major roles in the critical debates of the era, weighing into the public space of the republic with discourses on Boulangism (a thwarted coup), the Panama Canal scandal, and the critically important Dreyfus Affair. The *petit* press set a standard, as copycats of Millaud's industrial journalism wrapped Paris in newsprint. By the turn of the century "four greats," the five-centime newspapers with over one million circulation, dominated the daily press: *Le Petit Journal, Le Journal, Le Matin* and *Le Petit Parisien*. As the twentieth century dawned, *Le Petit Parisien* of Jean Dupuy (later senator and minister) correctly bragged that it had the world's highest newspaper circulation, 1.5 million. Most dailies had to drop their cost to 5 centimes to meet reader expectations. The small-circulation old-style press of opinion and commentary that had dominated the century saw its influence on the wane, although it remained a force through World War I.

By 1914 Paris dailies had shrunk to about eighty. But the figure sounds less impressive when one considers individual titles. The "four greats" and *L'Echo de Paris* at nearly a million represented two-thirds of the city's circulation. These five dailies actually sold more papers in the provinces than in the capital. The "prestige dailies" such as *Le Figaro,* for a cultured audience, and *Le Temps,* the Third Republic's paper of record, each sold 25,000 to 30,000 copies to the country's opinion leaders.

Even smaller in circulation were the dailies run by every major politician to disseminate his ideas. While circulations hovered in the low thousands, their readers were influential indeed. *L'Aurore*, directed by Clemenceau, published the famous pro-Dreyfusard *"J'Accuse"* of author Emile Zola that rocked the country in 1898. Beyond this press and the specialist dailies noted above were about thirty dailies at any given time that came and went without much notice, printing as few as 1,000 copies. Political extremists expressed their ideology in these newspapers, but only a few faithful read them.

The Power of Money

The press had become both cheap and free. The 1881 law, however, said nothing about control from another quarter, money. As journalism moved from artisanal to industrial in France, capitalism's influence became the chief concern. Chasing financial survival in a hypercompetitive world of inexpensive papers and scarce advertising, French journalists discovered the temptations of bribery and blackmail.

This era's French journalists were probably more prone to unethical money schemes than their colleagues in Europe and America. Why? The answer seems to lie in the place given to advertising in nineteenth-century French society. The Havas agency early on acted as an intermediary between journalism and advertising. For many advertisers the costs outweighed the utility of the service. Merchants favored catalogs and posters. French consumers also seemed to prefer this publicity, perhaps repelled by the naked capitalism of the often ugly newspaper ad during this golden age of Paris poster art.

Joining merchants and readers in resistance to advertising were journalists themselves, who had little fondness for ads, even though they helped to pay their salaries. The wall that developed between journalists and advertisers was thick in France. The Third Republic's declaration that the press had a duty to inform and educate served as affirmation to journalists that they were part of a noble mission. Particularly the *presse d'opinion* perceived their mission to be incompatible with claims of sellers that supposedly sullied pages. Unlike *The Times* of London, which filled its entire front page with ads, many French newspapers relegated them to the back page, a virtual bulletin board for merchants who wished to pin up virtual posters, kindly offered as a virtual public service.

Distrust of advertising was not without foundation. In France, advertisers often represented society's margins. These promoted the dubious powers of medications for all kinds of ailments, including those considered shameful in that century, syphilis, gonorrhea and cancer. French society found these claims disrespectful, even offensive.

Advertising by the 1880s separated into four distinct approaches. The "English style" was a simple announcement, today called a want ad. Display listings were larger and included several typefaces, occasionally small engravings. These were cheapest, because they were thought least effective. The *réclame* style, a paragraph or small story sprinkled among other articles, extolled the virtues of a product. Because it could be mistaken for an article, it was considered more persuasive, so it cost more. Also available was the longer "inspired article." This positive review of a product was an endorsement secured by an undisclosed subvention from the merchant. The last two reaped the most criticism.

Financial advertising, such as publicity for banks and stock or bond sales, was separate from other commercial ads. These appeared in specialized financial inserts or financial newspapers, after 1860 a significant component of Paris journalism. As industrialization produced more capital, successful entrepreneurs looked for new investments. Financial journalists provided opportunities by evaluating stocks and extolling new ventures. It was in this domain that press corruption took root in the Third Republic. Before the 1880s economic corruption was uncommon, but the triumph of press freedom in France ironically left feeble dailies to eke out their existence in a fiercely competitive industry. In 1867 Paris had 21 dailies, the provinces 57. By 1880 it was 60 and 190. Weeklies and monthlies grew at the same rate. Advertising did not. In 1865 the average ad ratio filled 30 percent of a French newspaper's space; in 1885, it filled only 10.3 percent. An economic slump only partly explains this drop. More to blame was the growing rivalry for a stagnant advertising budget. By 1914 the British press had five times the advertising of the French press, the United States, twenty times.

In French journalism, if money corrupted, lack of money also corrupted. Two great financial scandals dragged the press into a crisis of credibility from which it never really recovered. The 1890s Panama scandal involved payments by the Panama Canal Company to newspapers and politicians in an attempt to gain support for the high-risk public bond issues required to capitalize the construction. After the company foundered, it was discovered that 126 newspapers and journalists had enjoyed financial support totaling 12 to 13 million francs. The second scandal developed when documents revealed that Russia's czarist government had paid the French press to encourage support for and investment in its shaky totalitarian system before World War I.

Careful analysis by modern historians has shown this supposed "abominable venality," its common label in the period, was not quite what it appeared. Much of the money that went to journalists actually paid for advertising — 80 percent of it in the Russian case. Other money paid for inspired articles. Whether this was unethical is still debated today. It is true that French journalists did pocket bribes, and French editors, particularly those controlling the financial press, often engaged in blackmail. Most common was the financial journalist who threatened to publish a column warning investors to sell a particular stock, unless a financial institution paid him off. In sum, was much of the French press during this period corrupt? Undoubtedly. How corrupt? Probably not as much as presumed. Bribery and blackmail were not enough to keep any newspaper in business for long. Reasonable advertising sales were still essential. And without a strong stable of readers, sufficient advertising became impossible. In the end, it was the power of readers to accept or reject a publication that determined its success.

The Press on the Eve of War

By 1914 French journalists published some of the world's most inventive newspapers. Their political power reflected close ties to government, a relationship that had been established more than a century before. Their extraordinary variety reflected the enormous appetite in France for publications, at this time the world's highest reader rates. Circulations had reached a record matched nowhere else. On the downside, the French press during the Third Republic became one of Europe's most viciously polemical, attacking politicians, capitalists, other journalists or society in general, fearing no consequence beyond the supposedly noble challenge of a duel. Moreover, the advent of the *petit* press that sold for nearly nothing and the acceleration of competition for limited advertising sometimes drove newspapers frantic for funds toward the dark forces of bribery and blackmail.

World War I would put an end to the dynamism. In August 1914 the government reinstituted censorship beyond anything seen since the Bourbons. The war killed journalists in the trenches just as it killed Frenchmen from every corner of society. Before it was over, 1.3 million French soldiers would be dead. Post-war France would never recover the confidence and solidarity of the *Belle Epoque*. French journalism after 1918 was a scapegoat for pre-war "venality" and wartime *bourrage de crâne*. Roughly translated as "eyewash," critics accused war newspapers of publishing lies and overly optimistic news that misled the country about the true nature of the conflict. World War II proved to be the *coup de grace*. Charles de Gaulle's liberation government in 1944 decided to eliminate all "collaborationist" titles, seize their assets, and establish a new French press. The legacy of the nineteenth century had finally come to an end.

Bibliography

Research on post–French Revolution press history has enjoyed a revival since the 1990s with the publication of several important studies and establishment of the Société pour l'histoire des medias in 2000 (www.histoiredesmedias.com). The bibliography below includes the most recent work, except for the Bellanger et al. volumes, still the standard reference. There is no history of the French press during this period in English.

Bellanger, Claude, Jacques Godechot, Pierre Guiral and Fernand Terrou. *Histoire Générale de la Presse Française*. Volume II, 1815–1871, and Volume III, 1871–1940. Paris: PUF, 1969 and 1972.

Charle, Christophe. *Le Siècle de la Presse (1830–1939)*. Paris: Editions du Seuil, 2004.

Chauveau, Agnès, and Philippe Tétart. *Introduction à L'Histoire des Médias en France de 1881 à Nos Jours*. Paris: Armand Colin/HER, 1999.

Delporte, Christian. *Les Journalists en France 1880–1950. Naissance et Constructon d'une Profession*. Paris: Seuil, 1999.

Delporte, Christian, Michael Palmer and Denis Ruellan, eds. *Presse à Scandale, Scandale de Presse*. Paris: L'Harmattan, 2001.

Eveno, Patrick. *L'Argent de la Presse Française des Années 1820 à Nos Jours*. Paris: Editions du CTHS, 2003.

Feyel, Gilles. *La Presse en France des Origines à 1944. Histoire Politique et Matérielle*. Paris: Ellipses, 1999.

Jeanneney, Jean-Noël. *Une Histoire des Médias des Origines à Nos Jours*. Paris: Editons du Seuil, 2001.

Martin, Marc. *La Presse Régionale des* Affiches *aux Grands Quotidiens*. Paris: Fayard, 2002.

———. *Trois Siècles de Publicité en France*. Paris: Odile Jacob, 1992.

Schlosser, Fabrice. *Les Legendes de la Presse*. Lyon: Aléas Editeur, 2002.

Germany
Mass-Circulation Newspapers Shaped by an Authoritarian Setting

Ulf Jonas Bjork

When the *American Review of Reviews* published a series of articles about the world's newspapers between 1904 and 1906, the piece devoted to Germany began by noting that press freedom there was less than in France and far less than in Britain and the United States. It is telling that the American magazine chose to lead with that observation, for German journalists worked under legal conditions that their colleagues in the United States would have considered appallingly restrictive. Even today, those familiar primarily with the development of American journalism are likely to find the history of the nineteenth-century German press strange and anachronistic, the long and twisted story of newspapers struggling for rights that their American counterparts had long taken for granted. Moreover, the Germans seemingly never quite succeeded in securing those rights, and the 1800s saw several instances of press freedom expanding in Germany only to be restrained once more by the authorities. It is symptomatic, too, that the German press of the nineteenth century did not produce any particular journalist who could be credited with taking up the cause of press freedom and leaving a clear-cut record of enlarging it; instead, it can be argued that the one person who stands out in the history of the press in Germany in the 1800s is not a journalist but a government official, Otto von Bismarck, whose legacy was a comprehensive policy for controlling and manipulating the press. It should be stressed, however, that the history of the German press during the era is also one of newspapers adapting to narrow legal circumstances and in many instances thriving in spite of them.

Germany (Bjork)

The difficult relationship between press and government was a major reason why Germany, the country that had invented the printing press and played a pivotal role in the early history of newspapers, did not lead when it came to the development of the modern mass-circulation newspaper, which emerged much later there than in the United States, Britain and France. There were other reasons as well, such as peculiar structures for delivering and financing newspapers and a general unwillingness among publishers to embrace innovations. Even in the early 1900s, foreign observers commented on how old-fashioned German newspapers seemed to be in appearance, size and relationship to readers.

The *American Review of Reviews* was not alone in characterizing the German press as less free than its counterparts in Western Europe and North America in the early 1900s, as its assessment was echoed by others at the time and is still essentially confirmed by modern historians, German and foreign. Summing up the development of newspapers in Germany in one of the major works about that country's nineteenth-century press, historian Kurt Koszyk stresses that German society as a whole evolved in the shadow of authoritarianism in the 1800s, which had profound consequences for the press in the Central European region that in 1871 became the unified Germany. Either willingly or by force of law, newspapers functioned as a tool of the authorities, whether those authorities were the German Confederation of the first half of the 1800s or the imperial government of the last quarter of the century. Government management of the press was sophisticated and complex, ranging from censorship and prosecutions for libel to financial subsidies and control of information sources. These policies had tangible results for the reach of German newspapers, for their news content and for the status of journalists.

For that reason, a great deal of attention must go to the century-long fight for press freedom and to the governmental response. Although the discussion here encompasses various regions, the main focus is on developments in Prussia, the largest German state and the one that was instrumental in the eventual unification of the country.

The First Years of the 1800s: A Press Limited in Scope and Freedom

Germany entered the nineteenth century with papers in major cities such as Berlin, Königsberg, Cologne, Hamburg, Leipzig, Augsburg, Breslau and

Frankfurt. Typically, gazettes found fertile ground in communities where trade was a major source of revenue and where commercial concerns created a demand for information and intelligence. In the great port city of Hamburg, for instance, the *Hamburgische Correspondent* circulated an estimated 30,000 copies in 1800, a figure that made it the most widely read paper in Europe.

These papers were exceptions. Although many in other cities were longstanding institutions that could trace their origins back half a century or more, their influence was limited by their small circulations, both in number of copies and geographical range. Most had 2,000 or fewer readers almost exclusively in the hometown and the region surrounding it.

Strict government censorship also determined the content of the press. The two newspapers published in the early 1800s in Berlin, the capital of Prussia, offered readers official reports, minor provincial items and miscellany from abroad; discussion of political events was avoided so as not to attract the attention of the censors, and editors found an outlet for critical writing only in reviews of concerts and plays.

The Press as a Weapon: Johann Joseph Görres and the Rheinischer Merkur

The strict censorship practiced by officials across Germany in the early nineteenth century was rooted in a view of the press that was almost exclusively negative and devoted to suppression. Somewhat paradoxically, it took the occupation by a foreign army to change the relationship between the government and the press. As French armies conquered large parts of Germany during the Napoleonic wars, Germans were introduced to a new and different official perception of the press. Napoleon was not averse to prohibiting newspapers critical of him, but the French emperor also valued the press as a force in shaping public opinion. Even more important, his use of newspapers to carry propaganda for him and France compelled his German adversaries to adopt similar tactics.

The need to counter Napoleon's efforts inspired the journalist who traditionally has been credited with giving the German press a political voice, Johann Joseph Görres. Initially a radical who was enthusiastic about the Enlightenment and the revolutionary ideas emanating from France, Görres turned into a fierce opponent of the French and their emperor after he witnessed France's occupation of the Rhineland and the policies Napoleon pursued there. Consequently, this pioneering German journalist saw as essential the fostering among Germans of a patriotism that would spur opposition to France. To achieve that goal, Görres envisioned a press that expressed the opinion of the public along the lines of English papers, not like current German ones which he accused of being backward and falling short of their true purpose.

In the turmoil surrounding the final years of Napoleon's continental empire, Görres' vision coincided with the aims of Prussia and other opponents of the French emperor. As Napoleon's troops were driven from the Rhineland in 1813, the Prussian government wanted to neutralize pro–French sympathies in the area, and an eager Görres was entrusted with that task. His tool was a newspaper called the *Rheinischer Merkur*. Issued between 1814 and 1816, the *Merkur* under Görres' editorship became known both in Germany and abroad for its polemic and well-written editorials.

As long as Napoleon remained a threat, Görres and his paper were preoccupied with resistance to France, but when the French Emperor was conclusively defeated in 1815, Görres turned his attention to his homeland, criticizing officials and conditions there. That swiftly put the *Merkur* on a collision course with the authorities who soon banned it in a number of smaller German states and, finally, in Prussia itself.

A Return to Repression: The Carlsbad Decrees

The demise of Görres' newspaper was a sign that German governments were returning to a view of the press predating Napoleon. That outcome was even more evident three years after the last issue of the *Merkur*, when a uniform press law was passed by the German Confederation. Created in the wake of Napoleon's defeat, the Confederation was an unwieldy entity consisting of thirty-five monarchies — including the large countries of Prussia and Austria — and four free cities. Decisions by the Confederation Diet required unanimity or a significant majority, so it was largely ineffective. Yet there seemed to be general agreement among the Diet delegates that the press needed to be strictly controlled. Consequently, the so-called Carlsbad Decrees of 1819 reintroduced government pre-publication censorship in the member states of the Confederation after the brief period of liberalization that had followed the fall of Napoleon. To a large extent, the Decrees were part of an international reaction to the turmoil caused by revolutionary and Imperial France, reflected also in the passage of the repressive Six Acts in Britain the same year and by similar legislation in France shortly afterwards.

In addition to re-establishing censorship, the Carlsbad Decrees stipulated that journalists whose papers had been suppressed be barred from working within the press for five years. The law required newspapers and magazines to print the names of the editors responsible for their content, holding out the possibility that anonymous publications would be seized by the authorities and their originators fined or jailed.

The Confederation's justification for these severe measures was typical of press systems with an authoritarian perspective. The officials present at Carlsbad noted that they were mindful of "the troubled movement and fermentation of emotions prevalent in large parts of Germany" that had resulted in a political murder and an assassination attempt. As to the reason for the unrest, the officials had little doubt: it was the "abuses of the press," particularly "the mischief" practiced by newspapers, journals and pamphlets.

Since the German Confederation was merely a loose federative structure, it fell to each Confederation state to put the Carlsbad Decrees into practice. Only a month after the Decrees were announced, Prussia revived its old censorship law and created a new agency, the Ober-Zensur-Kollegium, to enforce it. In Württemberg, government censorship was legally reintroduced, ending a brief period of relative freedom in that kingdom. Member states could also go further than the Carlsbad Decrees, which Prussia did in 1822 by enacting a stamp tax on newspapers. That, too, was a weapon that had counterparts in both France and Britain.

The 1820s and 1830s: Adaptation and Resistance by the Press

Independent papers soon devised ways to adapt to this restrictive press environment. The content of the *Augsburger Allgemeine Zeitung*, Germany's leading gazette, shows how the Carlsbad Decrees played out in the type of news offered readers. In a typical 1823 issue, for instance, the *Allegmeine* opened with official decrees from abroad and with official reports from foreign royal courts, but dealt with German matters only toward the end. In the realm of domestic news, the paper merely noted that the Diet of the German Confederation was in session in Frankfurt. The only item possibly controversial reported unrest among the students at the University of Jena in central Germany, but the *Allgemeine* stressed that the university administration was cooperating with the local government and with all professors "of good judgment" to suppress such movements and had expelled seventeen students. The story added, in a sympathetic note, that most of these young men were among the most excellent of the university's students and that their parents held "esteemed official positions in various state governments."

The Carlsbad Decrees were to remain in force for thirty-nine years, but they quickly encountered resistance. As so often would be the case in nineteenth-century Germany, calls for reform were inspired by events abroad. One of the first challenges arose from the July Revolution in France in 1830. The ousting of reactionary King Charles X symbolized a triumph for democracy. Germans noticed that one of the triggers of the uprising was an attempt by the king to limit press freedom. The spirit and ideas of the 1830 Revolution found a receptive audience across Germany. In Baden, a southwestern state on the French border, the legislature in 1831 passed a new press law that abolished censorship, and Bavaria also relaxed its censorship shortly afterwards.

The Baden law took effect in 1832 but was almost immediately rescinded as the Confederation Diet put pressure on the Baden government. The Diet, concerned that events in France had caused riotous incidents across Germany, directed censors within its jurisdiction to be particularly vigilant in monitoring dailies, whose coverage of domestic conditions could weaken confidence in local governments and fuel rebellion.

How effective such declarations were is a matter of debate. Historian Abigail Green notes that enforcement of government censorship was not uniform across Germany, despite the assumption of the Carlsbad Decrees that they would set a federative standard. She also points out that censors took the audience into account when deciding whether to suppress materials. More educated and wealthy readers enjoyed greater freedom than the public at large, for instance, as the Carlsbad Decrees applied only to publications of less than twenty pages. Above all, Green stresses, censors found it difficult to cope with an ever-increasing volume of printed matter. Between the 1820s and the 1840s, the number of newspapers published in Germany doubled, and the sheer quantity of material that landed on the censor's desk made comprehensive enforcement difficult.

Literature as a Weapon: Heinrich Heine and Young Germany

The rapid increase of printed matter may have made it difficult for government censors to be effective across the board but did not prevent them from pursuing high-profile cases. In the wake of the July Revolution they trained their sights on a popular but controversial author, Heinrich Heine. Heine, who had already made a name for himself as a poet and travel writer in the 1820s, left for France in 1831 and began contributing articles about events there to the *Augsburger Allgemeine Zeitung*. He was excited by developments in France, and his columns soon attracted the eyes of government officials. At first, the authorities allowed the publication of Heine's letters, mainly because the *Allgemeine Zeitung* was Germany's most influential paper in the 1830s, and both the Prussian and the Austrian governments sought to maintain good relations with its publisher, Johann Friedrich Cotta. Judging from complaints from Heine, Cotta's editors also made the author's work more palatable to the authorities by deleting particularly sensitive passages. In 1832, however, a representative of the Austrian government told Cotta personally that Heine's contributions in the Augsburg paper had to end, and the author should instead turn to books to disseminate his views.

The censors likewise soon scrutinized the output of Young Germany, a literary movement founded by a group of writers inspired by Heine. Young Germany members believed that literature should serve politics and espouse liberal ideas, so newspapers became an important outlet for them. Initially, the authorities targeted papers that published Young Germany articles, but in 1835 the Confederation Diet moved against the group. Asserting that its purpose was to use "belles-lettres writings accessible to all classes of readers in order to attack Christian religion, disparage current social conditions and destroy morality," the federal legislature directed governments of all member states to apply stringently, against the authors, publishers, printers and distributors of works belonging to the Young Germany literary school, all relevant laws addressing abuses of the press. Given his experience with government censorship, Heine, who was specifically named as a banned author in the 1835 Diet directive, came to see freedom of the press as particularly important. Despotism, he commented, first suppressed freedom of the press, then freedom of speech, and then, finally, freedom of thought.

The Early 1840s: Resisting Censorship and Testing Its Limits

Actions such as the prohibition of the works of Young Germany increasingly put the spotlight on censorship itself. There were also signs of public opinion turning against the general idea and practice of censorship, such as an 1832 mass meeting at Hambach Castle that attracted 30,000 participants who demanded liberty of the press. Clearly alarmed at such sentiments, the authorities responded by banning public meetings and suppressed the *Deutsche Tribune*. Its editor, J.G.A. Wirth, was one of the Hambach speakers and had proposed a national association for the support of a free press.

What a free press should cover, however, was less clear. In some ways, German newspapers had already changed compared with earlier decades. From France came the feuilleton, which soon became a staple of the German newspaper. French influences were also responsible for an increase in business news and for the introduction of serialized novels in German papers. For many liberals, however, the main purpose of newspapers was to debate political issues, and what German papers still lacked in comparison with their counterparts in England and France were political editorials.

There were some stirrings to add editorials in the so-called Vormärz period between 1830 and 1848. In Baden, another new press law, passed in 1840, allowed newspapers to discuss "internal political events" as long as the tone was respectful. The statute was tested almost immediately by Joseph Fickler, publisher of the *Seeblätter* in Konstanz. It was Fickler, argues historian Elmar Fetscher, who introduced editorials along French and English lines in the German press, offering readers a reasoned and balanced discussion of political matters. The *Seeblätter* publisher sought to get away from the academic and convoluted style typical of leading papers of the age without resorting to the polemic style he felt was too close to agitation and inevitably attracted the attention of the censors. He wrote in clear and direct language, hoping that the style would engage the great mass of readers. Content, of course, would have to pass the censor's muster. What Fickler discovered after publishing articles critical of neighboring Bavaria and favoring German reunification was that the authorities had decided to allow political discussion as long as it was expressed in a reasoned and courteous way.

Prussia: The Promise and Reality of Press Freedom

Baden was a small and unusually liberal state on the fringes of the German Confederation, but its relaxation of censorship was part of a softening attitude across Germany in the early 1840s. Even in Prussia, home to some of the most stringent restrictions, the accession of new monarch, King Frederick Wilhelm IV, led to a relaxation of censorship in 1841. The new conditions set for newspapers by government in Germany's largest kingdom were similar to those in Baden. The royal censorship decree of 1841 instructed officials that articles should be cleared for publication if they had "good intentions" and sought to examine the truth in a moderate way. Press freedom expanded further in 1842, when the government altogether exempted lithographs and etchings from censorship. This move unleashed a deluge of political cartoons, many of which opposed censorship itself.

The loosening of official control of the press led to the reappearance of letters from Paris by Heinrich Heine in the *Augsburger Allgemeine Zeitung* and brought another influential German writer, Karl Marx, to the forefront. Asked by liberals in Cologne to assume the editorship of the *Rheinische Zeitung für Politik, Handel und Gewerbe,* Marx began his career as an editor in 1842 and soon increased the paper's readership to more than 3,000, making the *Rheinische Zeitung* known in Germany and abroad.

The radical tone of Marx's articles annoyed the Prussian government, which was already signaling that it was reining in the press. In October 1842 it announced its duty to muzzle the "bad" part of the press in order to prevent further deterioration. Marx fell victim to that campaign three months later, when the *Rheinische Zeitung* was banned. Because his writings had been so widely noted, his fate at the hand of the authorities generated a slew of anti-government cartoons. They prompted the government to rescind the exemption for illustrations along with the short-lived toleration of well-intentioned discussions of the truth. Heine's contributions to the *Allgemeine Zeitung* were next. The celebrated poet remained in France, and Marx, warned that he might be arrested, went into exile there as well.

By 1844 the Prussian censors were more active than ever. Between 1830 and 1840 they had banned an average of thirty publications every year; for 1844 the corresponding figure was fifty-five. In one sense, however, the campaign of suppression backfired, as it focused the public's attention even more on the issues of censorship and press freedom. As an example, the repressive 1840s witnessed the birth of a poetic genre devoted exclusively to excoriating censorship and the officials engaged in it, the so-called *Censoriad*.

The Revolution of 1848 and Its Aftermath: An End to Censorship

As the 1840s were drawing to a close, events in France would once again stir up emotions in Germany. This time, the impact on the country's newspapers and journalists would be profound. When word spread across the German Confederation in February 1848 of yet another revolution in France, emotions pent up for more than a decade found expression in direct and resolute action. In March the news from France caused civil unrest in Berlin, forcing the government to make an official declaration of press freedom in Prussia and to abolish censorship. In April 1848 the German Confederation Diet in Frankfurt followed the lead of Prussia, and also Austria, and formally rescinded the twenty-nine-year-old Carlsbad Decrees, ending pre-publication censorship across the Confederation's territory. Several triumphant opposition writers commemorated the occasion by making their last contributions to the Censoriad genre, offering poems with titles such as "The Last Censor" and "The Dead Censor." Enthused by a general sentiment that press freedom had finally arrived, political newspapers sprang up overnight, bringing the total number to more than 230.

Unfortunately, the time of official benevolence toward the press proved short-lived, as it so often had been before. Government reaction both to the March Revolution itself and to the issue of press freedom was swift and severe. In fall 1848 the military ended the Berlin uprising, and the authorities quickly began to move against the wave of radical political papers that the revolutions had spawned. Even as the counter-revolution rolled back virtually all the reforms enacted since March, government officials realized that public opinion would not tolerate a return to pre-publication censorship. That particular means of controlling the press was dead.

The German Press at Midcentury: Limited in Reach and Ambition

While the end of censorship after 1848 marked a turning point in the history of the German press, resulting in a changed relationship between government and newspapers, there is little doubt that journalism in Germany still lagged far behind its counterparts elsewhere. It was not an integrated part of a political party system as in France, and it was even further away from the commercial and politically independent press that was emerging in Britain and the United States.

The reasons for the slower development of the modern newspaper in Germany went beyond direct government interference with press freedom. The examples of Baden and Württemberg illustrate this point well, for the political systems in the two border states were notably less restrictive than elsewhere in the German Confederation. Both had attempted to abolish censorship before 1848, and they acted swiftly to end it conclusively following the demise of the Carlsbad Decrees. Yet in neither state did a large and influential newspaper appear. Neither Baden nor Württemberg had a city big enough to sustain the urban culture necessary for mass-circulation newspapers to thrive. The slow process of industrialization in southwest Germany also meant that the region lacked a large homogenous working class to provide the mass readership that large-circulation papers required to be economically viable.

There were also other impediments to the development of an independent press on the English or American model. These barriers existed not only in states like Baden, but, according to historian Elmar Fetscher, across Germany. The most important handicap was political fragmentation, the result of a German Confederation so loosely structured that its members retained a great deal of autonomy. Because they controlled their own borders, the Confederation's postal system increased fees, sometimes as much as fivefold, when printed matter crossed states.

Adding to the political fragmentation was the mentality of *Kleinstädterei,* a parochial outlook prevalent across Germany which meant that average readers took little interest in events beyond their home communities. Publishers who strove for a wider view, to argue for a greater sense of German unity and national consciousness, had little response from their readers. Thus, the majority opted for simply reflecting the prevailing outlook. That decision, in turn, limited their appeal to readers beyond their hometowns, which kept the circulation of the typical mid-century German newspaper to a few thousand copies.

Unlike their penny-press colleagues in New York, who ever since the 1830s had seen circulation as the real measurement of success and had eagerly adopted technologies that could increase the number of copies, German publishers had little interest in expanding readership. It is paradoxical that two of the technological innovations that made true mass-circulation possible, the steam-driven printing press and newsprint made from wood pulp, were pioneered by Germans, Friedrich König and Gottfried Keller, respectively. Neither found a receptive environment at home but had to go abroad to find publishers eager to adopt their innovations. König went to London, where *The Times* inaugurated his press in late 1814. Even after his success outside Germany he discovered that German publishers were more interested in hand-driven presses than in steam-powered ones, as the small circulation of their papers did not necessitate large-capacity machines. Almost thirty-five years would pass between König's London sale and the general use of steam printing presses in Germany.

1850s Prussia: A New Era of Repression — and a Brief Liberalization

If the mentality of publishers and readers was one reason for the slow development of the German press, continuing government restrictions were even more significant. That was most evident in Prussia. Because of that kingdom's size and importance in Germany and the role it would play in the creation of a unified German state, developments there in the 1850s merit a detailed examination. The press freedom declared in Prussia as the 1848 revolution broke out had been officially enshrined in a new constitution in December, but a revision of that document in 1850 made it abundantly clear that the liberty given to newspapers and other publications by the government had limitations. While censorship was gone, restrictions could still be imposed by legislation; the focus of the authorities had merely shifted from prior restraint to post-publication sanctions.

In 1851, barely a year after the constitution was revised, a press law was enacted that gave the Prussian government wide powers to control the press. All newspaper publishers were required to have a government-issued license, a so-called trade concession, and they had to submit a copy of each issue beforehand to the police. Publishers of newspapers had to pay a security deposit (a measure possibly borrowed from France, where caution money had been in effect since 1820), and if the author of an offensive piece of writing could not be identified, the editor or publisher responsible for the publication would be liable in the author's place. Only in one aspect was the law a substantial improvement on the pre–Revolutionary era: actions of both police and state prosecutors against newspapers were now subject to review by the courts.

In addition to the tools of the press law, the government had the criminal code, where one paragraph made it an offense to attack "the reputation of the government and the existing order" and another prohibited the dissemination of fabricated or distorted facts as well as libel and derision that subjected government institutions to hatred and contempt. Finally, the authorities could penalize newspapers by economic means. Besides the burden imposed by the security deposit, newspapers in 1852 were subject to a stamp tax calculated on the consumption of newsprint, a measure intended not only to raise revenue but also to make newspapers more expensive and to hold down their circulations.

Those circulations had soared in the wake of the 1848 Revolution. In

Cologne, the circulation of the *Kölnsischer Zeitung* grew by 80 percent to 17,400 between February and April 1848, and Berlin's *Vossische Zeitung* increased by 20 percent to reach 24,000 during the same period. The stamp tax and the generally harsher official climate of the 1850s took their toll on these figures: by 1852 the Cologne paper had lost 7,400 readers, while its Berlin colleague had seen its circulation shrink by 13,000.

To survive economically, newspapers had to adapt to the new, less permissive environment in Prussia. One way of doing so was to avoid discussing domestic politics and to concentrate on foreign affairs. Events abroad could even offer editors an opportunity to allude to conditions in Prussia. Such was the case of the Crimean War, which the Berlin press framed as a conflict pitting liberal, progressive England against reactionary, authoritarian Russia. Such approaches appeared to be effective. In Berlin, for instance, the liberal papers began gaining readers again in the mid-1850s, although not on the spectacular scale of 1848.

The leading papers of the Prussian capital, like most papers in Prussia and elsewhere in Germany in the latter half of the nineteenth century, were characterized as "liberal," a designation that went back to the 1830s. It never connoted a partisan press similar to that of France, however, because press ties to liberal party groupings was never particularly strong. By the time the first liberal political organizations appeared in the 1860s, the newspapers that they sympathized with had existed for decades, and the subsequent instability of these organizations and their frequent splits into factions did little to stimulate a close relationship with newspapers. In fact, historian Jörg Requate argues that the term "independent," which often accompanied "liberal" as a label for newspapers, should be interpreted as independence not only from government but also from political parties. Instead of party affiliation, the term liberal referred to a broad political philosophy espoused by the papers' editors.

In 1858 that liberal philosophy was given a boost by a change of government in Prussia that signaled the end of the "Reactionary Era" of the decade. Legislation affecting the press was the same, but officials made a point of distancing themselves from the "abuses" of power of the previous years. The press almost immediately understood the ramifications of this posture. Publishers wasted no time using it to their advantage. In Berlin, the *Volks-Zeitung*, which since its founding in 1853 had survived by convincing the authorities that it was politically harmless, shifted its focus to previously off-limits domestic politics. The paper had clearly tapped into a need among readers, for its 1858 circulation of 10,000 soared to 26,000 within three years, making it the largest gazette in the capital.

Unbeknownst to the *Volks-Zeitung* and its competitors, the government's attitude toward the press was about to shift once more, and, as so often before, in a negative direction. The event that precipitated that change was the appointment of a new Prussian prime minister, a man who was to cast a long shadow over the development of German journalism: Otto von Bismarck-Schönhausen. Before dealing with the impact of Bismarck's rise to power, it is necessary to consider conditions elsewhere in Germany.

Across Germany, a Tradition of Control

Much of Germany had witnessed the same kind of conservative reaction to the 1848 Revolution as had occurred in Prussia. Officials everywhere voiced similar concerns that the newly liberated press was a tool for unrest and dissent. As noted above, the Confederation Diet had abolished the Carlsbad Decrees in 1848. When it passed a uniform federal press law in 1854, it was clear that pre-publication censorship would not under any circumstances be reinstituted. Even so, state governments could use a number of ways to control the press. As in Prussia, editors could be prosecuted for libelous remarks or writings inciting treason or resistance to authority, and publishers were required to have a government concession in order to print and distribute a newspaper. Somewhat mitigating was that the federative law had followed the Prussian example of subjecting government actions to the review of the courts. Because officials also had learned that repressive measures often generated negative publicity, they were somewhat reluctant to employ them. For that reason, governments across Germany began seeking other ways to master the press. States such as Hanover and Saxony established official newspapers and, unlike Prussia, found them fairly useful. There was no longer any way in which governments could prevent an independent press from criticizing official policy, noted a Saxon official in 1857, so it was necessary for them to sponsor their own journals to defend their positions.

To reach that goal, the authorities set out to ascertain what had made the independent liberal newspaper so popular. In states such as Saxony and Württemberg, they eventually concluded that it was good news reporting that attracted readers. Here, government organs had a major advantage, as they had unique access to officials. Inherent in the nature of official gazettes was that this information be presented from the government's viewpoint, which required crafting articles with subtlety. The civil servants in charge of these papers appeared to assume that readers automatically discounted much of what was published in them, so bias could not be too blatant. Moreover, polemics had to be avoided, not only because of the impression they left with readers but also because these organs represented the dignity of the government.

Since German newspapers borrowed freely from one another, officials also tried to plant pro-government articles in independent newspapers. Many independent papers were eager to print government news and some, even to tone down their opposition if offered that news. If that tactic did not work, the authorities turned from the liberal press to smaller provincial newspapers. In Saxony, for instance, local papers in dire need of revenue received monopolies on government advertising in exchange for espousing pro-government views.

When successful, these policies gave a state real dominance of the press in the years around 1860. In Hanover, for example, an 1862 estimate put a little more than half the papers under direct government influence and another quarter under that influence less regularly.

Bismarck's First Years: The Clock Turns Back

Developments in states such as Saxony and Hanover in the early 1860s paralleled those in Prussia in a number of ways. Officials still had access to a wide range of instruments to manipulate the printed word yet increasingly opted for more subtle methods to do so. Alternatively, Bismarck's view of the press and his initial techniques of controlling it were a continuation of traditions not only in his native Prussia but also in Germany at large.

Journalists' first encounter with the new prime minister did not bode well. Within weeks of taking office, Bismarck began work on a new, more restrictive press law, which went into effect in June 1863. The order empowered the police to prohibit, either temporarily or indefinitely, newspapers whose publishers had been given two official warnings. Police suppressions could not be appealed to the courts but only to the Prussian Cabinet, and to justify a ban, the authorities merely had to declare the content of the offending publication a "danger to public welfare."

Used to several years of far looser reins, the liberal press of Prussia lodged a formal protest against the new rules, only to find them applied immediately. When several papers were issued a first warning, the general press reaction was to fall silent and adapt to the new policy. As it turned out, the order did not last long. After the Lower House of the Prussian legislature reconvened in the fall, its liberal majority swiftly voted to rescind the emergency order.

If Bismarck's far-reaching attempt to curtail press freedom had failed, his next steps left no doubt that press freedom had once again narrowed. The new prime minister had all the tools of the 1851 press law at his disposal and displayed no hesitation about employing them. Issues of several leading opposition papers were confiscated. Others had their government concessions withdrawn, and were thus legally unable to print, or had their postal privileges denied. In Königsberg in eastern Prussia, the leading liberal paper, the *Hartung'sche Zeitung*, was taken to court 100 times between 1862 and 1864.

Bismarck Shifts from Control to Manipulation

Even under these adverse conditions, the liberal press continued to increase in circulation. That fact made Bismarck realize that restrictive measures were not sufficient to control the opposition press. Consequently, he also pursued the time-honored practice of tying some newspapers closely to the government through financial support. Moreover, Bismarck soon showed himself a master of what modern mass-media scholars call agenda-setting. As he began his big project, the reunification of Germany (accomplished by three short and decisive wars between 1864 and 1871), he was able to shift press attention away from domestic issues to larger German ones. On these matters Bismarck and the liberal press found common ground, since both favored a firmly unified German state without Austrian participation and a stronger sense of German nationalism.

Despite his successful cooperation with the liberal journals during reunification, Bismarck remained profoundly suspicious of the press as an institution. He held the classically authoritarian view that politics was the concern of the ruler alone because only he and his officials understood the context of political events and had access to the information essential for correct decisions. Further, he thought that government was not obliged to conduct its affairs in the open and that to allow newspapers to report on or criticize the actions of officials was absurd, since writers were ill-informed and lacked experience in government service.

Bismarck was particularly annoyed that journalists in the late 1860s were able to increase their opportunities to discuss matters of state. Liberal members of the diet of the North German Confederation, the cohesive political entity that replaced the old German Confederation in 1866, were able, for instance, to limit the scope of libel in the Confederation's criminal code, giving editors considerably more leeway to discuss religious and political issues. Equally important was that the new legislation replaced the laws of individual member states, which in most cases were considerably stricter.

The 1870s: Rules for the Press in the German Empire

The North German criminal code became imperial law after reunification in 1871, and three years later the new Empire passed a comprehensive press statute that replaced the local laws of member states. The new legislation did not represent a substantial expansion of press freedom, although it abolished the security deposits that publishers had to post with government as a guarantee for "good behavior" as well as the stamp taxes designed to curb newspaper circulation.

Shortly after the press law was enacted, the imperial government emphasized that the freedom enjoyed by newspapers was still heavily restricted. In the eighteen-month period after the passage of the statute, a record number of prosecutions were started, many initiated by the chancellor personally. The extent to which individual editors became pawns in the struggle between the press and the government is well illustrated by the case of the *Berliner Zeitung*. The imperial press law had kept the provision of its 1851 Prussian predecessor that made editors personally responsible if the authorship of an article could not be ascertained. Since German papers favored a tradition of printing articles unsigned, editors were responsible for the entire paper. Bismarck's personal feud with the *Berliner Zeitung* sent all three men who were its editors between 1878 and 1882 to jail for months and fined them substantial amounts.

Although prosecutions such as the ones against the *Berliner Zeitung* were highly visible and served as warnings to other papers, the press law eventually proved to be less effective than Bismarck had hoped. The relatively small imperial bureaucracy found it difficult to initiate the number of prosecutions needed to check the rapidly growing independent press, and prosecutions inevitably generated negative publicity. For these reasons, Bismarck concentrated on the manipulation of the press that had proven so successful in the 1860s.

Germany (Bjork)

Bismarck's Methods of News Manipulation

A particularly effective tactic employed by the chancellor was to appropriate symbols of patriotism and national unity and make himself their exclusive guardian. He consciously constructed an image of himself as the most important symbol of the new empire, the one man who put the welfare of the nation ahead of partisan politics and self-interest. He achieved such success that many Germans found it inconceivable that anyone but Otto von Bismarck could be chancellor. By overseeing a copious output of printed matter that glorified his work and person, such as his private letters, political correspondence and official speeches, he shaped opinion. His first authorized biography appeared in 1879, written by the editor of an official government newsletter, and several more were to follow before he was dismissed as chancellor in 1890.

Abetting Bismarck's goal of dominating the flow of news in Germany were his roles as unifier of Germany and leader of the new empire, both of which made him an unsurpassed generator of news. For any journalist reporting on domestic politics and foreign affairs, there was simply no way around him. Bismarck realized early that the need for news driving much of the large independent press could be exploited in his favor. He had a particular fondness for using the tradition of anonymity in the press as a way to get points across without making it evident that he was the leak, attributing the information to "sources close to the chancellor."

The run-up to the 1870 war with France provided a concrete example of how Bismarck manipulated information to rouse public opinion and accomplish broader political ends. In what turned out to be a decisive step toward war, French Emperor Napoleon III forced a German prince distantly related to Germany's Emperor Wilhelm I to renounce his candidacy to the throne of Spain. Not content with that outcome, Napoleon also sent his Berlin ambassador to Wilhelm to make the German Emperor guarantee that the candidacy would never be revived. Declining that request in a formal but polite manner, Wilhelm sent a telegraphic account of the meeting to Bismarck, who, sensing an opportunity to provoke a war, recast it as a tense encounter where each party had offended the other. The chancellor sent his version to the *Norddeutsche Allgemeine Zeitung*, where its publication stirred up public opinion on both sides of the border and helped pave the way for open conflict.

On a day-to-day basis, Bismarck's use of the press typically involved the supply of news rather than outright manipulation. Through an elaborate system of government press offices and official newsletters, the German government of the 1870s dangled a rich supply of information before the eyes of newspaper publishers. In one package, they could, if they supported the chancellor, receive news summaries from Berlin, reports from various government departments, bulletins from German diplomats abroad, editorials on foreign affairs and stock market reports. None of this material made any pretense of being detached and objective, however, but clearly reflected the government's views.

Bismarck's Press Machinery

The primary channel for relating such views was the Literary Bureau of the Prussian Ministry of the Interior, an agency that employed as many as a dozen journalists in the 1870s. Almost as important was the Central Bureau of the German Foreign Office, whose employees, often journalists, got their article outlines from Bismarck who also corrected their final drafts. He also decided whether the completed article should be sent to specific papers that he had selected or be slotted for distribution to the general press through the Literary Bureau.

Beside the apparatus for placing government-friendly news in independent liberal newspapers, Bismarck opened channels directly to readers. On the national level, the government published an official newspaper called the *Deutsche Reichs- und Preußische Staatsanzeiger*. A number of local counterparts, called *Amtsblätter*, carried government news and official advertising. Such advertising was a vital source of revenue for many smaller papers, and Bismarck frequently made it clear that advertising went as a favor to sympathetic publishers. To supply government news to the local press, the chancellor established a central source of suitable and thoroughly reviewed material, an official newsletter called the *Provinzial Correspondenz*. It was based in Berlin, and its articles could be reprinted or quoted by the provincial newspapers that had access to it.

The newsletter that supplied the press with news became a favorite weapon of Bismarck but, besides the *Provinzial Correspondenz*, he had another important publication at his disposal. The *Oldenburg Correspondenz*, which originally was an independent publication, offered Reichstag reports and general government news. Its founder, journalist Karl Oldenburg, soon became closely connected to Bismarck and was eventually paid a secret government salary. In an arrangement that exploited the growing press need for timely material, Oldenburg's newsletter received official stenographic notes of speeches and other Reichstag proceedings and printed important government news far ahead of papers that had their own parliamentary correspondents. In return, Oldenburg was obligated to report all government statements in full, which meant that speeches by opponents were related in short, heavily edited passages.

As suggested above, there were papers that did not require economic incentives to throw their support behind the chancellor but did so because their owners were in Bismarck's camp already. Not surprising, Bismarck prized these semi-official publications, notably the *Norddeutsche Allgemeine Zeitung*, a Berlin paper with a circulation around 7,000. The chancellor clearly valued the close connection between himself and papers such as the *Norddeutsche Allgemeine*, but he also sought to keep that connection secret. The attempt was largely a failure; both the liberal press and the public soon came to regard the paper as a conduit for Bismarck. That caused him problems because he was regarded as responsible for the entire content of the paper rather than for only articles he had contributed. Thus, after a series of rash pronouncements in the *Norddeutsche Allgemeine*, the government subjected it to pre-publication censorship.

The 1880s: Bismarck's Power Over the Press Wanes

If the 1870s marked the high point of Bismarck's control of the German press, the 1880s, the last decade of his long tenure, saw a gradual decline of that control. One reason was that he became more openly confrontational in his dealings with liberal newspapers. As a result, those that had previously endorsed his policies began to distance themselves from him. In the 1881 Reichstag elections, the government took aim at liberal papers, banning them from railway stations and army barracks and prohibiting public employees from reading them.

Despite such harsh measures, the conservative election victories that Bismarck had envisioned did not materialize, leading him to investigate why these campaigns had failed. A major reason was that the elaborate communication system that he had established in the 1870s had lost its effectiveness. Rather than providing a steady stream of uniform and officially approved news and views, the multitude of press offices of the imperial bureaucracy increasingly reflected rivalries between ministries and agencies and so offered a variety of opinions. Lack of control was also evident in official publications such as the *Provinzial Correspondenz*, whose content, much to Bismarck's dismay, was no longer reviewed by bureaucrats before it was sent out. The practice of rewarding loyal publications with valuable government news was also in disarray, as a large number of the papers that received bulletins from the Literary Bureau were fierce opposition sheets. Although the problems were obvious, Bismarck made no real effort to revive his once-effective system for manipulating the independent press, choosing instead to supply news to official local papers.

Bismarck's hold on the press may have loosened after 1880, but his policies had affected newspapers in Germany profoundly. Long after he was gone, the German government continued to rely on some of the methods he pioneered, such as catering specifically to local gazettes and inserting government-produced articles in independent but friendly papers. Moreover, into the new century, newspapers and their editors lived with the threat of becoming defendants in both criminal and civil trials.

Bismarck's years in power had also left his mark on the attitude of journalists. Buffeted by the chancellor's openly hostile attitude and by the continuing threat of legal action yet used to a copious supply of vitally important if slanted government news and opinion, many liberal editors were battle-weary. A number of them opted for withdrawal from politics, resulting in many German papers taking a neutral or apolitical stance. By World War I, half the newspapers in the country characterized themselves as non-partisan.

The Prosperous Press of an Empire — and Its Problems

One of the problems that frustrated Bismarck in his attempts to control the press was the steady growth of newspapers. By 1885 the total number of dailies and weeklies was more than 3,000, but almost 90 percent had circulations of only a few thousand. Even the largest newspapers were small in comparison with leading French, British and American papers. As late as 1870, four decades after newspapers in New York began to pursue a mass readership, circulations of 35,000 made the *Kölnische Zeitung* and the *Volks-Zeitung* widely read papers in Germany; fifteen years later, the *Berliner Tageblatt* could boast of 70,000 readers — although that figure apparently included late-day extras published after the main edition.

Publications with a mass readership did exist, but they were magazines. As early as 1833, Johann Jakob Weber had launched the *Pfennig-Magazin*, an illustrated weekly patterned on the English *Penny Magazine* that soon attracted a readership of 60,000. Twenty years later, Ernst Kiel founded *Gartenlaube*, a magazine with a broadly liberal outlook that contained articles highlighting technological and scientific progress as well as poetry, prose and history. By 1875 *Gartenlaube's* circulation had reached 500,000.

Several factors made it difficult for newspapers to achieve such a large audience. The structure and outlook of gazettes remained intensely local, just as it had been in the 1840s, with a great majority of them circulating in their neighborhoods where there was little competition. The *Kleinstädterei* that had characterized large parts of the press was still a powerful force, and even after reunification it took at least a decade for Berlin to establish itself as a national center of government, business and communication.

Peculiar arrangements within the newspaper industry, moreover, tended to prevent gazettes from becoming the highly successful business ventures that they were in Western Europe and America. First, because of regulations that banned street sales, distribution was almost solely by subscription. Sales as well as delivery were not handled by the newspapers themselves but by independent companies or the post office. Consequently, newspaper publishers knew little about their readers and had little incentive to increase circulation. Just as they had been reluctant to adopt new printing technologies, publishers resisted trying new distribution methods. The Deutsche Journalistenag, (the German Journalists' Conference) the first professional journalism organization, voted overwhelmingly in 1871 to reject the idea of selling newspapers in the streets or from newsstands, as such methods were "unseemly." Similar hesitation was evident when it came to layouts that might have broadened readership. Big headlines were rare in German papers until war news seemed to necessitate them after 1914, and pictures were few. The continued use of Gothic type also contributed to an old-fashioned look.

A second impediment to newspaper growth in Germany was the organization of the advertising industry. The lucrative task of locating potential advertisers and finding space in the press to promote their products had not fallen to newspaper publishers but to independent advertising agencies. Newspapers signed long-term contracts with these agencies, leasing out space in their columns and receiving payment that was regular but low. Initially, publishers tended to favor such arrangements because they guaranteed a steady income. As industrialization took off in the later decades of the nineteenth century and spurred a growth in advertising, it became evident that the papers' relationship to the advertising agencies put them at a disadvantage.

Just how profitable advertising could be was evident from the career of Rudolf Mosse, who had begun as an advertising salesman for the *Gartenlaube* magazine in Leipzig. Mosse's work was pivotal for the success of the magazine, and in the late 1860s he left *Gartenlaube* and moved to Berlin to put his experience to good use there. In 1867 he founded his own advertising agency. By the late 1870s it had absorbed most of its competition and had most of Germany's leading newspapers as clients. Mosse became a millionaire from this venture and even tried newspaper publishing. He launched the *Berliner Tageblatt* in 1871, which in the course of fifteen years became Germany's largest paper.

The final barrier to an expansion in newspaper readership was the restrictive system of news distribution. In Germany as elsewhere in Europe and America, agencies selling news had first appeared around 1850. The important role these agencies played in the flow of news from abroad and within Germany quickly became evident to the Prussian government, which at one point even considered starting a state-run telegraph service to counter their influence. Instead, Bismarck opted for tying an existing agency closer to the government. In 1866 intervention by King Wilhelm I resulted in substantial private loans for the financially troubled Wolff agency, which was in danger of being acquired by foreign competitors. Bismarck later bound Wolff even closer to the government with a substantial official loan and the guarantee that its bulletins would have priority on the state-run telegraph lines.

In return for Wilhelm's and Bismarck's benevolence, the agency gave the government a great deal of influence over appointments to its board of directors. It also agreed, secretly, to give news generated by authorities extra prominence in its bulletins, without revealing its source. The agency's comfortable arrangement with the government enabled Wolff to outdistance its competitors and attain a virtual monopoly on telegraphic news within Germany. Its central role in the German news-distribution system was further solidified when it joined the European news cartel in the 1870s and became responsible for delivering news from Germany, Scandinavia, Russia, the Balkans, Austria and the Netherlands to its partners Havas in France and Reuters in London.

To the large independent liberal newspapers, Wolff's dominating position was one of considerable concern. Its monopoly allowed the agency to charge rates that publishers considered excessive. The quality of its information was another issue, as Wolff usually employed state telegraph operators who were not journalists and did not, according to press representatives, understand news values. Finally, despite the secrecy surrounding Wolff's 1869 agreement with the Prussian government, editors and publishers soon realized how beholden the agency was to the authorities and recognized that its news frequently had a pro-government bias. To dilute Wolff's influence, the Deutsche Journalistenag at one point proposed forming a cooperative news agency modeled on the Americans' Associated Press, but the idea failed to attract interest and capital.

A Press Resistant to Change

The failure of the proposal to establish a cooperative news service was, in one sense, indicative of a general attitude among German journalists toward independent news-gathering. To some extent, that attitude had its roots in the repressive and manipulative policies of the government, which encouraged the use of officially disseminated news and discouraged the active gathering of information by reporters even when such activities were allowed. It is noteworthy, for instance, that only one German newspaper had a correspondent in the new Reichstag in the 1870s; all the others eschewed such first-hand coverage and instead relied on the *correspondenz* newsletters put out by Reichstag members and private persons, the most important of whom was Karl Oldenburg. Publications of this type were thriving in the last decades of the 1800s, and by 1914 they numbered almost 1,000. Another practice that indicated no interest in active news-gathering was the republication of articles from other newspapers. Although the use of scissors and paste tended to be heaviest among the financially weak local papers, large wealthy dailies practiced it as well.

Editors resented the way that the telegraph services slanted news toward timeliness and brevity and priced its delivery too high. Newspapers reacted by developing a particularly German style of writing that favored opinion, interpretation and argumentation, a style that made the editorial department rather than the news pages the linchpin of a paper. As Requate notes, the hallmark of German journalism in the late nineteenth century was the "leading article" that radiated learning, and the reporter, so central in the development of British and American journalism, was a marginal figure in Germany.

The Social Standing of Journalists

Even if reporters received little respect in Germany as the 1800s drew to a close, the nineteenth century nevertheless witnessed the emergence of journalism as a distinctive occupation. Before 1800 the contents of newspapers were typically put together by printer-publishers, but after the turn of the century writers began to emerge who were divorced both from the production side and from ownership. This kind of writer, of whom Johann Joseph Görres is probably the best example, was often referred to as a publicist. A survey of biographies of journalists active in the 1800–1848 period revealed that journalism was not their primary occupation. As historian James Retallack commented, many were in journalism because their main occupations, as librarians, postmasters, government officials or lawyers, had brought them into contact with printed matter.

After 1830 more writers viewed newspaper work as a primary career, but it was a career with different levels. Publishers, in the early nineteenth century, had begun to divorce themselves from the tasks of writing and editing and to concentrate on the managerial and financial sides of their enterprise. Writers, on the other hand, increasingly were employees and, as such, expected to defer to the opinions of employers, a presumption strengthened by the custom of anonymity of authors. Editors were somewhere between publishers and writers and, known by name, could often command respectable compensation for their work.

Newspaper writers were not well paid, probably because their work earned them little respect. A common stereotype, expressed by both Bismarck and Emperor Wilhelm II, was that they were people who were good for nothing else, restless young men who had left school before graduating. Critics faulted them for writing "newspaper German" and claimed that gossip-mongering, sensationalism and political naïveté were prerequisites for their occupation.

To counter such negative perceptions, professional associations such as the Deutsche Journalistenag discussed examinations for prospective journalists to weed out those unfit for the field. A number of German universities and private institutions offered instruction in newspaper work around 1900, and those interested in that field could also read several journalism manuals. The formation of associations such as the Journalistentag was another way that journalists sought to enhance their status, and by the turn of the century such organizations were numerous.

The Growth of a Party Press

One reason for the large number of professional journalism organizations was that many were formed to represent the political affiliation of individual journalists. That, in turn, was an indication of the growth of a party press in Germany in the latter half of the 1800s. As noted above, the large group of newspapers that labeled themselves liberal could not be said to constitute a segment of the party press, as their ties to party groupings was loose at best. A party-affiliated liberal press as such barely existed, and papers that tried to function as voices of specific liberal parties frequently found it difficult to survive, particularly in the 1870s.

The organs of other political parties, more akin to partisan newspapers in other countries, were never able to challenge the independent liberal press in strength and numbers. To the right was a cadre of conservative papers, on whom Bismarck could depend for support of his policies. Despite the chancellor's insistence that it was independence from government that made this group of papers particularly valuable, it soon became necessary to subsidize most of them in order to guarantee their survival. Even with funding, their numbers, around sixty in the mid–1880s, and circulations remained small. The exception was Berlin's *Kreuz-Zeitung*, which thrived because it applied the methods of the successful liberal press to a conservative publication. Although its circulation never exceeded 12,000, its readers tended to be powerful, such as Emperor Wilhelm I himself. The independence of the *Kreuz-Zeitung* eventually caused Bismarck headaches, however, as it became his frequent critic from a right-wing perspective. The paper's exposés of the business dealings of some of his associates resulted in lawsuits against the editor and in government confiscation of some issues.

Another group of party newspapers was created by political groups representing Germany's Catholics. With Austria excluded in Bismarck's reunification, Catholics suddenly found themselves in the minority, with almost no voice in the leading press. As Bismarck commenced the Kulturkampf in the early 1870s to curtail the influence of the Catholic Church in Germany, the Church's adherents responded by founding their own press, one that grew to more than 200 papers by 1885. While a national Catholic paper called *Germania* had surfaced in 1872, most Catholic journals were small, and their total number was a minute share of the 3,000 papers in the mid–1880s.

If Bismarck failed to curtail the rise of the Catholic press, he was more successful in suppressing the newspapers of a third group that began organizing a party press in the last third of the nineteenth century, the Social Democrats. The world's first social democratic party, born in Germany in the 1860s, had quickly comprehended the need for its own organs. Exactly how large this press was during Bismarck's years in power is difficult to determine, as it was subject to constant harassment by the authorities. An internal party survey named seventy publications in 1875, but a party veteran who subsequently wrote about that time thought the number was closer to forty. Whatever the number was, it became irrelevant in 1878 when Bismarck secured legislative approval of an emergency order that banned all socialist publications. The order was renewed several times while he was in office, and only after his downfall were Social Democratic papers free to publish in Germany.

А Mass-Circulation Press Arises

The relatively small size of the genuinely party press compared to broadly liberal newspapers, and the tendency of many of these papers to espouse "impartiality" in their political views, gave the German press of the late 1800s a decidedly apolitical character. That trait was further reinforced by the appearance of a new type of newspaper that did not consider politics particularly relevant.

This so-called *Generalanzeiger* was pioneered by August Scherl, who had spent time working for a company that sold inexpensive literature door-to-door. During that time he acquired a sense of what publications seeking wide circulation should contain. Inspired by French and American newspaper models, Scherl launched the first issue of the *Berliner Lokal-Anzeiger* in 1883, hoping to win as many readers as possible. He was particularly intent on capturing an audience that the existing Berlin newspapers had left untouched: the small tradespeople and workers who had recently moved to the city.

To do so, Scherl served up sensational human-events news from the rapidly growing German capital, along with sports, serialized novels and recipes. He commanded that the writing style be simple and concise, that contents stress information instead of commentary, and that editors keep the paper's perspective apolitical. Advertising was an essential component of the paper, with department stores and variety theaters especially eager to reach the readers of the *Lokal-Anzeiger*. Everyday people also made heavy use of its classifieds, both placing and reading them.

In sharp contrast to the publishers of existing papers, Scherl paid intense attention to promotion. His first issues were distributed free of charge to 200,000 Berlin households that he had selected from the city directory, anticipating that this move would build reader interest in the new publication. Initially a weekly, the *Berliner Lokal-Anzeiger* started publishing daily in 1885; its readership reached 123,000 in 1889, and by 1893 it was Berlin's largest paper. By 1900 it had passed the 200,000 mark.

Keenly aware of Scherl's success, one of his competitors, the Ullstein family, launched a similar publication, the *Berliner Morgenpost*, in 1898. Unlike Scherl, the Ullsteins were already well established as newspaper publishers and owned two respected liberal Berlin dailies, the *Berliner Zeitung* and the *Berliner Abendpost*. Both showed signs of weakening in the 1890s, however, prompting the company to explore new journalistic avenues. Four years before launching the *Morgenpost*, the Ullsteins had acquired a failing illustrated

An engraving from the *Berliner Illustrierte Zeitung*, 1891, illustrating street sales in Berlin, still a novel concept in Germany at this date.

weekly magazine, the *Berliner Illustrierte Zeitung*, which they resuscitated by abandoning the prevailing practice of distribution through subscriptions in favor of single-copy sales in bookstores and at newsstands. The same distribution process was applied to the *Morgenpost*, which became an almost immediate success, claiming 100,000 readers within eight months of its first issue. By 1900 it had overtaken Scherl's paper in circulation and reached the quarter-million mark.

When a government ban on street sales of newspapers was lifted in 1904, the Ullsteins decided to start yet another popular newspaper, the *BZ am Mittag*, which was sold to the public by uniformed newsboys. A newspaper created to be read not in the home but in transit or in cafés and offices, the *BZ am Mittag* offered a roundup of court and police news, stock-market reports, reviews of plays and cabarets and sports stories. Its editors paid great attention to layout and typography. Striving to make the paper as easy to read as possible, they used the front page to showcase the rest of the paper. It too soon became immensely popular with Berliners, attaining a circulation of 125,000 in the years before World War I. With the rise of the *Lokal-Anzeiger,* the *Morgenpost* and the *BZ am Mittag,* Berlin and Germany at last had a popular press.

Contemporary Views

The status of German newspapers and German journalism in the early 1900s compared to their counterparts elsewhere is particularly well portrayed in the observations of contemporaries. One of these was Swedish journalist Fritz Henriksson, who offered a harsh assessment of the Berlin press and its journalists in a 1901 book. What struck Henriksson as particularly problematic about his German colleagues was their lack of professional solidarity, which led to incessant infighting. Rather than taking a united stand against the government, for instance, Berlin editors curried the favor of officials at the expense of colleagues. Their fawning attitude toward those in authority did them little good, however, and only served to reinforce the already low respect for their occupation.

Henriksson was also appalled at the apparent lack of interest in newsgathering. Rather than engage in active reporting, Berlin journalists contented themselves with "lean and meaningless" releases from government press bureaus or with material from the *correspondenz* newsletters, whose streamlined bulletins contained the local city items and crime and accident news that newspapers in other countries collected themselves. What little reporting Berlin papers did was on staged events involving the imperial court, which produced what Henriksson sarcastically termed a mass of nothingness enveloped in a plentitude of turgid phrases. With so little in the way of solid information on which to base their articles, Berlin editors filled their columns with speculation. The papers did contain articles about science and literature, Henriksson acknowledged, but these were produced by academics, not journalists.

As for the newspapers themselves, Henriksson considered them old-fashioned, with unappealing and confusing layouts and small formats. While journals in Paris and London were truly national papers with large audiences outside their home cities, the papers of the German capital had few readers beyond Berlin, making them provincial in character. German distribution methods struck the Swedish journalist as equally antiquated. The lively street vending that was such a major part of newspaper life in the United States, France and Britain was altogether absent, leaving readers to subscriptions or newsstands and tobacco stores. The new category of newspaper represented by the Berliner *Lokal-Anzeiger* did not impress the Swedish journalist. He contended that the main characteristics of Scherl's paper were its total lack of opinion and its hyperbole on the activities of the imperial family and high society.

Fourteen years after Henriksson, American journalism professor Walter Williams echoed the Swede. Although Williams' views were more detached and academic in tone, he too was struck by the "dull" appearance of newspapers and their weakness in gathering news. The social standing of journalists was considerably lower in Germany than in France and Britain, Williams claimed, quoting a statement by Bismarck that reporters were mere "ink-sparrows." Finally, the American had grave reservations about the continued presence of government subsidies to the press, which he considered a barrier to newspapers becoming true organs of public opinion.

The negative tone of Henriksson's and Williams' accounts was not unique to foreigners. Similar assessments appeared in Germany. A 1908 book by Robert Brunhuber, one of the first academics to study the press methodically, praised the newspapers of Germany for their honesty, thoroughness and love of truth but thought they showed dullness, lecturing and servility. Like Williams, Brunhuber worried about the implications of official press manipulation for democracy, citing the close ties between the government and the monopolistic Wolff agency in telegraphic news. Brunhuber was also concerned about the role played by the numerous *correspondenz* newsletters, whose offerings from news summaries to editorials threatened the independence of papers by making them more uniform in content.

In two respects, Brunhuber went beyond Henriksson and Williams. First, he was greatly troubled by the repressive tools still at the government's disposal under the 1874 imperial press law. He fervently hoped that the abuses of police power that had surfaced during the highly publicized prosecutions of newspaper editors in the early 1900s meant that police harassment of the press was a thing of the past, but he was apprehensive about a section of the criminal code that allowed the authorities to prosecute journalists for exposing social problems.

Second, the pioneer researcher was deeply suspicious of the motives of the owners of the large mass-circulation dailies who he suspected were putting their business interests ahead of journalism's democratic obligations. Deeming the encroachment of capitalism on the editorial mission of the press a grave danger, he wanted journalists to recognize that they were the only protection against the peril.

Brunhuber's last point clearly pertained to the rise of the commercialized mass-circulation newspaper in Germany around 1900, and the frequent references in his book to conditions abroad are evidence of his awareness that this genre was an international phenomenon. In Germany as elsewhere, the new papers assumed that low price and general-interest content attracted the widest possible audience. Even with a heavy reliance on advertising to bring in revenue, the large financial investment essential to produce and distribute a mass-circulation newspaper meant that publishing increasingly was a corporate venture. That trend worried Brunhuber and others, who claimed that profit was taking precedence over the obligations to inform and enlighten. Eager to please advertisers, some German publishers had supposedly suppressed news, such as workplace accidents, that reflected badly on business and industry.

Some German press critics thought that advertising had another effect. They reckoned that the large newspaper in their country was becoming "Americanized" insofar as advertising drove editorial content and catalyzed expanded operations to achieve economies of scale. The result, claimed critic Walter Hammer, would be to sell everything, from the editorial to the smallest local news item, just as he believed was true in the United States.

The comparison with foreign papers and the concern about foreign influences notwithstanding, it was obvious that the German press in the early

1900s substantially differed from its counterparts in France, Britain and the United States. Most important was that the framework within which even the most successful papers operated was still authoritarian. Living with the threat of a wide array of government sanctions, the press tended, with some notable exceptions, to shy away from political discussion generally and criticism of government specifically. By the outbreak of war in 1914, many papers were swept up by the boastful nationalism of Wilhelm II, so few of them offered arguments for resolving the conflict. Even Scherl's *Berliner Lokal-Anzeiger*, launched on the premise of being apolitical, had moved into the Emperor's camp.

Another difference between the German press and its kin elsewhere was that it was still fundamentally local in character. Although large newspapers of the *Generalanzeiger* variety had appeared in cities other than Berlin once the success of the *Berliner Lokal-Anzeiger* was evident in the capital, most of the 4,200 newspapers that were published in Germany in 1914 were small; even after the war, publications circulating to only a few thousand accounted for two-thirds of all papers. In that sense, little had changed despite the 1848 Revolution, Otto von Bismarck and the rise of the large modern commercialized newspaper.

Bibliography

Brunhuber, Robert. *Das deutsche Zeitungswesen*. Leipzig: G.J. Göschen, 1908.
Engelsing, Rolf. *Massenpublikum und Journalistentum im 19. Jahrhundert in Nordwestdeutschland*. Berlin: Duncker u. Humblot, 1966.
Fetscher, Elmar B. "Censorship and The Editorial: Baden's New Press Law of 1840 and the Seeblätter at Konstanz." *German Studies Review* 3 (1980): 377–394.
Fritzsche, Peter. *Reading Berlin 1900*. Cambridge, MA: Harvard University, 1996.
Frölich, Jürgen. "Repression und Lenkung versus Pressefreiheit und Meinungsmarkt. Zur preußischen Preesegeschichte in der Reichsgründungszeit 1848–71." In *Kommunikation und Medien in Preussen vom 16. bis zum 19. Jahrhundert*. Ed. Bernd Sösemann. Stuttgart: Steiner, 2002.
Green, Abigail. "Intervening in the Public Sphere: German Governments and the Press, 1815–1870." *Historical Journal* (Great Britain) 44 (2001): 155–175.
Henriksson, Fritz. *Från det moderna Tyskland: Studier, bilder och intryck*. Stockholm: Bonnier, 1901.
Keyserlingk, Robert H. "Bismarck and Freedom of the Press in Germany 1866–1890." *Canadian Journal of History* 11 (1976): 25–42.
_____. *Media Manipulation: The Press and Bismarck in Imperial Germany*. Montreal: Renouf, 1977.
Koszyk, Kurt. *Deutsche Presse im 19. Jahrhundert: Geschichte der deutschen Presse Teil II*. Berlin: Colloquium Verlag, 1966.

Münster, Hans A. *Geschichte der deutschen Presse.* Leipzig: Bibliographisches Institut AG, 1941.
Retallack, James. "From Pariah to Professional? The Journalist in German Society and Politics, from the Late Enlightenment to the Rise of Hitler." *German Studies Review* 16 (1993): 175–223.
Reuveni, Gideon. "Reading Sites as Sights for Reading. The Sale of Newspapers in Germany Before 1933: Bookshops in Railway Stations, Kiosks and Street Vendors." *Social History* 27 (2002): 273–287.
Rieger, Isolde. *Die Wilhelminische Presse im Uberblick, 1888–1918.* München: Pohl, 1957.
Smith, Anthony. *The Newspaper: An International History.* London: Thames and Hudson, 1979.
Stangerup, Hakon. *Avisens historie i de lande, der skabte den: England, Frankrig, Tyskland og USA.* Vols 1–2. Copenhagen: Politiken, 1973–74.
Walchner, Martin. *Entwicklung und Struktur der Tagespresse in Südbaden und Südwürttemberg-Hohenzollern.* Sigmaringen: J. Thorbecke, 1986.
"What the People Read in Germany." *American Review of Reviews* 30 (1904): 210–12.
Wilke, Jürgen. "Gewalt gegen die Press: Episoden und Eskalationen in der Deutschen Geschichte." In *Unter Druck gesetzt: Vier Kapitel deutscher Pressegeschichte.* Ed. Jürgen Wilke. Köln: Böhlau, 2002.
Williams, Walter. "The World's Journalism." *The University of Missouri Bulletin* 16 (1915).

The "Fourth Estate"
British Journalism in Britain's Century
E.M. Palmegiano

Introduction

The "glory of the Nineteenth Century is the Press" wrote John Eagles in an 1854 article in the renowned *Blackwood's Edinburgh Magazine*. His judgment was not unique. Britons before and after Eagles accurately perceived the press as an influential force at home and abroad. Between 1815 and 1914 it became the most powerful public medium of communication in the kingdom. During that time the press displayed a breadth that is extraordinary. Its output, approximately 36,000 separate titles, explains contemporaries' sense of the press as significant and verifies its transformation from elite to democratic institution. Abetted by the networks of telegraphy and empire, the globalization of news and common formats in use today developed. Shifts in production and financing, writers and readers also shaped the nineteenth-century press and set the stage for that of the twentieth-century.

"The history of Journalism is still unwritten" said an unknown author in the popular *Chambers's Journal* in 1850. The statement is valid in the early twenty-first century, for no modern history exists on the British press in the decades between the end of the Napoleonic Wars and the beginning of World War I. Many studies have appeared, but they are narrower. The same is true for those done in the era. Works such as Alexander Andrews' *The History of British Journalism* (1859), James Grant's *The Newspaper Press* (1871), Mason Jackson's *The Pictorial Press* (1885), and H.R. Fox Bourne's *English Newspapers: Chapters in the History of Journalism* (1887) are not only incomplete but replete with contradictions. Memoirs and letters are abundant but obviously biased. Data on circulation and evidence on readership are either unavailable or unreliable. A good source is the press itself where the British tried to describe what this medium was and how it achieved power.

The nineteenth century was the birth of modern journalism, but this name did not initially apply. Not until 1833 did Gibbons Merle, a peripatetic newspaper editor, muse in the *Westminster Review* that "journalism is a good name ... for the intercommunication of opinion and intelligence ... by means of journals."

The first newspapers emerged in the seventeenth century, most of them bulletins on political and religious controversies associated with the English Civil Wars. These so-called "mercuries" spewed propaganda in texts and illustrations from woodcuts, while John Milton penned his *Areopagitica* in defense of press freedom. After 1695, when censorship formally died, newspapers blossomed despite taxes and restrictive legislation.

Most eighteenth-century gazettes, usually with one page of news and advertisements, came and went. Small audience papers, however, could have an impact. Daniel Defoe's *Review* was the progenitor of the social commentary in the *Spectator* of Joseph Addison and Richard Steele and the political in the *Register* of William Cobbett. The trial of John Wilkes for statements in the *North Briton* highlighted the scope of press liberty, and the paragraphs of Junius in the *Public Advertiser* were a prototype for the political columnist. In the era of the American Revolution the *Morning Chronicle* and the *Morning Post*, great London dailies, began. *The Times*, the giant of the nineteenth century under the direction of John Walter, II and III, commenced in 1785 as the *Universal Daily Register* before adopting its new name in 1788. Magazines, some with news and many with book reviews, flowered by 1730. The most famous was the *Gentleman's Magazine* partly because its principal writer was for a time Samuel Johnson and partly because its pages paraphrased legislative debates.

Parliamentary reporters had to rely on memory since taking notes was a misdemeanor until 1783. Thereafter, shorthand and team coverage made a verbatim record possible. Before 1815 the press also gained access to the courts, and the French wars, finishing that year, produced the phenomenon of second and even third editions.

Journalists worked hard chronicling Parliament and suffered hardships tracking domestic riots and military campaigns. Yet the public in 1800 considered the press disreputable because scribes were unskilled in news-gathering and writing or unsparing in their commentary. Connection to the press was so embarrassing that many contributors preferred anonymity. Their status did not improve with the establishment in 1802 of the *Edinburgh Review*, although its authors exhibited appreciable knowledge and style. The *Edinburgh*, which ran throughout the century, marked the arrival of quarterlies that used review of a book as an excuse to discuss questions of the day.

In 1815 the chief public media were the pulpit, pamphlets and street ballads. Journalism existed as a division of literature, albeit one of inferior rank. Newspapers were separate from other periodicals only because Parliament in 1712 imposed a tax on publications that carried news. A stamp on each issue indicated payment of the duty. During the eighteenth century the stamp duty steadily increased, accompanied by tariffs on paper and advertising. These imposts, later dubbed "taxes on knowledge," were high enough to silence many fringe tribunes, but laws on seditious and blasphemous libel inhibited every publication. While the London press was in the pay of government and its opponents, local weeklies and Scottish and Irish gazettes tended to echo the capital. Sporadic and typically unstamped sheets in urban centers targeted causes. Newspapers outside London were often a sideline for printers and were equally often without currency and coherence, acceptable grammar and readable print. These publications reinforced the notion that newspaper personnel were mere "scribblers," a stock epithet of the era. Contributors to other serials, from cheap, amusing but irregular squibs to expensive reviews on politics and literature, were frequently from other fields.

Within the next hundred years this scenario changed dramatically. By 1914 penny and even halfpenny dailies were popular; London newspapers were independent of direct political funding if not political slant; quality local heralds were ubiquitous, and serious quarterlies were unfashionable. Taxes had ended, and magazines for every conceivable taste had sprouted. Journalists had formed associations and had started to specialize.

Themes in the Press

Several themes are discernible in the press, 1815–1914. Until the 1830s journals were intensely partisan. Those for the wealthy were the organs of party, Tory (Conservative) and Whig (Liberal), or faction, Radical (reformist). Those directed to the lower classes, particularly the inhabitants of the new factory towns, were voices, sometimes revolutionary, for the disenfranchised. From the 1830s the goal of the press for the educated was to assist them in conceiving their own ideas. As Alan J. Lee underscored, this aim accorded with liberalism's theory that a marketplace of opinions would result in reasoned conclusions and radicalism's theory that information would catalyze political and social revisions by law, not violence. As the number of autodidacts swelled, papers addressed to workers concentrated less on inciting rebellion and more on acculturation. This emphasis confirmed the conviction that the principal role of the press was instructor, a dominant view until the 1880s. By then everyone had some schooling and most men could vote, so journalism reflected this more democratic world. Whereas earlier journals could manipulate untutored minds in a battle for power, later ones could blur the truth and debase the language in a race for wealth. The first strategy categorized readers as pupils; the second, as consumers. Although research, notably by Joel Wiener, has demonstrated that the shift was not abrupt, others at the moment and after regarded it as a metamorphosis in content and layout.

Jeremy Black and Lucy Brown noticed related trends. Black called attention to the gradual disengagement from official financing. Many newspapers never abandoned party loyalty, and after the advent of a local political press in the 1870s many had party sponsors, but the press increasingly looked to advertising for revenue. This source did not reach American proportions because the British were slow to link it to circulation. When that happened, dependence on advertising seemed to the British, as to the Americans, as insidious as the bribes once proffered by government. Only in the 1890s did the kind of centralization conducive to advertising and eventually labeled monopoly surface. For most of the century, however, newspapers remained in the hands of families or syndicates of friends who served buyers and sellers well.

Lucy Brown elucidated how location affected content at mid-century. London newspapers typically spotlighted Parliament, the empire and nations of consequence. Country gazettes reported little outside their environs except what they purloined from London papers, albeit journals in bigger towns were less guilty as time passed.

Speed was another factor that determined content. As audience demands for immediacy and variety escalated, a production process that could rearrange and print quickly more if shorter columns was essential. Technology — faster presses, cheaper paper, telegraphy and the telephone — was important as competition deepened. The pressure of time, nevertheless, went beyond machinery. Readers feeling "rushed" no doubt accelerated the demise of the annual and the decline of elite serials. Perused and sometimes penned by powerbrokers, the latter gave way to monthlies, which in turn lost ground to weeklies that were equally cerebral.

Other commonalities show in an analysis of journalists. In the early 1800s newspapermen, according to Brown, were typically self-taught artisans, poorer members of the middle class and clerical families, or Irish. Newspapers also attracted mercenaries, men without pretensions to learning but ready to author scurrilous personal attacks on a political party's enemies for money. Many free-lancers came to the press for temporary income. Trainees for the professions and aspiring novelists and poets, a cadre that George Gissing's novel *New Grub Street* vividly portrayed, wrote for newspapers and magazines. For magazine contributors active in other careers, press pay was supplemental. Gradually, women tried journalism because it was one of the few venues open to them thanks to anonymity.

Anonymity provoked unremitting controversy. Backers defended it as a pillar of journalism's moral authority, a safeguard for whistleblowers and an opportunity for novices. A minority before 1850 responded that anonymity deprived journalists of decent salary and job security, sheltered the biased and incompetent, permitted libel without recourse, and concealed deception when a scribe published the same article in several places or contradictory articles on the same topic. Although signature won and respect for journalists heightened during the century, people always suspected them of spying on society, culling secrets from the willing informer or stealing them from the reluctant. Without agreement on whether they were in a profession or craft, had an avocation or even vocation, journalists would not formalize criteria for education, self-regulation or state certification by 1914.

No survey of British journalistic motifs would be complete without reference to readers. H.W. Massingham, a distinguished newspaper editor, estimated in a 1910 article (*Contemporary Review*) that in 1840 only about one in fifty could read, but one in six had access to a weekly and one in 500, to a daily. The rich ordinarily subscribed to newspapers and magazines. Others bought or shared issues. In coffeehouses, taverns and even workshops, there was someone who read aloud newspapers. They also went from farm to farm.

Who readers were is harder to ascertain. Richard Altick examined the problems of identifying them, but the journals themselves contain some clues. A prospectus is an ideal audience barometer. Price, language and subject matter point to wealth, education and class. A publication's orientation — religion, gender, age, occupation, interest — likewise is an indicator of its readers. Letters to the editor are particularly useful to profile scanners of general newspapers and miscellanies.

Because it was common for a long time to share periodicals, discovering the reasons for readers' choices is more difficult. Nonetheless, everybody wanted news and views, and many, recreation. Since industrialization often distanced individuals from familiar environments and customs, readers counted on journalism to explain their different world and how to react to it or to distract them from it.

Growth in the Face of Restraint after 1815

By 1815 the spread of industry sired towns and a few large cities as the populace migrated to areas with jobs. Poor living and working conditions sparked newspapers of revolution, as the *Black Dwarf*, answered by those of counterrevolution, as the *White Dwarf*. Social distress propelled protests, among them a famous demonstration, the so-called Peterloo Massacre, in 1819. Government reacted to it with laws, two directed against the press. One placed heavier penalties on seditious libel. Thus, when Richard Carlile's *Republican* in 1819 published a report of the Peterloo Massacre, he was fined and imprisoned and his shop, shuttered. A second statute raised the stamp duty and ordered printers to pay, like the French, a security deposit in advance. Parliament did not repeal this supposed safeguard against circulating libel until 1869. The legislation in fact spurred unstamped and therefore illegal sheets. To escape prosecutions initiated by officials anxious to quell unrest, these papers typically resorted to surrogate editors.

The higher stamp did not hurt the top London dailies, among them the *Morning Chronicle, Morning Herald* and *The Times*, whose price and content already put them beyond the pocket of most people. They established their reputations by disseminating reliable news during the 1800s Napoleonic campaigns. The metros centered on politics and finance but had paragraphs on the law courts, the police and the arts. They might have something from abroad written by an expatriate and from the country, but London newspapers were not about the capital's neighborhoods. Advertising was on the first page, and an editorial, called a leader from the leaded line that divided it from other text, dealt with grave concerns. Leaders, fairly recent additions, had to be judicious. Unless a paper was in the pay of government, editorials might result in prosecution for seditious libel. Gazettes that rejected official subsidies recruited skilled "leader-writers" in hope of avoiding indictment. For example, Thomas Barnes, editor of *The Times* (1817–41), retained talented men by paying them well. Newspapers had no departments, but assignments to Parliament and the courts were routine. Other news came from "penny-a-liners," free-lancers who rushed to accidents and crime scenes. Paid by the line, they elaborated on stories and penned on paper called "flimsy," which created multiple copies, in order to earn more money. Submitting a piece to every daily, and London had thirteen by 1832, had the potential to reap a tidy sum for one report. After *The Times* in November 1814 switched to Friedrich König's steam press, its competitors did the same. This innovation meant not only timelier news but clearer printing.

Weeklies in the 1820s ran the gamut from the young Tory-subsidized *John Bull*, notorious for its coarse tirades, to the older *Observer*, circulated on Sunday since 1791 and famed for its illustrations. The *Literary Gazette*, the half-newspaper, half-magazine launched in 1817, had higher ethical and literary standards than the other two. William Jerdan, its editor (1818–50), sent a column to local papers, an antecedent of syndication. Two weeklies that opened in 1828, the *Athenaeum* and the *Spectator*, were more sophisticated. The *Athenaeum* focused on literature and the arts, winning accolades for excellent criticism. The *Spectator*, with an incisive style, explicated politics and societal topics with exceptional independence.

Outside London, the press was not uniform. Large towns might have several newspapers, some of distinction. By the early 1830s Liverpool and Manchester each had eight weeklies, one of which was the *Manchester Guardian*, later a commanding daily. Country districts usually had two weeklies, one for each of the major parties, Tory and Whig. Addressed to the landed wealthy, local gazettes used scissors and paste to pirate news from London papers and appended community gossip and advertising. Printer-editors might cover country meetings solely to get printing jobs.

Scotland had a number of profitable newspapers, among them the *Aberdeen Journal* and the *Glasgow Herald*. The *Scotsman* would be as good as most in London after Alexander Russel took the helm in 1849. Ireland, with more constraints due to religion and economics, situated its press chiefly in Dublin and Belfast before Charles Gavan Duffy's *Nation*, the voice of Young Ireland, became the symbol of nationalism in the 1840s. Wales, torn between the Welsh and English languages, more slowly nurtured a press. And even the Channel Islands had a few newspapers, which by the 1840s listed advertisements for illegal lotteries.

Well before 1830 other costly periodicals, such as the *Quarterly Review*, *Blackwood's Edinburgh Magazine* and the *Westminster Review*, rivaled the *Edinburgh Review*. Until mid-century they disseminated countless literary and political diatribes as well as groundbreaking essays. This prose was one way men who attained literary stature, such as T.B. Macaulay and J.S. Mill, started their careers. The *Westminster* is notable for publishing a series (1829–30) by Gibbons Merle on newspapers throughout the kingdom.

Many serials were merely conduits by which publishers such as Henry Colburn promoted, "puffed" was the Victorian term, books issued by their firms. For the wider public, every religious sect had an organ, and in 1822 the *Mirror of Literature, Amusement, and Instruction* pioneered the inexpensive illustrated periodical.

Pivotal Innovations, 1830–1850

The 1830s were a watershed for British history and the British press. In 1832 Parliament extended suffrage to males of the middle class. They joined the already enfranchised landed nobility, but both groups accounted for a small percentage of the population. The wealthiest of the new voters were captains of industry who believed that social stability was a prerequisite for successful capitalism. Many were self-made men who saw upward mobility as a tool to defuse dissent from below. The aristocracy, content with its privileges, also wished to deter rebellion. Both ranks soon regarded the press as an ideal medium to stifle discontent by modifying unacceptable behavior or diverting workers from it.

Legislative changes in the 1830s even more directly hit the press. A long and heated debate occurred about the "taxes on knowledge," mainly the stamp duty. Although most of the approximately 550 unstamped penny weeklies in circulation were apolitical, supporters of the stamp feared that repeal, or even reduction, would flood Britain with sedition, blasphemy and attacks on property. Working-class advocates of repeal contended that cheap papers would enable their disenfranchised class to air grievances and to learn politics. Middle-class foes of the stamp said that access to information was imperative for rational judgment, essential for laborers' eventual citizenship and immediate repudiation of violence. A respectable cheap press would turn the masses from fascination with catastrophe and crime to ratification of contemporary cultural and moral values. Such a press would also end the economic domination and intellectual discrimination of the stamped and therefore too expensive newspapers.

While the middle class drafted over a hundred petitions and attended numerous meetings, workers defied government by buying the unstamped. As Joel Wiener documented, Henry Hetherington's *Poor Man's Guardian* sold

10,000 weekly, 1831–32, and John Cleave's *Weekly Gazette*, 40,000 each number, 1835–36. Poor sellers who flooded urban streets were arrested and frequently jailed for violating the Hawker's Act, 1743, prohibiting sale of unlicensed sheets. When William Carpenter (*Political Letters and Pamphlets*), John Doherty (*Poor Man's Advocate*) and other publishers challenged the press laws, they faced incarceration and destruction of their equipment. Prosecutions against the unstamped skyrocketed in the 1830s. Finally in 1836 Parliament dropped the stamp tax on newspapers to one penny, paper and advertising duties having previously been lowered. Concurrently, the amount of the security deposit and fines for selling unstamped papers increased. In the same year Parliament created a postal system that allowed mailing of newspapers around the country without charge. By 1838 circulation jumped to 53 million, 15 million more than in 1836.

Paralleling these statutory amendments were other milestones. For ten months in 1832, Eliza Sharples Carlile edited *The Isis*, a radical, women's weekly and a harbinger of those at the century's conclusion. In 1834, two years after it began, *Chambers's Journal* published a history of newspapers, one more likely to reach the middle and lower classes than Merle's earlier essays in the *Westminster Review*. In 1836 owners of local gazettes founded the Provincial Newspaper Society to monitor advertising practices, especially those that victimized small proprietors. If they overcame startup expenses, higher than in London where printing equipment and compositors were readily obtainable, they could survive on modest advertising and subscriptions. Journalists were apparently more in peril because in 1837 owners created a Newspaper Benevolent Association to aid the most distressed. And in 1838 Henry Vizetelly was the first to get a press pass from the police to cover a public ceremony, the coronation of Queen Victoria.

The juncture of legal and cultural circumstances caused a modest boom for newspapers. For example, London, dailies averaged about ten and weeklies thirty in the 1830s, and fourteen and seventy-five in the 1840s.

Circulation data is foggy because newspapers did not have to release such statistics. Further, people continued to share gazettes, by joint subscription and the post or in social settings. In the capital, private clubs kept newspapers for gentlemen, and coffeehouses served legions. Renting a newspaper, although technically illegal, was possible because the vendor could subsequently mail it to the country. Notwithstanding this commingled circulation, estimates for *The Times* suggest that it went from about 10,000 copies in 1830 to 40,000 in 1850. These totals were paltry compared to others. In the 1840s the *Northern Star* published 60,000 weekly. It was the organ of Chartism, a movement that sought the vote and other political reforms to expand worker participation in government. Even more substantial was the tally for the *Family Herald*, an inexpensive miscellany that allegedly distributed about 125,000 weekly in 1849, seven years after its inception. Circulation of local tribunes was ordinarily small, constrained by the cost of the stamp and by the railroad that delivered London journals rapidly. The country persisted in culling from metropolitan dailies but slowly incorporated original editorials.

The Times, nicknamed the "Thunderer" because of the bluntness of its editorials, emerged as the paramount journal in the 1840s. By 1850 its revenue, according to Joseph Hatton (*Journalistic London*, 1882), onetime London correspondent for Chicago's *Morning News*, was equal to the richest German state. The newspaper epitomized "public opinion." John Delane, the editor (1841–77), maintained a high standard of writing by hiring educated men. He introduced the feature article by outsiders and spearheaded campaigns to rectify social abuses. Others of the capital's morning newspapers gained notice for their bitter political partisanship, witty reporting, moral influence or intellectual acumen. The evening dailies, such as the *Standard* (dating from 1827), published an edition at four and a second at six. Because of errors in fact and imprecision in style, they had fewer sales and less status than the morning press. They did, however, include abstracts from the late mail and from the financial markets.

Among the weeklies, the *Weekly Dispatch* (launched in 1801) and the recent *Family Herald* exemplified public emphasis on respectability but in different ways. The *Dispatch* offered an abundance of news, and the *Family Herald* scattered humor, adventure and poems among short essays. The *Herald* excelled in answers to correspondents asking for all manner of information and advice on social conventions. Readers relied on these public responses for much of the century. Absent national schools, skilled laborers and the lower middle class who aspired to social mobility had few other means to discover the mores of society.

The 1840s witnessed important innovations, domestic and international. In 1842 the first newspaper that prioritized the visual, the *Illustrated London News*, appeared. With ballooning sales, it limited advertising and soon carried tinted woodcuts and engravings by good artists. Although not inexpensive, it required little concentration and reached a circulation of 100,000 within a decade. Meanwhile, a flurry of railroad construction sped distribution, well coordinated by the firm of W.H. Smith, and telegraphy sped news-gathering. Previously, top newspapers expended large sums to get the news first. For example, London editors ordered reporters to arrive at the coast before steamers docked, board them offshore by private and pricey boats, then race by express trains to the office, jotting down en route copy on overseas news. Telegraphy transformed not only the collecting but also the character of news by homogenizing it once news agencies arose. Because telegraphy was in private hands until 1870, telegrams were expensive. Their fees and other expenses related to publication doomed proprietors who were speculators hoping for quick profit. People admired shrewd enterprise, but they wondered if financial venturing in journalism would subvert its honesty and further tarnish its reputation.

Newspapers grew steadily, but magazines climbed faster after 1830 with over one hundred commencing in each decade until the 1880s. Many died young, but some had long tenures: among these were the costly *Fraser's Magazine* (1830–82) and *Dublin University Magazine* (1833–80) and the cheaper *London Journal* (1845–1928). *Tait's Edinburgh Magazine* (1832–61) was unusual insofar as its editor, 1834–46, was a woman, Christian Johnstone. In the 1840s *Punch*, the most famous of the humor serials, started its lengthy run with literature and art that reaped prosperity and clout. John Leech was one of its eminent artists. Specialized monthlies as diverse as *Alexander's East India Magazine* and the *Ladies' Cabinet* and light miscellanies surfaced. The swarm of maternity magazines did not threaten fashion gazettes that targeted rich women. Readers of the *British Mothers' Magazine* were not the same as those of the *New Monthly Belle Assemblée*. What the maternal guides did was denote a societal mood swing about the fundamental role of women.

Fans of abolition of taxes frequently cited the *Penny Magazine* (1832–45) as proof that low price did not necessarily correspond to crude content. Charles Knight, its publisher, recollected in 1854 (*The Old Printer and the Modern Press*) that the *Penny*'s predecessors were obscene or brainless. Alternatively, the *Penny* had good woodcuts and diagrams alongside poems, tidbits lifted from others and small articles. At its height, it circulated 200,000 copies weekly. Like its kin, such as *Chambers's Journal*, the *Penny* spoke to workers and the lower middle class, many of them anxious to apprehend, not to challenge Victorian norms. The *Penny* and its brethren encouraged men to adopt the values associated with capitalism, such as hard work and moderate living, and women, to manifest traits then deemed appropriate for femininity, such as passivity and piety.

As autodidacts and graduates of private schools burgeoned, they went to penny reading rooms open until late in the evening, Mechanics' Institutes and, after the Public Libraries Act (1850), to those places to read. Urbanites perused the *Penny* or its progeny for practical information, mostly about jobs and job training, and for relaxation, poring over everything from hobby manuals to adventure serials. These sites provided access to many titles that were otherwise unavailable to the lower classes. What Altick catalogued as the democratization of culture, others have tabbed social control accomplished by decisions about what to put on the shelves.

The lower class also purchased penny periodicals, clipping from them reproductions of paintings to hang on their walls. Workers were not the only ones interested in art. The 1830s were the apogee of the annual. These beautifully illustrated publications had little good literature but were very expensive, intended to affirm the discernment and status of female buyers. Notwithstanding their audience, few had female editors. An exception was Countess Marguerite Blessington, who garnered a hefty income from this occupation.

Early Generations of Journalists, 1815–1850

Most journalists were not so fortunate in the years from 1815 to 1850. Irregular and insufficient pay, which socially marginalized them, made journalists unlikely cultivators of intellect and taste. Small newspapers outside London usually had a staff of printer/owner/editor and reporter/gofer. Editors ranged from ignorant amateurs with few business skills to knowledgeable and competent managers, but even the most qualified earned far less than their London counterparts. When the lone reporter, gaining experience from sundry assignments, moved to a better paper, he left work to another neophyte. For example, H. Findlater Bussey remembered in 1906 (*Sixty Years of Journalism*) that at thirteen in 1844 he was a reporter for his father, editor of the *Preston Chronicle*, and accompanied him from job to job. The senior Bussey shuttled between metro and local papers and his son, between both and news agencies.

Things were not much better in London, at least for editors of weeklies. These overworked men plowed through every report and letter in contrast to their colleagues at the dailies. Reputedly despots, Delane and his confreres, busy in conversations with powerbrokers, supervised production. Since most editors gave orders verbally, their administrations are hard to assess. The top men seemed to set the bar for dispassionate reporting if not commentary. Above all, they knew their readers' priorities and employed those who could write on subjects tailored to subscribers.

Only the biggest dailies had large staffs. At the pinnacle were the well-paid Parliamentary reporters and leader-writers. The first had a tradition of excellence. From the late eighteenth-century's William Woodfall, nicknamed "Memory" because he never depended on notes, and continuing through the youthful Charles Dickens, these men were for a long time the only ones to hold the title reporter. Originally, many were Irish famous for their wit and audacity, but by the 1840s newspapers enlisted educated "gentlemen" deemed more capable of understanding complex legislative debates and of exercising tact in choosing what to record. Reporters penned under pressure because officials demanded timely detailed accounts of Parliament and, when it was not in session, of Members' speeches in their constituencies. Writing in shifts, reporters needed about three hours to transcribe their shorthand or flesh out their remembrances. Not until the 1850s did they have comfortable seating in the House of Commons and space nearby to unwind.

Leader-writers, the editorialists, toiled at the other extreme. They typically wrote at home, going to the office only to get topics from editors and to return with copy. Their columns on public affairs were supposed to be logical and straightforward. An assignment could pose an ethical predicament when a theme conflicted with a writer's beliefs. Because of the reverence for the anonymous editorial "we," editors expected leader-writers to echo a paper's overall policy but tolerated some difference in perspective. Journalists who advocated signature were disdained as ambitious celebrity seekers who would be happy only at prestigious journals.

Before 1850 the more sophisticated newspapers had subeditors, men designated to review the submissions of penny-a-liners and to cut and coordinate items from local papers that might fit a broader audience. Subeditors, renowned throughout the century for efficiency and calm demeanor, also checked submissions of foreign correspondents, literally letter-writers living outside Britain. They culled news from another nation's gazettes and from its government departments. Before telegraphy, they had to decide whether a breaking story was important enough to warrant the cost of an express train or the risk of a carrier pigeon. Because of the sensitivity of their position, they rarely meddled in foreign politics for fear of alienating their sources.

The same cannot be said about authors in magazines. Free-lancers who were men of stature did not hesitate to judge people and conditions in and out of Britain. Some writers were politicians, some novelists, some experts in a field. Although many remained — and remain — unidentified, names circulated by word of mouth and in advertisements for their books or the journals for which they labored. Those known to an editor, directly or by reputation, might be commissioned to pen an article, paid by the sheet. The best serials lived on commissioned essays; the rest relied on voluntary submissions. Magazines regularly offered guidelines for the benefit of potential contributors, but newspapers never broadcast such tips. The advice was sensible: select a subject suitable for the journal; write in a legible hand in black ink on one side of good paper; plan to be edited but not to be published swiftly; do not harass editors. Because of the proliferation of periodicals, there were many openings, but lesser offerings tended to pay sporadically and to disappear overnight. Nevertheless, internal evidence suggests that women without other options for income entered this arena. Reputation came, even at mid-century, primarily by publishing a signed collection of one's articles.

Journalism at Midcentury

The 1850s began the heyday of journalism, one that lasted until about 1880. Journals mushroomed for every interest, the arts and the trades, high fashion and household management, imperial life and world politics, public health and private hobbies. Magazines could delight with sports, tales, poems and pornography, or they could demean. The racing press, with a subtext on gambling, covertly paved the way to the Victorian version of immorality. Racist missionary serials overtly stereotyped indigenous peoples, and misogynous ladies' monthlies subtly or not underlined women's irrationality. Some organs were condescending, urging workers to be "genteel" in imitation of gentility; some quarterlies were nearly incomprehensible when they reverted to ancient Latin and Greek; some miscellanies were charming, such as those of short fiction and intriguing correspondence, and many were merely ordinary, the stuff of amusement or curiosity. Among the noteworthy were the innovative proto-feminist *English Woman's Journal* (1858–63), edited by Barbara Bodichon and Bessie Rayner Parkes, and the *Saturday Review* (1855–1938), prominent because of its scathing social commentary and the *esprit de corps* of its university-educated staff. *Household Words* (1850–59), edited by Charles Dickens, disseminated insightful essays and satire and trained many successful journalists. It also anticipated the modern soap opera, closing the weekly episode of sometimes very good serialized novels with a cliffhanger that left readers to speculate about the likely outcome. Yet when contemporaries stressed the power of the press, which they did constantly after mid-century, they meant newspapers. The "citadel of freedom," "one of the chief pillars of civilization" and the "real rulers" were exuberant but not exceptional appraisals of gazettes.

Exemplified by F. Knight Hunt's book, *The Fourth Estate*, published in 1850, the newspaper came of age in that decade. Knight, the editor of London's *Daily News* (established in 1846), knew the business from the inside. Shortly after his text appeared, Parliament effectively ended all duties impacting newspapers: advertising in 1853, the stamp in 1855 and paper in 1861. The outcome was the birth of penny morning dailies, the first the *Daily Telegraph* in 1855. By then the London morning press, headed by *The Times*, sustained the notion that a newspaper should be careful and clear, accumulating and organizing facts responsibly. Using anonymity to present a journal's stance, editorials should be informed evaluations of major issues, done with common sense and in forceful writing. *The Times* attracted readers who admired its willingness to measure each societal concern on its merits and infuriated those who construed impartiality as inconsistency.

Many proponents of the stamp warned that a penny press would emulate American newspapers, which they considered inferior in content, layout and language. This threat did not materialize. Although the *Daily Telegraph* had graphic details from the Divorce Court and objectionable advertising for unregulated baby care, the penny papers did not break radically from the past. After all, the "Agony" classifieds in *The Times* transmitted heart-wrenching notices about lost relatives and cryptic messages to lovers. Apart from this human interest, neither the fledgling nor the prestigious London daily was casual reading.

Three leaders usually occupied one column each. Without paragraphs, these editorials necessitated close attention. Reports on finance, Parliament and international politics still took up most of the inner space interspersed by more and more telegrams. Foreign news coming by ships from the Continent and elsewhere and then from the ports to London by fast trains often had to wait for the second edition, published at noon. Only a Parliamentary sketch interrupted heavier matter.

The *Telegraph* later enlarged sales, following the lead of the *New York Herald* in Henry Stanley's search for Dr. David Livingstone, but by the 1850s newspaper revenue came about equally from sales and advertising. The newsboy was busy delivering morning gazettes to subscribers, then hustling the rest at railway stations. At twilight this entrepreneur acquired enough copies by ingenious and informal exchanges with buddies to fill orders for late mailing to the country where shops peddled papers to non-subscribers. Advertising, more significant as firms expanded that budget, never reached the proportions of the United States. Although *The Times* was the first to run a full-page advertisement, the paper grew sales more by highlighting national moments, such as with engravings of the funeral of the Duke of Wellington, the hero of the Napoleonic wars. Balance was crucial because too many advertisements signified that a daily was not serious.

The Sunday press was the long-time favorite of workers mesmerized by its police reports. Among the most popular Sunday publications were the low-priced *Lloyd's Weekly Newspaper* and *Reynolds's Weekly Newspaper*. *Lloyd's* purportedly had a circulation of 170,000 in the 1850s, about three times that of *The Times*. It supplied the masses with news, editorials and answers to questions and attempted to conform to Victorian ideals. By contrast, *Reynolds's* exhibited a passion for crime that appalled commentators. The measure of offensiveness was obviously class-bound since *Reynolds's* allegedly sold over 300,000 copies weekly. Because their jobs ordinarily precluded reading a newspaper except on Sunday, workers eschewed penny dailies for decades. Their choice of a Sunday journal also made it difficult for working class papers, from the general *Beehive* (1861–76) to the specialist *Co-operator* (1860–71), to prosper.

Without the stamp, Londoners at last had gazettes about London. So-called parish papers blossomed in every district after 1855. One, the *Clerkenwell News*, matured into the broader *Daily Chronicle*. The country press, however, was the chief beneficiary when the stamp went. Newspapers multiplied, numbering approximately 375 in 1855 and 1,225 in 1885.

Penny dailies, where text from magazines and sports reports complemented editorials and local news and advertising, particularly snowballed. Onlookers opined that the majority were ably conducted and fairly written, less petty about people and more sensible about politics than many London weeklies. The largest locals paid a London correspondent to write a "London Letter" that charmed more than enlightened the reader, but they too pilfered items — from the capital, competitors and even colonial and foreign journals. This habit discouraged originality but did not erode trust. Unlike their big-city brethren, country editors were well-known. Many were men of honor, and a few would enter Parliament, as did T. Wemyss Reid (*Leeds Mercury*), where they sat with proprietors, among them Joseph Cowen

(*Newcastle Chronicle*). Several organs were the property of educated capitalists who held them as investments; that is, not all owners were yet in the business of newspapers. Affiliations were closer to informal connections of relatives and friends than to formal corporations. Nevertheless, an advantage of this joint venturing was that it was an avenue to more advertising.

In the years after the legislation on taxes, government affected the press in other ways. From 1858 to 1865, Henry John Temple, Viscount Palmerston, was prime minister. Lord Palmerston was probably the first man to hold that office who comprehended the value of good public relations, in the modern sense, with the press. Previous bribes and prohibitions seemed worthless to Palmerston who realized that he could manipulate the press, testing policy by leaking it to a reporter or making an editor a confidante. While such maneuvers raise ethical dilemmas, they validate journalism as a social institution.

The ultimate proof that journalism was a force came from an unlikely direction. The London of mid-century was a sanctuary for foreigners who were *persona non grata* in their home states. Many of these residents, among them Karl Marx, supported themselves by writing for newspapers. Perhaps the most extraordinary was Alexander Herzen, whose London-based *Kolokol* was said to be the most popular paper in Russia where it circulated in secret. That this journal could spring from England is bizarre in light of the fact that in the 1860s the government prosecuted Irish gazettes that it linked with the revolutionary Fenian movement.

Journalists in the Peak Years

If the 1850s initiated the apogee of the British press, the decade likewise witnessed the first steps toward clarifying the role of journalists. Since the 1830s journalist had come to mean a person connected to periodicals. With easy entry, breadth in assignments and many participants who prioritized their other jobs, the field was hard to define. From mid-century through the 1870s people referred to it as a vocation or a profession; by the 1880s, as an avocation or a profession and by the 1910s, as a craft or a profession. Traditionalists were loath to remove journalism from literature. Writers in better reviews revered style and despised deadlines, favored treatises to fragments, and put thinking about ahead of amassing facts.

For magazines and reviews, the word journalist applied to publishers, editors and contributors. The last category welcomed the occasional stray from other fields searching for income and the frequent free-lancer. Authors could be female or male even when anonymity slowly gave way to initials, pseudonyms and then signatures. Harriet Martineau, who penned essays for elite serials and editorials for the *Daily News*, thought that anonymity was a blessing for women because it permitted them to discuss matters supposedly beyond female competency and to earn a living in an occupation that might otherwise be closed to them. The extent of women in journalism is hard to gauge because evidence about them is scarce or indirect. For example, an 1858 article (*Englishwoman's Domestic Magazine*) on "literary women" merely mentioned that females wrote two-thirds of *Chambers's Journal*.

In London, the dailies of the 1850s differentiated journalism by detaching the literary from the management side. The literary encompassed an editor, one or more subeditors, leader-writers, Parliamentary and other reporters and correspondents on salary. The editor was even more a director. He oversaw everything and specified editorials still done off-site. He also met with owners, more often after 1855 when the competition of the penny press threatened profits, which the wages of skilled typographers further reduced. As rivalry deepened, proprietors tended to take a greater hand in managing and writing. The conscientious editor was equally under pressure as telegrams increased and increasingly arrived close to press time. Failure to meet train schedules meant angry country subscribers. The subeditor, by now akin to a city editor in the United States, scrutinized telegrams and other copy and worked with the printer on layout, but it was the editor who decided content.

Among the staff was the Parliamentary corps, more staid as they aged. Some, like Charles Dod, manager of *Times* men, stayed for thirty years. Other personnel had assignments to the law courts, the police, the royals, finance, sports and theatre. Music, art and book reviewers might be outsiders who were no insurance against bias. Nonetheless, their work was preferable to critiques by overburdened and unlettered staffers mandated to fill space. Reporters had to report, hopefully scooping their colleagues on the crimes and accidents previously covered by penny-a-liners, whose numbers were dropping. Their ingenuity, bordering on lying, discredited them, and their verbosity rendered them obsolete. Penny-a-lining was reputedly a haven for lackadaisical ex-reporters wasted by alcohol, ambitious tyros and semi-literates trapped by trite vocabularies. In contrast to this grubby characterization was another, of capable, vigorous and dedicated reporters with greater job mobility.

Special correspondents referred to two breeds: "our own" were writers ready to go anywhere to write on anything; others were stationed abroad, always in Paris and usually in New York. Papers with few specials received much of their news from Reuters. P.J. Reuter formed his news agency in the late 1840s in France and relocated to London in 1851. His service allowed other papers to compete with *The Times*, which had myriad overseas scribes, and readers to have a common experience of news.

One branch of the specials evolved further in mid-decade. The war correspondent was formally born in the Crimean War (1854–56), a struggle that pitted the British and their allies, the French and Turks, against the Russians. William Howard Russell of *The Times* penned scathing articles on the British military. Long before his time, newspapers dispatched chroniclers to the scenes of revolution and war. James Perry, the man behind the *Morning Chronicle*, was in Paris in 1791 and Henry Crabb Robinson of *The Times*, in Spain in 1808. Harriet Ward, arguably the first female war correspondent, wrote on Southern African struggles in the 1840s and 1850s for the *United Service Magazine*.

Russell, however, was the first to be at the front with access to telegraphy. His columns kept both the public and officials up-to-date on events and raised questions about the role of the war correspondent in a society with a free press. The fundamental issues were how much access the reporter should have to military men, planning and activities, and what should be the correspondent's credentials. Debate about this journalist continued well beyond World War I. In the interim, the Victorians listed as job qualifications energy and enterprise, linguistic and riding abilities, and above all, bravery. The men who covered the Franco-Prussian War, 1870–71, seventeen from the *Daily News* alone, were soon heroes. Archibald Forbes especially enhanced the paper's reputation with his reporting. Readers relished correspondents' exploits, such as riding all night to reach a telegraph station or transmitting material by carrier pigeon when no station was near. While the growing dependence on telegraphy changed war correspondence from lengthy, tardy description to abbreviated scribbling on breaking news, the feats of the war correspondent won him mythic fame and commensurate salary.

Some journalists were apparently not so blessed. In 1864 owners replaced the old Newspaper Benevolent Association with the Fund to assist needy journalists. Anonymity still left most without status, although the 1860s brought more jobs at country papers and news agencies. The *Newspaper Press*, commencing in 1866 as "a Medium of Intercommunication between all Parties

THE

NEWSPAPER PRESS;

𝔗𝔥𝔢 𝔓𝔯𝔢𝔰𝔰 𝔒𝔯𝔤𝔞𝔫:

A MEDIUM OF INTERCOMMUNICATION BETWEEN ALL PARTIES
ASSOCIATED WITH NEWSPAPERS,

AND

A RECORD OF JOURNALISTIC LORE.

EDITED BY

ALEXANDER ANDREWS,
AUTHOR OF "THE HISTORY OF BRITISH JOURNALISM," Etc.

VOLUME I.

London:
E. W. ALLEN, 11, AVE MARIA LANE.
MDCCCLXVII.

The Newspaper Press—Volume I (1866–67): Title page. (P.P. 6481.e. [Shelfmark] By permission of the British Library.) This journal advertised itself as a means to facilitate communication among newspaper people.

Associated with Newspapers, and a Record of Journalistic Lore," broadcast benchmarks for journalists. Among these were working to short deadlines, long hours and relatively early entry to the field. These signposts marked the occupation off from more leisured periodical writing.

Another difference was that, unlike newspapers, magazines in the 1860s were abandoning anonymity. Disciples of signature denied that an unknown writer, invested with a journal's authority, could guide a reader. They insisted that anonymity was unfair because it forestalled an honest forum and shielded irresponsible scribblers. Enemies of a "star" system retorted that ego had no place in journalism, that collective and not individual wisdom led readers to truth, an unusual argument in a society that otherwise prized individualism.

Maturity of the "Modern Marvel"

The 1860s and 1870s were the acme for journalism, what *Chambers's Journal* in 1873 tagged a "modern marvel" that was everywhere. For example, in 1879, London alone had twenty dailies and 405 weeklies. The arrival of the midbrow monthly, which incorporated serial fiction and essays, gave each side a vote on authorship. *Macmillan's Magazine*, scion of the noted publishing firm, in 1859 opted for signature. The *Cornhill Magazine*, edited by novelist W.M. Thackeray and printing the novelist Anthony Trollope, in 1860 clung to anonymity. The intellectual reviews, the 1865 *Fortnightly* and the 1866 *Contemporary*, chose signing. Perhaps the quarrel was irrelevant since all of these titles lasted beyond 1900. The bulk of periodicals were unconcerned. Organs of general knowledge and moral counsel, such as *Leisure Hour* (1852–1905) and *Good Words* (1860–1906), were the mainstay of much family reading irrespective of their decision on the matter. And publications for the professions and for the trades were multiplying as people defined or refined identity. Sports offerings were more extensive, and illustrated and religious publications were as sought after as ever. Meanwhile, Emily Faithfull's Victoria Press startled onlookers by employing women compositors to produce the *Victoria Magazine* (1863–1880).

By 1865 monthlies issued about 2.5 million copies per year but soon faced competition from innovative newspapers. In 1868 Thomas Gibson Bowles resurrected an eighteenth-century formula. His weekly *Vanity Fair*, with caricature by Carlo Pellegrini, was the model for the nineteenth-century "society journal." Thriving on gossip that was originally discreet but shortly moved to a license that bred libel suits and their attendant publicity, the society journal dismayed a few as it captivated the many.

Simultaneously, the *Pall Mall Gazette*, a significant evening daily priced at twopence, surfaced in 1865. Frederick Greenwood, the first *Gazette* editor and once editor of the *Cornhill*, postulated that scholarly yet trenchant articles would appeal to cultured readers, so he recruited skilled *Saturday Review* staffers. The *Gazette* also was a trailblazer in descriptive writing, from "A Night in a Workhouse" (1866), and occasional notes, one or two pithy sentences on a timely topic.

Country journals thrived in the 1860s, among them weeklies that provided essential information about employment, goods, services and rites of passage (births, marriages, deaths) in the area. Some papers were quite small, but dailies like the *Scotsman* and *Manchester Guardian* were formidable, each printing 25,000 to 40,000 copies. They could afford Parliamentary reporters, whereas many rural sheets suffered from editors who published inconsistent editorials and novices who could barely find, much less record news.

Locals commonly maintained a party tie because politics engrossed their subscribers and lent papers importance when Parliament was not in session, when Members spoke in their constituencies. The political bond was never strong enough to interfere with business. For instance, editors sometimes refused to print a candidate's speech unless he also took advertising. They might publish book reviews to secure the advertising of publishers, but it was monopoly of a district's advertising and news, together with a low price, that floated the typical local herald.

Country gazettes benefited greatly from a decision by Parliament in 1870 to nationalize telegraphy. The action was partly the result of lobbying by the Press Association, the 1868 offspring of the Provincial Newspaper Society. The Association, though predated by the Central Press created in 1863 by some country owners, sent news to local papers thanks to an agreement with Reuters. Drawing copy from agencies might propagate less reliable information but lowered the cost of collecting it. To ensure accuracy, the foremost journals outside London had their own wire service. Because the legislation on telegraphy dropped production costs, more dailies appeared in the next decades. Receiving news as quickly as London, they could compete with the metros, but evidence suggests that sophisticated country readers continued to subscribe to London dailies for their commentary and coverage of international events.

By the 1870s the effect of an unstamped press was evident in the capital. In 1861 *The Times* published 70,000 per day; the *Daily Telegraph*, 130,000. By the 1870s the gap was wider, with *The Times* down to about 60,000 and the *Telegraph* up to about 190,000. Besides the absence of the stamp duty, technology was significant in factoring price and thus sales. Even as the paper duty ended in 1861, a shortage of quality rags forced newspapers to switch to cheaper wood pulp in paper manufacture. Also in the 1860s the web-fed rotary press sped printing, and the full operation of the Atlantic cable, the transmission of news. The Hattersley machine improved composing but was inferior to the American-designed Linotype of the 1880s.

As important as these developments were, they were overshadowed by a critical legal decision. *Wason v. Walter* (1868) protected the fair reporting of Parliamentary proceedings from libel. According to Lucy Brown, giving constitutional place to this reporting engendered pride among Parliamentary reporters and indirectly enhanced the stature of all journalists. Coupled with a trend to employ the better educated, journalists' status and pay jumped commensurately. They won an even greater victory in a case noticed by Alan J. Lee. In 1874 John Vaughan, editor of the *Liverpool Leader*, successfully pleaded that journalists could shield their informants. While these decisions touched journalism directly, another legal occurrence had greater implications for it.

Changing Audiences, Changing Formats after 1870

In 1870 Parliament passed a law mandating national compulsory education. Enactment was partly a byproduct of the 1867 statute enfranchising many lower class men. Even as that bill was moving through Parliament, Members complained that democracy without education was dangerous. Within a generation the national system would train multitudes. Although its test of literacy was the reading of a newspaper, many contemporaries decried the effect of these millions on journalism. Historians have divided on the subject.

The Victorians saw literacy as a prerequisite for intelligent voting. They assumed that the newly educated would engage in the same intellectual analyses as the previously enfranchised, namely using facts and opinions in newspapers as the bases for making independent political choices. This assumption overlooked the realities that many gazettes were intensely partisan and that many people regarded the newspaper as gospel. Much to the distress of observers, the students of compulsory education did not seem inclined to imitate their idealized forebears. Rather, they fancied fast reads sandwiched between the stresses of life and work. The halfpenny evening dailies, from the

Echo in 1868 onward, probably crested in the 1870s because they had the latest telegrams and updates on the financial markets and sports. Unlike their statelier morning kin, they were hawked on the streets by loud, agile, uniformed newsboys. Those who wished to skim the more expensive morning dailies without subscribing could still rent one for an hour, have it mailed by a friend, or go to numerous reading rooms and libraries. They could also scan *Public Opinion*, which after 1861 summarized in thirty-two pages selling for twopence, eighty world heralds.

The chief issue by the 1880s was not the availability of newspapers but their content and layout. Scribes christened changes already in progress "New Journalism," a phrase of Matthew Arnold in 1877 (*Nineteenth Century*), but disagreed about what it was. They did concur that the press was no longer a teacher. Proponents of New Journalism declared that instruction was unnecessary because of compulsory education and critics, that national schools graduated a literate but unthinking population whom the press mirrored. Traditionalists asserted that the press should mentor readers, not indulge their prejudices, but this function had overtones of class differentiation unpalatable in the wake of democracy.

The catchword for New Journalism was sensationalism. How the Victorians characterized sensationalism was another matter. One view was that it amplified the accepted role of the journalist as public watchdog by more dramatically spotlighting the worst social abuses. The best example of crusading was "The Maiden Tribute of Modern Babylon," an 1885 series on child prostitution by W.T. Stead in the *Pall Mall Gazette*. A year after, Stead spelled out the idea of journalistic responsibility in his "Government by Journalism" (*Contemporary Review*). In that essay, he portrayed an editor as "the uncrowned king of an educated democracy," able to speak for the populace but also able to prioritize a policy and to invent a controversy.

Another perception of sensationalism was that it intruded into private lives by borrowing the interview from the United States and by making "society" journals prosperous. As newspapers lessened Parliamentary coverage, they showcased stories about the famous, or soon to be. The elaborations on persons rather than ideas could be witty and picturesque in the hands of a master, such as G.A. Sala, once a rookie at *Household Words*. While such pieces resembled those in the Sunday and women's presses, to readers who paired curiosity about the personal with intimacy, the style was discomforting. Intent on checking any inference of effeminacy, champions reassured that the "crisp" language in political sketches branded New Journalism as masculine. The *World* and *Truth* were emblematic of the weeklies that cropped up in the 1870s and after, a genre that allegedly blended French frivolity and American flippancy. Their gossip was sharp but not vulgar; their satire, reckless but never seditious.

A third concept of sensationalism had to do with layout. News pushed advertising from front pages in order to capture street sales. Bold headlines, short and snappy paragraphs and the 1889 "stop press" catered to those in a hurry. Parliamentary summaries or the chat of Members, more but briefer stories and trivia seemingly lured those uninterested or unprepared to invest time in analysis. Clipped "leaderettes" bumped decorous but dull "leaders" by thoughtful writers. Readers who wanted in-depth studies had to peruse weightier magazines and weeklies. Popular diction, slang to some, supplanted correct grammar and graceful sentence structure.

Symbolizing this school was *Tit-Bits*. This very profitable paper started by George Newnes in 1881 was a model for those whose main goal was volume sales. He solicited ideas for copy and letters seeking advice from readers. Replicating this technique, the young Alfred Harmsworth (later Lord Northcliffe) began *Answers to Correspondents* in 1888. He invested its profits in a string of other small periodicals, such as *Comic Cuts*, before mounting a foray against the dailies. In 1894 Harmsworth bought the *Evening News* at the behest of Kennedy Jones, a journalist with an option to purchase it. They tested techniques in the *Evening News* that Harmsworth would soon implement elsewhere.

Established publications slowly adjusted to New Journalism. The country press, still solid because of price, news agencies and local focus, devoted more space to sports. As the politics of democracy spread, the parties launched papers, the Liberals initially more successful than the Conservatives. Gazettes with a weekend edition carried serial fiction. Illustrations and then photography enlivened texts and advertisements. Once-authoritative elite reviews and magazines lost ground because they did not take up the whim of the moment and their articles had too many pages. By the 1890s pensive readers were even turning from sober weeklies to stately evening dailies.

One of the outstanding neonates was the *Westminster Gazette*, dating from 1893. Among its founders were E.T. Cook, ousted editor of the *Pall Mall Gazette*, and J.A. Spender, who directed the *Westminster* for over twenty years. Its benefactor was Newnes, who in 1891 had added the well-illustrated *Strand Magazine* to his holdings. The *Westminster*, a sheet unique for its green paper, was small but influential. Cook disliked the tone of New Journalism but recognized the benefits of a front page with an incisive editorial and other columns with concise but penetrating opinion. He and then Spender made the *Westminster* a paradigm for this species of newspaper before World War I.

The 1890s were transitional years in other ways. In that decade periodicals substituted sociology and socialism, science and pseudo-science for earlier themes of theology and literature. Faith, however, was perennially in vogue, and art revived. Magazines for juveniles, once religious and then instructive as Kristen Drotner noted, were more entertaining and more gendered. Boys' and girls' serials looked different and emphasized differences. Boys' journals, such as Harmsworth's *Boys' Friend* (1895–1927), contained adventure tales that connected manliness and bullying in contrast to the uplifting *Boys of England* (1868–99). Many publications for girls focused on love, a keynote also of ones aimed at their mothers. Most women selected monthlies that sanctioned customary behavior and penny illustrated weeklies that paraded the aristocracy rather than organs that discussed female education, employment and especially suffrage. Even the relatively moderate *Women's Suffrage Journal* (1870–90) was no match for traditional favorites. Men liked the *Illustrated Police Budget* to supplement the Sunday gazettes and the evening halfpenny for its news and sports. W.T. Stead probably understood that the host of choices might overpower readers inclined to skim because in 1890 he edited and then bought out Newnes' *Review of Reviews*.

Senior journalists lamented New Journalism, sure that there were too many mistakes of fact and too many lapses of integrity in editorials and financial and sports columns. Patrons deemed New Journalism successful capitalism because business had to come first for the press to serve the public. While everyone reaffirmed the preeminence of the press, the tension between the old and the new intensified before 1914.

New Journalism, nonetheless, did not eliminate basis commonalities. Amendment of the law impacted all. The Newspaper Libel and Registration Act (1881) was a modification of Lord Campbell's Act (1843) that permitted truth as a defense in criminal libel if the story was in the public interest. The 1881 legislation tightened the requirements for prosecution and, not incidental, mandated registration of newspapers and their owners. Yet lawyers could take advantage of newspapers slips, prevailing on owners to pay rather than go to court. Concurrently, the National Association of Journalists, begun in 1886 by proprietors, promoted journalism as an occupation worthy of recognition.

Journalists Unsure of Their Identity

What surprised some Victorians was that employees did not organize. One obstacle was that, even by the 1880s, they still did not agree on who they were. By then the term journalist subsumed anyone connected to a newspaper and could stretch to regulars at magazines. Those anxious to throw off the mantle of residual bohemianism disputed that journalism was a trade but had trouble justifying it as a profession. Many did not consider it their principal employment, although public respect for it was higher and shared experiences fostered collegiality. A consequence of this uncertainty was that journalists did not firm up prerequisite training for journalism. Qualification in a specialty was appropriate if it was a craft, and credentials and a test for certification, if it was a profession. Absent consensus about the nature of their work, journalists went in two directions before World War I.

The first was the customary apprenticeship. It purportedly enhanced an instinct for satisfying the public, provided hands-on experience, and honed skills. A local reporter in the 1890s usually earned less than an average printer, but salary was secondary to variety in assignments that sharpened observation and writing. Because enthusiasts of this route presumed that journalists inherently had persistence, common sense and tact, they reckoned that reading in general and of the how-to manuals bursting into print was sufficient schooling. The ideal career went from local weekly to regional daily to London reporter, but writers on good country dailies could become department heads, subeditors, even editors at those papers. Otherwise, increasing one's income was problematic. Retailing news to smaller papers was less possible as news agencies hired their own corps and Parliamentary reporters spun imaginative paragraphs on politics for the locals. Alternatively, there was room for the industrious, as Henry Lucy typified. In the 1870s he owned *Mayfair*, oversaw *Daily News* reporters in Parliament, acted as London correspondent for twelve country papers, and penned articles for sundry periodicals. He authored columns, from 1880 to 1909 for the *Observer*, and, as "Toby, MP," from 1881 to 1916 for *Punch*. Ironically, when more journalists entered the House of Commons in the 1880s, they were generally not Parliamentary reporters but leader-writers.

The second track that journalists followed before 1914 was formal education, in journalism at King's College (London) or Birmingham University, or in a specialty, as illustration. Recently initiated, the university option was slow to enroll students before the First World War.

Division about preparation demonstrates journalists' ongoing ambiguity about their identity. Distinctions within the field evidence another dimension of their confusion. The *Quarterly Review* in 1908 distinguished the "journalist" as "a man who seeks to influence public opinion" from "the invaluable and indispensable person who purveys 'news'." But only five years later, T.H.S. Escott, a long-time journalist, contended (*London Quarterly Review*) that journalist and leader-writer were not synonymous because the editorialist had passed from critic to expositor of news harvested from telegraphy and telephone. Parliamentary reporters, at their zenith in the 1860s and 1870s, remained among journalism's nobility if they became editors, but by the 1900s agencies furnished enough legislative data to satisfy most readers. Few comprehended that press reliance on agencies' abrupt summaries abetted error and a herd mentality.

Another barrier to organization, besides the variant perceptions of journalists about their work, was anonymity, by the 1880s the bugbear of newspapers. English editors were proud of the "we" that they claimed warranted their independence in contrast to the French, whom they frequently derided. *The Times* and its peers held that signature prompted readers to forego thinking, leader-writers to pen for applause and reporters to suppress sordid items for money. Many magazines retained anonymity from habit or from the desire to protect the controversial author.

The 1890s were, irrespective of journalists' dithering, critical years for them. In 1890 an Institute of Journalists received a charter. Acknowledging that journalists were of many minds, the Institute construed journalism broadly. The association articulated a code of conduct and recommended educational standards, from basic work in literature, history and geography to study of languages, economics and libel law. However, the Institute did not set threshold requirements for the practice of journalism and did include owners, so its ability to monitor behavior was doubtful and to negotiate wages, nonexistent. Its principal effect was to divorce journalism from disreputability.

Five years after the Institute's charter, the Society of Women Journalists was born. A social rather than an economic group, it sponsored lectures and other events and kindled camaraderie. One female who did not participate was Elizabeth Banks, an expatriate American who commuted back and forth across the Atlantic. She made her name in the British press with "In Cap and Apron," published in 1893 in the *Weekly Sun*. For this series Banks toiled as a maid. Because investigative journalism was relatively recent and relatively unreceptive to women, most called her a "stunt girl." Her career specifies the general bias women encountered in journalism. People guessed that they lacked the judgment for subediting and editorializing, the stamina for reporting, the sophistication for interviewing, the training for illustration and the vulgarity for snooping — all necessary for success at a daily. They might find employment at country heralds, religious periodicals and weeklies eager for new blood, but their best option was women's publications, where they had ready access and a fair earning potential. Yet there were many exceptions, among them Flora Shaw, the first permanent female staffer at *The Times* and its Colonial Editor, 1893–1900, and Emily Crawford, a superb interviewer who was the Paris correspondent for the *Daily News* after her husband's death in 1885.

Even males apparently realized the tenuous nature of their occupation because in 1900 a cadre founded the Northern Society of Journalists. It was the first alliance of journalists without proprietors and the forerunner of the National Union of Journalists (1907). The National Union would deal with labor questions, although it had no history in 1914. Until it became effective, journalists were pawns of owners who could move them from gazette to gazette in an overcrowded market where their salaries lagged behind those in other professions.

A Mass Medium and Commercial Enterprise

As the century faded, there was no doubting that graduates of national schools preferred entertainment to tutelage. Big papers were brash; small could be quirky, such as *Shafts*. "Old" journalists grumbled that both types pandered to depravity in order to thrive; "New" averred that it was the duty of a free press in a democracy to sell cheaply what the majority craved, that it was the liberty of that press which enabled them to do so without interference, and that reading ephemera was better than not reading. Whatever the force of this logic, it did not neutralize the blatant commercialism that the arrival of the *Daily Mail* signaled in 1896.

The *Daily Mail*, Harmsworth's brainchild, was the first major morning halfpenny paper in Great Britain. In the 1890s the *Morning Leader*, whose inspiration was Paris' *Petit Journal*, and the evening *Star* had the same price but not the success of the *Mail*. It was a triumph for Harmsworth, who soon built a newspaper empire. The *Mail*, with its news abstracts and other tricks of New Journalism, appealed to the busy or unconcerned. Critics thundered that it epitomized papers wherein subeditors rewrote telegrams, thus doctoring the facts, and scribes penned news as stories. The first accusation was much graver. It implied that editors subordinated truth to sales or to agenda-setting. Confirmation of the implication seemed to come during the Second South African War (1899–1902), when one of the journalists credentialed for the front was the young Winston Churchill. The war, an imperial struggle between British and Dutch settlers in South Africa, sharply divided the nation. When the *Daily Chronicle* fired H.W. Massingham as editor because his shift from pro- to anti-war diminished circulation and the *Daily News* reversed its stance on the conflict under new owners, observers bemoaned the greed and insincerity of newspapers. This grumbling notwithstanding, the conduct was no different from before, only more transparent. Anonymous leader-writers often suppressed their beliefs to keep their jobs, and news selection always distorts reality. In 1900, for example, military-censored telegrams made instantaneous war news less accurate than lengthy, less supervised reports by mail.

The second apprehension about the halfpenny, that its accounts resembled fiction more than fact, was irrelevant for audiences beguiled by human interest, by persons rather than issues. Readers of 1900 without severe wants had little tolerance for editorials on public policy. As the authority of the editorial "we" evaporated, alteration of leaders and abridgment of news accelerated. Prioritizing immediacy meant eliminating any context for events, thus depriving readers of any basis for reasoned opinion. Reports of Parliament were cut back or cut out. In their stead went paragraphs full of platitudes and emotional slogans. Wars, crimes and natural disasters made excellent copy as they perpetually had. A gruesome murder was a guaranteed hit on the placards of street vendors, as the *Star's* earlier coverage of Jack the Ripper proved. Rumors and false alarms generated multiple editions. Pageantry of all sorts, from the royals to sports, also sold. Sports were so popular that, according to Tony Mason, these columns occupied one of the *Daily Mail's* eight pages.

A halfpenny's editor did not count on spectacles to occur naturally. He commissioned stunts, from physical endeavors to undercover probes, in order to tantalize buyers. Exposés boosted profit, even if in their details they hampered law enforcement. For those in a rush, headlines caught the eye, and photographs and trite cartoons simplified the facts. If such contents did not entice purchasers, newspapers sponsored competitions for prizes of all sorts. Adversaries classified contests as incentives to gambling, unwholesome if no longer immoral. What Albert Cave in 1907 (*Contemporary Review*) scorned as "journalistic Hooliganism" was smart business because, to enter, readers had to submit a coupon from a halfpenny's pages.

The *Saturday Review* in 1899 ridiculed the formula as "penny-in-the-slot journalism" needing eighty seconds at most of "intellectual persistence," but all the devices worked. Within a year *Daily Mail* circulation reached 200,000 and more than doubled by 1899. It represented the victory of New Journalism, but Harmsworth's *Evening News* was already moving beyond, mimicking the American "yellow press."

Harmsworth's ventures caused some talk of monopoly, notably when similar ownership patterns developed in the country. Long-held family papers were less able to match older London dailies that increasingly published news of the entire nation and sent stereotypes that impinged on local control of content. Consolidation of ownership offered a broader domain to advertisers, and their agencies permitted sellers to trade promises of space for editorial product endorsements.

The capital's morning press did not break off its extended romance with politics, but its role as counselor was incompatible with anonymity. Calls for signature were louder, but hoping that it would generate writing sufficient to insulate the elite papers from the onslaught of the mass press was futile.

The notion of the reading public as a mass was not bad insofar as it propelled the general gazette. People were still scanning monthly magazines in free libraries and religious serials in adult Sunday schools, but they were buying newspapers. In urban areas, the lower middle class picked up the one penny and the blue-collar, the halfpenny. In the country, men chose the one-penny weekly for news, the evening halfpenny for racing tips and results, and both for advertisements. Women, notably in London, were reading dailies, growing their circulation from a million in 1890 to 3.5 million in 1910.

The Press Barons

In the years between the death of Queen Victoria in 1901 and the onset of the Great War, the press stayed the course set in the 1890s. Led by Harmsworth, there were more consolidations that certified the press as a business first and foremost. By 1907 he owned the *Daily Mail*, *Evening News*, *Weekly Dispatch*, *Observer* (also a weekly) and the *Daily Mirror*, which he established in 1904 for women. The significance of the *Mirror* lies not in its gender orientation or even in its original weakness but in its size. Inspired by some discussions with Joseph Pulitzer, Harmsworth fathered the tabloid. Although its circulation was over a million by 1914, it was not his greatest coup. That came in 1908 when he purchased *The Times*, and with it cachet. Meanwhile, C.A. Pearson aped Harmsworth's strategy of investing revenue from a small periodical in a larger newspaper. He launched the *Daily Express* in 1900 and bought the *Standard* and *Evening Standard* in 1905. This template, obvious even in the country, effectuated a diminution in the number of newspapers by 1914, a circumstance particularly telling since there was a simultaneous rise in the number of readers.

Most papers adjusted to the trends. *The Times*, a trailblazer in faster and faster presses and utilization of the telephone, modified its content somewhat even before Harmsworth, albeit advertising remained on the front page. Moreover, the paper's prestige as ethical standard bearer endured even as Harmsworth steadily lowered its price. Fourpence after 1855, it dropped to threepence in 1861 where it was until 1911, twopence in 1913 and a penny in 1914. The *Daily News* and the *Daily Chronicle*, both with roots in the 1850s, went to a halfpenny in 1904. London's evening press lasted by publishing the most current statistics for sports betting. The affiliation of the press with gambling, troubling earlier, was an advantage now. The country tribunes carried local advertising alongside copy by wire from the Harmsworth organization and its peers, a variation of the old scissors. The era of the press barons had commenced.

The emergence of these men precipitated talk that truthful data and intelligent commentary were sacrifices at the altar of commerce as proprietors abandoned any charade of the press as a forum for public discourse. Collective reason seemed to have given way to collective emotion, logic to impression, thought to desire. Mirroring popular caprice hiked sales, but control of enough papers narrowed the breadth of news, or worse, let a few mold the opinion of the many readers to whom the press was pontifical.

If monopolies homogenized news, always dangerous in a democratic society, they also spawned more readable newspapers. Even devotees of "old journalism" admitted that its journals were dense in arrangement and intense in language. The new, with paper of lesser quality and smaller type, had clearer language, sparkling advertisements and no editorial sermons. Dull was definitely not the motto of the 1900s, but the interaction of newspapers was not one-sided. Newcomers recognized that perennially precise facts and occasionally good ideas could clothe a publication for profit in the moral cloak of the mid-century press. So, for example, in 1909 the *Daily Mail* added a signed editorial. The innovation was a cue not altogether appreciated at the time that Harmsworth could mobilize his papers to plot policy, which is exactly what he did during World War I. The onset of that conflict closed an age less for journalism than for society. Journalists had an inkling of how the struggle would affect them. In 1911 Parliament passed a new Official Secrets Act, clarifying issues previously discussed about war correspondence and anticipating others about the role of the press in a democracy at war. Coupled with the mounting sway of the press barons the law foretold a future in which periodicals might be muted for reasons of patriotism or orchestrated for reasons of propaganda and power. These outcomes were not what Victorians expected of the Fourth Estate.

Bibliography

Altick, Richard. *The English Common Reader: A Social History of the Mass Reading Public, 1800–1900*. 2d ed. Columbus: Ohio State University, 1998.

Beetham, Margaret. *A Magazine of Her Own: Domesticity and Desire in the Woman's Magazine, 1800–1914*. London: Routledge, 1996.

Black, Jeremy. *The English Press, 1621–1861*. London: Sutton, 2001.

Boyce, George, James Curran, and Pauline Wingate, eds. *Newspaper History: From the Seventeenth Century to the Present Day*. London: Constable, 1978.

Brake, Laurel, Bill Bell, and David Finklestein, eds. *Nineteenth-Century Media and the Construction of Identities*. London: Palgrave, 2000.

Brake, Laurel, Aled Jones, and Lionel Madden, eds. *Investigating Victorian Journalism*. London: Macmillan, 1990.

Brown, Lucy. *Victorian News and Newspapers*. Oxford: Clarendon, 1985.

Drotner, Kristen. *English Children and Their Magazines, 1751–1945*. New Haven: Yale University, 1988.

Hampton, Mark. *Visions of the Press in Britain, 1850–1950*. Urbana: University of Illinois, 2004.

Harris, Michael, and Alan Lee, eds. *The Press in English Society from the Seventeenth to the Nineteenth Centuries*. Rutherford: Fairleigh Dickinson University, 1986.

Jones, Aled. *Powers of the Press: Newspaper Power and the Public in Nineteenth-Century England*. Aldershot: Scolar Press, 1996.

———. *Press, Politics, and Society: A History of Journalism in Wales*. Cardiff: University of Wales, 1993.

Koss, Stephen. *The Rise and Fall of the Political Press in Britain*. 2 vols. Chapel Hill: University of North Carolina, 1981, 1984.

Lee, Alan J. *The Origins of the Popular Press in England, 1855–1914*. London: Croom Helm, 1976.

Mason, Tony. "Sporting News, 1860–1914." In *The Press in English Society from the Seventeenth to the Nineteenth Centuries*. Ed. Michael Harris and Alan J. Lee. 168–86. Rutherford: Fairleigh Dickinson University, 1986.

Onslow, Barbara. *Women of the Press in Nineteenth-Century Britain*. London: Macmillan, 2000.

Victorian Periodicals Review.

Wiener, Joel H. "How New Was the New Journalism?" In *Papers for the Millions: The New Journalism in Britain, 1850s to 1914*. Ed. J.H. Wiener. 42–72. Westport, CT: Greenwood, 1988.

———. *The War of the Unstamped: The Movement to Repeal the British Newspaper Tax, 1830–1836*. Ithaca, NY: Cornell University, 1969.

Coming of Age
The Growth of the American Media in the Nineteenth Century

Carol Sue Humphrey

In January 1815 Americans learned that an American army under the command of Andrew Jackson had defeated the British in the Battle of New Orleans and that the War of 1812 had ended with no loss of American territory. Although these events were not directly connected, most Americans believed that they were. Citizens rejoiced that the United States had successfully defeated Great Britain in war for the second time. They looked forward to a bright and glorious future. The American media joined in the celebration and also anticipated days of growth and success. And the journalists were correct in their assessment. Over the next 100 years, the American media expanded in amazing ways.

The Partisan Press

The newspapers that survived the War of 1812 differed very little in appearance from the papers of the American Revolution. Most were not big, with three to four columns per page in small type, and had few illustrations. The bulk of the news dealt with American politics and international affairs. Newspapers had begun to support particular political parties in the 1790s, and this trend continued after the War of 1812. In the years immediately after it ended, the Republicans (the party of Thomas Jefferson and James Madison) dominated the American political arena. Technically, there was no opposition. As the Republicans started to argue with each other, their disagreements slowly developed into a new two-party system, the Democrats and the Whigs.

In the 1824 presidential election, all of the candidates claimed to be Republicans, but they held a variety of views concerning issues that the United States was facing at the time. And, as had been true since the 1790s, these candidates turned to the press to get their ideas out to the American public. Each candidate had at least one newspaper supporting him. By the 1828 election, the two parties had organized more fully. The Whigs appealed to the middle classes and the Democrats, to working classes. Both parties used newspapers to urge Americans to support their platforms. Both parties likewise developed press networks throughout the country that proved very effective in reaching the American voter.

The majority of the political newspapers in the 1820s and 1830s preferred the Whig Party. Several of the top Republican papers switched to the Whigs rather than go with the Democrats. Topping this list was the *National Intelligencer* of Joseph Gales, Jr., and his brother-in-law, William Winston Seaton, and Peter Force's *National Journal*, both published in Washington, DC. Buttressing these two national papers were regional productions that preached the Whig platform throughout the country. The most important regional newspapers were Samuel Bowles' *Springfield* (MA) *Republican*, Thurlow Weed's *Albany* (NY) *Evening Journal*, and James Watson Webb's *New York Courier and Enquirer*.

The Democrats had fewer party newspapers than the Whigs, but they were better organized as a political party and thus did a better job of sending their message to the public. By 1828 the leading Democratic papers endorsed Andrew Jackson as the leading candidate of the party. The best Democratic papers were Amos Kendall's *Argus of Western America* in Frankfort, Kentucky; Duff Green's *United States Telegraph* in Washington, DC; and Francis P. Blair's *Washington Globe*, also in the national capital. The two most important regional papers were Edwin Croswell's *Albany* (NY) *Argus* and Thomas Ritchie's *Richmond* (VA) *Enquirer*. Among the influential second-level papers were the *Charleston* (SC) *Mercury*, the *Nashville* (TN) *Republican*, the *Baltimore* (MD) *Republican*, the *New Hampshire Patriot* (Concord), and the *Philadelphia* (PA) *Palladium*.

The editors of both the Whig and Democratic newspapers believed that their primary job was to sustain their political cause and to advocate their party's platform. They devoted a large amount of space to political discussions and debates about issues of interest to their readers. In doing so, they readily berated their opponents. Newspapers were full of invective and personal attacks aimed at the members of the other political party. Editors regularly referred to their enemies as "cowardly," "worthless," "incompetent," "insane" or similar epithets. This language caused papers such as the *Democratic Press* (Philadelphia, PA) to conclude (12 February 1825) that the campaign the previous fall had been "disfigured by passion and disgraced by violence."

Most editors, however, knew that their readers wanted news as well as political discussion. Most of the news related to foreign or national events. What local news editors printed generally dealt with crimes, disasters, marriages/deaths and local improvements. And politics remained the number one topic. Even after newspapers slowly moved away from direct connections to political parties, political news continued to be a mainstay of the American press.

Growing Numbers of Readers of Magazines and Newspapers

Alongside the newspapers, an assortment of magazines emerged. Magazines surfaced prior to the American Revolution and slowly but steadily grew in number during the following decades. Following the War of 1812, magazines proliferated so that by 1860 there were about 600 in the United States. They also varied more as editors tried to capture different segments of the American population as readers. Baltimore became a center of magazine publishing in the early 1800s. Hezekiah Niles established his prototype news magazine, *Niles' Weekly Register*, there in 1811. Shortly after, John Skinner founded an early agricultural periodical, *The American Farmer*, in 1819 and the first sports magazine, *The American Turf Register and Sporting Magazine*, in 1829. About the same time, Sara Josepha Hale launched the first successful women's magazine, the *Ladies' Magazine*, in Boston. She later went on to work for the most famous nineteenth-century women's periodical, *Godey's Lady's Book* of Philadelphia. Magazines also became a popular genre for reformers who used pages to publicize their goals. Abolitionist Benjamin Lundy began the *Genius of Universal Emancipation* and women's suffrage advocate Amelia Bloomer produced the *Lily* as forums for their ideas.

These magazines sought out an audience interested in a specific topic or issue, but most publications in the early nineteenth century were journals that featured popular literature. Leading this group was the *Saturday Evening Post*, founded in 1821. Equally important were the illustrated weeklies, such as *Gleason's Pictorial Drawing-Room Companion* and *Frank Leslie's Illustrated*

Newspaper, which became popular in the 1850s. The illustrated journals were the first periodicals to touch a truly mass audience, but all magazines developed techniques, particularly the use of illustrations, that would become important in newspapers in the coming decades.

This impact was significant because newspapers continued to be the predominant printed medium in the United States. Even before the influence of magazines, some editors were already considering changes in order to attract new readers. When proposing a new religious newspaper in the *Family Visitor* (8 October 1825), David Roper declared that "[a] thirst for newspaper reading prevails among all ranks of society throughout our country." Some editors modified content in order to lure a variety of readers. On 24 January 1824 the editor of the *New-York Mirror and Ladies' Literary Gazette* described a successful newspaper as "a bill of fare, containing a variety of dishes, suited to the different tastes and appetites of those who sit down at the entertainment. Politics are beef steaks, palatable to almost every one. Those who prefer them rare done, choose those from France. Electioneering is venison, Congress news is stuffed meats. Essays, humorous, speculative, moral, and divine, are a fine boiled dish, where, by a happy commixture in the use of bread, meat, and vegetables, a diet is obtained, nutritive, pleasant, and healthy. Ship news is a glass of grog at eleven. Poetry is custard. Marriages are sweet meats. Ballads and love ditties, plum pudding. Anecdotes, conundrums, and epigrams are spice and mustard. Sometimes here comes along a printer's dun — that is sour crust or cranberry tart."

One reason for expanding magazine and newspaper readership was the widespread literacy among Americans. By the early 1800s the majority of men and women in the United States could read. Many people approved this growth of a literate population because they believed it would enable Americans to be better informed about what was going on in the United States and thus would help to spread democracy and its benefits throughout the nation. For most Americans, newspapers were the primary source of the information necessary to be a good citizen and a useful way to influence public opinion. The editor of the *Washington Gazette* noted these advantages in the issue of 20 March 1822: "We every day witness the extensive and almost absolute influence of the power of the press over the minds of people ... Even the government of our union is so much swayed by the press, that it has not been inappropriately styled a government of newspapers." Visitors to the United States also commented on the increase in numbers and growing clout of newspapers. Probably the best-known assessment about the power of the press in the United States came from Alexis de Tocqueville in his *Democracy in America* (1:186–88): "In America there is scarcely a hamlet that has not its newspaper.... It causes political life to circulate through all the parts of that vast territory. Its eye is constantly open to detect the secret springs of political designs and to summon the leaders of all parties to turn to the bar of public opinion. It rallies the interests of the community round certain principles and draws up the creed of every party; for it affords a means of intercourse between those who hear and address each other without ever coming into immediate contact. When many organs of the press adopt the same line of conduct, their influence in the long run becomes irresistible, and public opinion, perpetually assailed from the same side, eventually yields to the attack. In the United States each separate journal exercises but little authority; but the power of the periodical press is second only to that of the people."

The Penny Press

The rise in literacy rates in the United States fueled other developments that encouraged newspaper growth. By about 1830 the Industrial Revolution in the United States had produced a clearly visible working class, and editors hoped to recruit readers from this class. At that time, there were about 1,200 newspapers published in the United States on a regular basis. Most still had political connections, and most were expensive. These circumstances changed after 3 September 1833, when Benjamin Day distributed the first issue of the *New York Sun*, the first of the "penny press" directed to the new working class audience. In that issue, Day told his readers that "the object of this paper is to lay before the public, at a price within the means of every one, all the news of the day, and at the same time offer an advantageous medium for advertisements." The urban industrial readers whom Day hoped to win wanted entertainment and information, and Day and other "penny press" newspapers tried to satisfy this need. Their editors used headlines and illustrations to grab the attention of readers and to keep that attention with livelier writing and stories that went beyond politics and international news to deal with crime and other so-called sensational topics. The "penny press" editors also broke with tradition by selling their papers one at a time on the street rather than insisting that readers purchase a yearly subscription. This change enabled even the poorest to buy a paper occasionally, whenever they could afford it.

The premier issue of the *New York Sun* had four pages. At first glance, it looked no different from the partisan papers that then dominated the media.

About a third of it was advertising, but almost half of it was filled with shipping, police and general news. Later issues had stories about ordinary people doing ordinary things or about alarming crimes and startling events. Probably the most famous series in the *Sun* has become known as the "Moon Hoax." In columns supplemented by illustrations the *Sun* dutifully reported the work of Sir John Frederick William Herschel, an astronomer who supposedly used a new large telescope to discover life on the moon. Descriptions of vegetation, forests, animals and human-like beings captivated readers. Later described by its author, Richard Adams Locke, as a satire on popular astronomy books that mixed fact and fiction, the Moon Hoax was a great boon for the *Sun's* circulation. More important, the overall success of the *Sun* showed that a general non-partisan newspaper would sell on the street to the general public and that a newspaper with lively and unpretentious writing could thrive. Benjamin Day's achievement set a new style and standard that would dominate the American media for years to come.

James Gordon Bennett

Day's first serious competition came from the *New York Herald*, edited by James Gordon Bennett, that initially appeared on 6 May 1835. Bennett yearned for success, tremendous success. He constantly told his readers that he was going to achieve it. He presented his ideas about newspapers and about his accomplishments within journalism in a later issue (28 February 1837) of the *Herald* when he said: "The daily newspaper press has been a mere organ of dry detail — uninteresting facts — political nonsense — personal squabbles — obsolete rows — tedious ship news — or meagre quotations of the markets. I have changed all this. I have infused life, glowing eloquence, philosophy, taste, sentiment, wit, and humor into the daily newspaper. I have shown, in eighteen months, that a daily newspaper conducted with power, knowledge, industry and genius, can be made the most powerful instrument of civilization and of improvement that the world ever saw. Shakespeare is the great genius of the drama, Scott of the novel, Milton and Byron of the poem — and I mean to be the genius of the newspaper press. Until this age the power and capacity of the daily press have never been discovered. It has never been applied to the great purposes of civilization, science, virtue, elegance, refinement, till the years 1836 and 1837." Furthermore, Bennett saw his numerous critics as proof of his triumph: "Guided by the light of genius, that like the bush of Moses in the wilderness, burns to the very heart but consumes not, I have broken out of the old ridiculous, foolish, empty path, and published a paper that has created a greater sensation in this country, than a war in Europe would have done, or even a revolution in France."

To attain this personal recognition and power, Bennett planned from the outset to establish a newspaper for everyone, read by everyone because it would avoid political entanglements. He declared his independence in the initial issue: "We shall support no party — be the organ of no faction or COTERIE, and care nothing for any election or any candidate from president down to a constable. We shall endeavor to record facts on every public and proper subject, stripped of verbiage and coloring, with comments when suitable, just, independent, fearless and good-tempered." Bennett meant to report news as briefly and clearly as possible. In the 19 August 1836 issue, he spelled out again his view of the press: "What is to prevent a daily newspaper from being made the greatest organ of social life? Books have had their day — the theatres have had their day — the temple of religion has had its day. A newspaper can be made to take the lead of all these in the great movements of human thought and of human civilization. A newspaper can send more souls to Heaven, and save more from Hell, than all the churches or chapels in New York — besides making money at the same time. Let it be tried."

James Gordon Bennett, founder of the *New York Herald*. This photo is a surviving portrait by the important nineteenth-century photographer Mathew Brady.

And Bennett did try to reach this goal. In his second issue, he promised to "give a correct picture of the world." But he shocked many readers as he put this plan into action. Bennett refused to use the proper Victorian terminology that most people expected to see in print. For example, he referred to shirts instead of linen and legs instead of limbs. He also covered crimes and the courts in such detail that his readers felt as if they were in the middle of the story, a sometimes unsettling sensation. Opponents attempted to undermine Bennett's efforts through boycotts, and he toned things down a bit, but he never gave in completely. Bennett also changed the newspaper business in other ways. He maintained a subscription policy that required payment in advance while at the same time selling individual copies of the *Herald* on the street. He introduced the "Personals" column and ordered advertisers to alter their ads frequently enough to keep them fresh and to give readers variety.

Bennett's most important contribution was a redefinition of the concept of news. Previously, editors and readers had not really worried about whether the information in newspapers was timely. Even in the 1840s stories often appeared weeks after an event occurred. Bennett wanted to publish news promptly. In 1838 he took advantage of the new steamship lines across the Atlantic to set up a network of European correspondents who would provide current news reports about events on the Continent. Three years later he created a corps of Washington correspondents to file more immediate columns on events in the nation's capital. Bennett likewise took advantage of the recently-invented telegraph to speed delivery of the news. His *Herald* inaugurated coverage of sports, business and women. In 1855 he hired Jane Cunningham Croly ("Jennie June") to write about "society." Croly's byline became famous as she penned articles about fashion, beauty and social gatherings. Bennett had a good understanding of the many types of stories that readers liked, and he determined to print them all.

Other Penny Press Editors

Another major "penny press" editor was Horace Greeley. Greeley had been a job printer for several years before joining the "penny press." He produced the first issue of the *New York Tribune* on 10 April 1841, six years after the *Herald* arrived. With the *Tribune*, Greeley entered a crowded New York City publishing world that already included about a hundred periodicals and twelve daily newspapers. Like Bennett, Greeley wanted to publish a paper for everyone. He thought that it was possible to produce a paper that enabled people to learn all they needed to know about critical current events. Greeley copied Bennett's creation of a stable of correspondents scattered across Europe and the United States. Among his many correspondents was Margaret Fuller, who reported on the Italian revolution of 1848–1849. Fuller was the first female foreign correspondent for an American newspaper. With correspondents like Fuller and others, Greeley developed a reputation for excellent news coverage. He also gave his readers more information by circulating lectures, poetry, serialized novels and book reviews. He hoped to differentiate the *Tribune* from other penny papers by ignoring more sensational items, such as those from the police courts and murder trials. Greeley also took strong editorial stands in favor of reforms such as abolition and prohibition. His crusading helped make the *Tribune* an influential paper during the middle years of the nineteenth century.

The last significant editor in the years before the Civil War was Henry Raymond, who founded the *New York Times* in 1851. Raymond had previously written for Greeley's *Tribune*, but he left in frustration because he felt overworked and underpaid. His purpose for the *Times* was to appeal to readers who did not like either the *Herald* or the *Tribune*. Generally more conservative and middle-class, these readers judged the *Tribune* too radical because of Greeley's support for abolition and prohibition, while the *Herald* was too nasty because of Bennett's refusal to abide by Victorian language conventions. Visually, the *Times* looked much like the competition. It had four pages of six columns each, with foreign and local news displayed on the front page. But the contents were often very different. Raymond hoped to champion "the public good" by praising what was worthwhile and criticizing what was not in the United States. Over the years, the *New York Times* earned a reputation for fair and accurate reporting with an emphasis on foreign affairs. Raymond, like his colleagues at other penny papers, intended to capture a mass audience, but unlike his rivals, he meant to do so without their sensationalism. By 1860 the *Times* was well-established, successfully competing with the other penny papers in New York. When Raymond died in 1869, the editors of *The Nation* (24 June) praised his efforts: "In the art of making a good newspaper, we need hardly say, he was a master. The *Times* under his management probably came nearer the newspaper of the good time coming than any other in existence."

Journalistic Developments to the 1860s

These "penny papers" shifted and sometimes raised the bar for the American newspaper. They produced cheaper papers that more people could afford to buy. They provided more consistent coverage of all sorts of news, including crime, finance, sports and scandals. "Penny press" editors regularly assigned reporters to cover certain stories, thus creating the basis of the later beat system where a reporter focused on a particular area or issue. Washington and foreign correspondents, whose origins were noted above, soon became common for any newspaper seeking a large audience. These reporters and correspondents developed the interview, later grudgingly adopted by the British, as a mechanism for gathering information. Most significant, the "penny press" publishers turned news into a commodity as they discovered that readers were more eager to buy news and information than they previously had been to buy opinion. Ultimately, the "penny press" became the first true mass medium in the United States.

These modifications sold papers, so other editors and publishers sought to emulate them. Newspapers in every major city in the United States copied the innovations in New York. Remodeling in writing style and content pulled in new readers everywhere. People liked the emphasis on sensational and human interest stories and the expansion of local news. Most gazettes continued to have some sort of tie to political parties, particularly at the local level, but they increasingly tried to report the news in a more neutral fashion — what would later be termed "objectivity." Editorials were clearly separated from news stories, and editors recruited correspondents to provide more on-the-scene reports from all over the world. Inventions in technology, discussed below, also enabled newspapers to grow in size and reach. By the middle of the nineteenth century, the newspaper business in the United States was complicated. The one-person shop was a relic of the past as the process of producing a newspaper involved more and more people. The preponderance of major dailies now needed a publisher, at least one editor, a handful of reporters, and a number of printers in order to get the paper out on time.

The burgeoning of newspapers also sparked improvements in mail delivery as that remained the most common means of dissemination. Between 1825 and 1861, several postal express systems arose in different parts of the country in order to speed delivery. Congress authorized a nationwide express service in the Post Office Act of 1836. But private express companies stayed in business, either competing directly with the Postal Service or functioning in areas not served by the post office. Probably the most famous private company was the Pony Express, which during 1860 and 1861 operated between St. Joseph, Missouri, and San Francisco, California. Resort to express companies by journalists declined after the completion of the transcontinental telegraph in October 1861. The telegraph had been increasingly used for the submission of news reports ever since its introduction in the United States by Samuel F.B. Morse in 1844. It became the most popular means for reporters to submit stories during the Civil War and remained so until replaced by the telephone in the late nineteenth century.

Another major development about mid-century, one that had tremendous implications for the future, was likewise related to the need to gather news from great distances. In 1848 the six chief newspapers of New York agreed to pool information in order to cover more ground and save money. The outcome of their decision was the Harbor News Association. At first it sent a news boat to meet incoming ships and then conveyed the information collected to the six newspapers. The group later branched out, sharing telegraphic news from Boston, Washington and other major cities. By 1858 the six adopted a new name, the New York Associated Press. This forerunner of the modern Associated Press showed how much material could be gotten when newspapers cooperated in gathering news, a practice that would greatly contribute to the timeliness and amount of news in journals across the United States.

By the 1840s direct ties between political parties and newspapers were declining, but that did not mean that political issues ceased to be of interest. In fact, the growing circulation of newspapers kept Americans well informed on key questions and so helped to fuel the heated controversy about slavery that would eventually lead to the Civil War. Writers in newspapers and magazines engaged in a war of words years before the fighting started. The initial arguments appeared in the 1820s when a number of slavery's opponents launched antislavery newspapers and magazines. The most famous of these journals, William Lloyd Garrison's *Liberator*, commenced in Boston on 1 January 1831. In this first issue, Garrison declared "I *will be* as harsh as truth, and as uncompromising as justice. On this subject, I do not wish to think, to speak, or write, with moderation.... I am in earnest—I will not equivocate—I will not excuse—I will not retreat a single inch—AND I WILL BE HEARD." Garrison's strong attack on slavery generated equally strong reactions. Southerners feared that his words would stir up slave revolts while northerners worried that he would destroy any chance of compromise on the slavery issue. Other antislavery editors, such as Benjamin Lundy, Lewis Tappan and Frederick Douglass, also sparked debates among Americans as the slavery question became more volatile. Challenging slavery in print could prove dangerous. Garrison was mobbed on several occasions and, in 1835, Elijah Lovejoy, editor of the *St. Louis Observer*, was one of the first American martyrs for freedom of the press when he was killed by a crowd as he tried to protect his press.

The Civil War and Journalism

By 1860 the argument over slavery had stoked an argument over the rights of the states versus the powers of the national government that ultimately erupted into war. The opening shots were fired at Fort Sumter in April 1861. During the next four years, most Americans on both sides of the fight looked to the papers for news about how the war was going. For the first time, reporters depended on the telegraph to get stories back to their newspapers. This quick transmission of news spawned numerous "extras" full of the latest details from the front. The focus on speed was not always an advantage. Haste could cause bad reporting, and the printing of rumor was common. On 27 May 1861 the *Baltimore Sun* summarized the attitude of most newspaper editors at the time: "Rumors of every kind multiply. Every hour gives rise to the most extravagant reports.... The press North and South seems to have entered upon a war of crimination and recrimination, and instead of calming the excitement and allaying unfounded prejudices, to rejoice in adding to the excitement of the moment." Most newspapers commonly used the column heading "IMPORTANT — IF TRUE." But Americans still snatched up the latest publication in order to find out the most recent details about the war, even if the press was primarily a purveyor of half-truths. After the war ended, a reporter stated in the 27 July 1865 issue of *The Nation* that "to print first, however incorrect and incomplete intelligence, was the height of ambitions."

The Civil War became the reporter's war. The emphasis on speed put the spotlight on reporters. Those for the Union Army were nicknamed the "Bohemian Brigade." As many as 500 reporters worked for northern newspapers during the conflict, and most of them lived on the edge of danger. Although the public considered them a bit disreputable, Americans still read their pieces because the reporters went to the front, ready to face the hazards of the shooting to get the story. New York sent out the most reporters. The *Herald* had over sixty in the field during the war. The *Tribune* and the *Times* commissioned fewer reporters, but the correspondents of each of the three papers strained to be the first to submit descriptions of the latest battles. The New York Associated Press (AP) dispatched the largest number of reporters. The AP already had a network of correspondents throughout the nation when the struggle broke out, so it merely added to this corps in the field once the fighting started. Because of the high rates the AP charged, a group of western newspapers formed their own news cooperative in November 1862. These efforts at joint news-gathering, which continued after the war, further modified how most newspapers acquired national and international news for their readers. Northern reporters also created headaches for American leaders. The journalists reported everything they learned, and their editors did not cut anything out of their stories. Thus, columns about troop movements and the strength of troops in the field appeared frequently. General Robert E. Lee and other Confederate officers customarily perused northern newspapers in the hope of gaining useful military intelligence.

Southern newspapers also sent reporters to cover the war, but they never numbered more than a hundred. The Confederate reporter faced many of the same problems as his northern counterpart, but they were much more immediate for Southerners because the war was nearer their homes. For example, communication difficulties plagued southern reporters because of the breakdown of telegraph and mail service as the fighting spread throughout their states. Southern newspapers also experienced manpower shortages because many employees left to serve in the army. Confederate reporters worked diligently to report the war and to boost public morale. Given the number of obstacles that they encountered, they did a pretty good job.

One of the big journalistic issues of the war for both the North and the South was how detailed should military information be in the newspapers. Generals tried to control what the media published, but they met with little real success. Officially, specific information related to troop movements and military plans was to be deleted from the telegraph dispatches of reporters. Actually, reporters found a plethora of ways to bypass the restriction. If they could not get the message on the wire, they turned to a special messenger or delivered it in person. Several generals expelled reporters from their camps in an effort to curb the dissemination of sensitive material. General William T. Sherman arrested Thomas W. Knox of the *New York Herald* for sending out two maps of the size and layout of Sherman's army during a failed attack on Vicksburg. Knox also wrote a story that portrayed Sherman as incompetent. Consequently, Knox was tried for spying, giving aid to the enemy, and disobeying orders. Sherman threatened to hang him. Knox was eventually found guilty only of disobeying orders. He escaped the more serious charges that carried the death penalty because Sherman could not prove that Knox had actually given information to the South. The reporter was discharged from the Army of Tennessee and told never to return. Southern generals had somewhat more success in limiting news because they refused to allow reporters to accompany the army during campaigns. Because the Civil War was the first

American conflict that applied large-scale censorship, everyone stumbled along, reporters determined to get news and generals equally determined to stop them. Ultimately, most efforts were ineffective. General Joe Hooker ordered reporters traveling with his army to use bylines, to sign all the pieces that they submitted to their papers. Reporters initially opposed the byline until they and their editors realized that it often increased readership as reporters secured national reputations. Still, Hooker's order did not become a common habit among reporters until several decades after he issued it.

The Civil War spurred not only a tremendous quantity of written reports but also the use of illustrations in the media. Illustrated news weeklies were first popular in the 1850s, but public interest in the Civil War motivated several publications to assign artists to the battlefront to draw for newspapers at home. The leaders in this area were *Frank Leslie's Illustrated Newspaper*, *Harper's Weekly* and the *New York Illustrated News*. Artists in the field sent sketches back to the home office where local artists fleshed out the drawings and transformed them into engravings for publication. What began as a rough draft ended as a detailed and powerful illustration of what happened in war. Improvements in the engraving process enabled publishers to put illustrations in print in a matter of days after they were received. Thus, Americans were able to read about *and* to see the war in detail.

The Civil War picture was not one of engraving alone. During the conflict, new technology emerged in the area of illustration. For the first time in the United States, photography captured a war for all to see. Morse had introduced daguerreotypes in the United States in 1839. By the time the Civil War started, the "wet-plate" process had developed, allowing photographers to carry their darkroom with them in the back of a wagon. An army of people photographed the Civil War. The most famous was Mathew Brady. Brady, a successful photographer before the conflict, took pictures at the first battle of Bull Run and then conceived the idea of making a photographic history of the war. He received the endorsement of Secretary of War Edwin Stanton but had to pay for the project himself. Brady invested approximately 100,000 dollars to hire and equip a crew of twelve photographers. These men followed the troops in black wagons that held all the equipment necessary to record what occurred on the battlefield. The photographs taken by Brady and the rest of his staff captured the horrors of war. They portrayed the dead and wounded in ways that drawn illustrations could never replicate. Because the technology of the 1860s did not permit printing photographs, those of Brady and others were put on display in major cities throughout the country. For

Americans, then and now, the photographs taken during the Civil War made the war real in a way that no story or drawing could accomplish. A writer in the 20 October 1862 issue of the *New York Times* said it all: "Mr. Brady has done something to bring home to us the terrible reality and earnestness of war. If he has not brought bodies and laid them on our dooryard and along our streets, he has done something very like it." Civil War photography pointed toward a new direction for wartime reporting. From this moment on, photographers would be an important and permanent part of every effort to report wars to the American public.

Altogether, the Civil War produced major changes in American journalism. Immediacy became the watchword for reporting of all sorts once reporters strove to get the story home as quickly as possible. In the future, Americans would assume that news about wars should be rapid. Civil War reporters also sought to go beyond specifics and to provide a "sense" of the war. War reports after 1865 would always push outside the perimeter of numbers to include discussions of personnel, both high and low rank, and of the impact of the event on the people involved. The Civil War likewise established the place of the visual in reporting. Because of the war's illustrations and photographs, Americans came to expect images as well as words in newspapers, indeed to count on them for an understanding of what was happening on battlefields and elsewhere. Finally, the Civil War raised issues related to national security that have never been fully settled. The tendency to publish all material incited debate about the proper balance between the right of the public to be informed and the need of the military to maintain secrecy, a controversy that continues to the present day.

New York Spurs Newspaper Growth

Following the Civil War, the more diversified industrial economy of the northern states came to dominate the economic and political life of the United States. And the center of this domination was New York City. The newspapers that ruled the New York press reflected the city's preeminence in wealth and power and benefited from it as well. Economic growth in New York helped its newspapers to sever their remaining ties to political parties. Advertising replaced politics as a source of income for newspapers throughout the country but seemed the most visible in New York. Although newspapers everywhere after 1865 became more and more independent of politicians and political parties, politics persisted as an important topic for newspapers because of the ongoing public interest in what government was doing. Editors did not abandon strong political opinions in their editorials, but more and more saw themselves as independent of party influence. Thus, they felt free to express their own views, to criticize a politician of any party when they thought his leadership was mistaken, rather than to echo party bosses.

The old guard New York editors, the overlords during the years of competition and war, slowly disappeared. Henry J. Raymond died in 1869, and both James Gordon Bennett and Horace Greeley succumbed in 1872. Replacing them were another generation of capable editors who developed the media even further. The most prominent of the new men were E.L. Godkin of *The Nation* and *Evening Post*, Charles Dana at the *Sun*, and James Gordon Bennett, Jr., at the *Herald*. These editors, and the others who joined the publishing ranks after the Civil War, relied on better technology to produce better newspapers. But, in many ways, they also adhered to tradition, following the practices of their predecessors. The focus of the gazettes remained entertainment and news that appealed to a wide audience. Even as the newspaper seemed more like big business, the editor still symbolized the press. The most successful publications were those that readers identified with particular men.

Probably the best example of this emphasis on personal style was Dana of the *New York Sun*. Dana purchased the *Sun* in 1868. He planned to increase circulation by concentrating on good writing and interesting news, so he hired the best writers he could find. Many of the reporters he employed were college graduates. Dana hoped to keep them by offering adequate salaries and training and the freedom to write as they chose, as long as what they wrote was interesting. Dana also enlivened the editorial page by adding "casual essays" on everyday life, essays he imagined would lure all readers. His focus on ordinary living may have inspired what constitutes one of the most famous editorials ever printed in an American newspaper. On 21 September 1897, the *Sun* published a response to a young reader's question about Santa Claus. Frank Church's answer, "Yes, Virginia, there is a Santa Claus" has been reprinted every year since then just before Christmas in newspapers all over the United States.

Dana's biggest competitor was E.L. Godkin, editor of both *The Nation* and the *New York Evening Post*. Godkin did not worry too much about the news sections of his papers. He always focused on the editorial pages. Godkin was a thoughtful intellectual who wrote forcefully because he wanted his columns to influence readers' ideas. In this endeavor he succeeded because the bulk of his subscribers were leaders of public opinion, such as clergymen and lawyers. Godkin urged them to work for change, and they urged the people they came into contact with to do the same. As a result, Godkin became an effective advocate for a variety of reforms in the late nineteenth century.

The last of the major editors in New York journalism immediately after the Civil War was James Gordon Bennett, Jr., who had inherited the *New York Herald* from his father. The younger Bennett realized that news had made the *Herald* profitable, a condition he naturally wished to maintain. During the 1870s the *Herald* was the leading newspaper in the United States in the amount, speed and thoroughness of news coverage. Bennett also had a good sense of what his readers wanted, and he tried to satisfy them. Much of the news reporting in the *Herald* was sensational in nature, but Bennett explored other ways to sustain reader interest. For example, the *Herald* financed Henry Stanley's triumphant search for the physician and missionary David Livingstone and published Stanley's reports on his adventures in Africa. Such efforts laid the groundwork for the "stunt journalism" that became so popular in the 1890s.

Moving to Big Business

Even though the noted editor with a personal touch was still significant, the conversion of the newspaper into a big business slowly transformed editors into employees, in many ways just like the printers and reporters who did the day-to-day work. As newspaper operations grew in size, stock ownership became a popular mode for raising money to finance a paper. For stock purchasers, making money generally outweighed the desire to shape opinion. New investors pushed publishers and editors to downplay politics in order not to offend any readers. This pressure occurred at the same time that selling advertising was crucial for profit. The prominence of advertising further reduced the sway of political parties because the needs of the parties and the desires of the advertisers often clashed. All of these adjustments in newspapers created stresses for many publishers and editors, particularly if they found it impossible to adapt. Gradually, as publishers and editors tried to maintain some equilibrium between newspapers as sources of information and businesses, profit came to the forefront.

Some of the earliest victories for proponents of the new approaches occurred away from the big cities of the East Coast. One of the first publishers to balance journalism as service and business was Victor F. Lawson. In July 1876 he bought a controlling interest in the *Chicago Daily News*. The paper was not doing well, but Lawson's personal combination of business and journalistic skills enabled him to turn the paper around financially. It quickly developed a reputation for fair reporting and editorial independence. Lawson and his editor, high school friend Melvin E. Stone, also paid attention to local news. This tactic, along with their determination to be evenhanded in presenting the news, gave Chicago a newspaper that readers liked and that business admired.

About the same time, Joseph Pulitzer also charted the same course in his *St. Louis Post-Dispatch*. He emphasized vigorous news-gathering and built advertising revenue by printing "Wants" without charge until the item desired was acquired. Pulitzer also promised to speak for the people in the pages of his newspaper. He ably summarized his ideas about the role of a newspaper in his statement of policies in the 12 December 1878 issue, one published not long after he purchased the paper: "The *Post and Dispatch* will serve no party but the people; be no organ of Republicanism, but the organ of truth; will follow no causes but its conclusions; will not support the 'Administration,' but criticize it; will oppose all frauds and shams wherever and whatever they are; will advocate principles and ideas rather than prejudices and partisanship."

Developments in technology soon had an obvious and significant impact on the newspaper business. The price of newsprint dropped dramatically by 1880 as it became possible to make paper out of wood pulp instead of cloth. Stereotyping made it feasible to produce plates for an entire page rather than having to set every item by hand. Other improvements in printing presses made it easy to move story deadlines closer to printing time. Newspapers also received news more quickly because of the extension of the telegraph in the United States and the installation of an underwater cable between Europe and the United States. All of these circumstances permitted publishers to reduce prices while at the same time producing more current journals. In many ways, systematization of newspaper production resembled the future assembly line in a factory.

"New Journalism"

The result of these modifications was to set the stage for one of the Golden Ages of American journalism, an era that marked the emergence of the modern media. Although often derided as the age of "yellow journalism," a more accurate label for what transpired in the late 1800s would be "new journalism." In general, "new journalism" signified a bold and energetic reporting of the news. Another of its characteristics was widespread use of illustrations. Stunts also became common as reporters undertook adventures, reporting vividly what they experienced. Editors and publishers were ever readier to spend money to acquire the news and to buy equipment to improve the quality of the finished product. High-speed presses, Linotypes, typewriters and telephones became a normal part of the workplace as publishers raced to outdo their rivals. The centerpiece, however, of the "new journalism" was its emphasis on news. Publishers of the 1880s and 1890s borrowed many ideas from the "penny press," and particularly from the older James Gordon Bennett. Then the later men expanded these notions to make a bigger and arguably better press. Bennett had underscored sensationalism, scoops and the twenty-four-hour news cycle. The "new journalism" publishers adopted his notions but took them a step further with big-letter headlines, action illustrations and popular crusades.

All of these efforts paid off in increased numbers. Newspaper competition exploded during the final decades of the nineteenth century. Dailies went from 971 in 1880 to 2,226 in 1900. Weekly and monthly newspapers rose by at least 50 percent. Technology fed much of this growth, but it also came from the urbanization of the United States. By the 1890s one-third of Americans lived in urban areas, and one daily newspaper circulated for every two people living in American cities. By 1900 almost 90 percent of Americans could read, which also encouraged newspaper growth. As newspaper prices once more dropped to a penny, more and more Americans purchased them on a regular basis.

Joseph Pulitzer

The person most responsible for producing the "new journalism" was Joseph Pulitzer. As noted above, Pulitzer's first venture in the newspaper business was his *St. Louis Post-Dispatch*. While in St. Louis, Pulitzer launched a number of newspaper crusades against corruption wherever he found it and calling for reforms. Pulitzer entered the New York newspaper market in 1883 when he purchased the *New York World*. In his first issue, published on 11 May, Pulitzer promised to print interesting news for everyone. He stated that the paper would "from this day be under different management— different in men, measures, and methods— different in purpose, policy and principle— different in objects and interests— different in sympathies and convictions — different in head and heart.... There is room in this great and growing city for a journal that is not only cheap but bright, not only bright but large, not only large but truly democratic — dedicated to the cause of the people rather than to that of the purse potentates — devoted more to the news of the New than the Old World — that will expose all fraud and sham, fight all public evils and abuses — that will battle for the people with earnest sincerity. In that cause and for that end solely the new *World* is hereby enlisted and committed to the attention of the intelligent public."

Pulitzer's concept of a brighter newspaper was one that was well illustrated. He quickly put his idea into practice by publishing a three-column illustration of the new Brooklyn Bridge. The *World* also was an innovator in the use of color and comics, primarily through the creation of the Yellow Kid, a character in the cartoon "Hogan's Alley." Pulitzer was also determined to produce a newspaper for the underdog. He avoided news pieces that seemed to demean the foreign-born and rejected the use of ethnic dialect writing in the *World*. He also supported stunt journalism because it fascinated so many readers. In 1887 he hired Elizabeth Cochrane ("Nellie Bly") to pretend to be insane in order to gain admission to the Blackwell's Island asylum. Her stories about unhealthy conditions and abuse of patients sparked an official investigation that subsequently led to improvements at the asylum. Nellie Bly undertook other such exploits, all of them bringing readers to the *World*. Probably the most famous stunt in American journalism was her around-the-world trip in less than eighty days to beat the record set by Jules Verne's fictional character, Phileas Fogg.

Pulitzer sponsored several crusades akin to Bly's exposé of conditions on Blackwell's Island. He advocated tax and civil reforms and prosecution of official corruption, all causes favored by the working

Joseph Pulitzer, publisher of the *New York World*.

poor. Pulitzer's public spiritedness probably peaked when he led a campaign to raise 200,000 dollars for a base for the Statue of Liberty, a gift from the people of France to celebrate the centennial of France's aid to the young United States in their revolt against Great Britain. When Congress did not act and a local citizens' committee organized to raise the money failed to accomplish its goal, Pulitzer mobilized the public, securing donations of pennies, nickels and dimes from untold numbers of immigrants. Obviously this drive raised the circulation of the *World*, but it also gave the ordinary American a sense of ownership of the new monument unveiled in New York Harbor in October 1886.

One of the most vigorous and ongoing of Pulitzer's crusades was against prostitution and the government officials involved in its protection. It is not clear whether Pulitzer truly wanted to eliminate vice and corruption or whether he only used the attack to augment newspaper sales — either served by the provocative headlines on the topic. Whatever the reason, this movement and his others helped his paper to prevail in New York. Within two years of moving to the city, he had established the *World* as its largest newspaper, disseminating over 200,000 copies daily. The *World* became the trendsetter for newspapers, the one to copy. For example, in 1884, the *World* acquired its own photoengraving plant, the first newspaper in New York to do so. Within ten years, every major daily newspaper in the country had a similar plant.

William Randolph Hearst

A number of publishers, resorting to a variety of strategies, tried to best Pulitzer, but no one tried as hard as William Randolph Hearst. Hearst had learned the newspaper business working on the family paper, the *San Francisco Examiner*. After triumphing at home, he looked around for new challenges. He bought the unprofitable *New York Journal* in 1895 and then proceeded to dominate the New York newspaper scene. Having inherited a fortune from his father, Hearst had the money to outbid Pulitzer for writers. He quickly recruited many of the *World's* best talents, including Arthur Brisbane, one of Pulitzer's top editors, and Richard Outcault, the creator of the Yellow Kid.

In many ways, Hearst sought to out–Pulitzer Pulitzer. The *Journal* engaged in more activism and more stunts and aggressively pursued news and stories. For instance, Hearst hired Winifred Sweet Black to be his counterpart of Nellie Bly. As "Annie Laurie," Black feigned fainting in order to investigate treatment by ambulance drivers and hospital workers. She later pretended to be a worker, taking a job in a cotton mill to get an inside story, and to be a member of the Salvation Army, laboring in a cannery for the same purpose. In the 13 October 1897 issue of the *Journal*, Hearst declared that it was the "journalism of action," which represented "the final state in the evolution of the modern newspaper." In the *Journal* of 28 September 1898, he reiterated his perception of the place of the press, saying that "the force of the newspaper is the greatest force in civilization. Under republican government, newspapers form and express public opinion.... The newspapers control the nation because they represent the people." By this time, the *Journal*, having passed the *World* in circulation, was preeminent in the American newspaper world. But this rank was not to last. In the mid–1890s the *New York Times* was a challenger for the top spot.

More Changes in American Journalism

In 1896 Alfred Ochs purchased the *New York Times*, then a second-rate newspaper that only sold a few thousand copies a day. Ochs quickly established the *Times* as the best alternative to the *World* and the *Journal*. Ochs consciously avoided the headlines and illustrations that characterized the "new journalism." He presented his paper as an alternative that avoided the excesses and sensationalism of the competition. In the 19 August 1896 issue, Ochs outlined his basic publishing principles: "It will be my earnest aim that the *New York Times* give the news, all the news, in concise and attractive form, in language that is parliamentary in good society, and give it as early, if not earlier, than it can be learned through any other reliable medium; to give the news impartially, without fear or favor, regardless of any party, sect or interest involved; to make the columns of the *New York Times* a forum for the consideration of all questions of public importance, and to that end to invite intelligent discussion from all shades of opinion." He summarized these ideas in the paper's new motto, "All the News That's Fit to Print," an indication of the tone he planned to adopt in its pages. Originally conceived as a marketing device, this motto became a permanent part of the front page in February 1897. In October 1898 Ochs gambled, lowering the price of the *Times* from three cents to a penny. The price cut was a desperate move to attract readers, a reduction many journalists deemed stupid. However, it proved to be very wise. Within three years, the *Times* circulation had quadrupled to

102,000. By 1908 it had climbed to 172,000. The paper continued to prosper, and Ochs' accent on straightforward reporting of the news was crucial in making the *Times* the nation's best daily.

Another development of the 1890s was the creation of a true newspaper chain. Publishers like Pulitzer and Hearst had owned several newspapers scattered across the country at the same time, but they concentrated their efforts only on one of them. The first real chain was the brainchild of Edward W. Scripps, whose family had been involved in newspapers in the western United States since the 1850s. The Scripps started their first newspaper, the *Detroit News*, in 1873 and followed it with other gazettes in Cleveland, St. Louis and Cincinnati. In the mid–1890s Scripps and his business manager established the Scripps-McRae League, the first genuine newspaper chain because Scripps played some part in all the newspapers within the League.

William Randolph Hearst, publisher of the *New York Journal*.

The Spanish-American War and Journalism

Critics have castigated newspapers of the late 1800s for their overemphasis on sensational stories and their efforts to influence government actions. Probably the best-known exemplar of both is the role of the "yellow press" in the Spanish-American War. Both Pulitzer's *World* and Hearst's *Journal* purportedly pushed the United States into war against Spain, a conflict that grew out of the Cuban rebellion against Spanish rule. Both Pulitzer and Hearst did support Cuban independence, and they did encourage American involvement, but they did not trick or force American leaders into declaring war. In early 1897 Hearst sent Richard Harding Davis and Frederic Remington to Cuba to spend a month with the rebels. They were unable to make contact, but their journey produced an enduring legend about the start of the war. Remington supposedly cabled Hearst to ask permission to return to the United States because nothing was happening. Hearst supposedly replied, "Please remain. You furnish the pictures, and I'll furnish the war." There is no evidence that these cables actually existed.

The final straw for American officials, one that led the United States to declare war, was the sinking of the *USS Maine* in Havana harbor in February 1898. Hearst and Pulitzer blamed Spanish authorities for complicity in the explosion and called on the American government to respond in some way. A number of editors accused Hearst and Pulitzer of stirring up trouble in order to boost circulations. Shortly after the sinking of the *Maine*, E.L. Godkin, in the 19 February 1898 issue of New York's *Evening Post*, criticized their actions: "Nothing so disgraceful as the behavior of two of these newspapers this week has ever been known in the history of American journalism. Gross misrepresentation of the facts, deliberate invention of tales calculated to excite the public, and wanton recklessness in the construction of headlines which outdid even these inventions have combined to make the issues of the most widely circulated newspapers firebrands scattered broadcast throughout the community.... It is a crying shame that men should work such mischief simply in order to sell more papers." Even if Godkin's judgment of their conduct was accurate, it did not prove that Hearst and Pulitzer were the engineers of war.

President William McKinley's administration was already considering intervention once diplomatic talks to settle the struggle between Cuba and Spain collapsed. When war came, the *Journal* and the *World*, as well as many other newspapers, covered it in as much detail as possible. As usual, Americans were interested in the activities of their military forces. But the conflict also was costly for the "yellow press," both in dollars and in decline in reputation. Readers tired of its sensationalism and flamboyance about the same time that more conservative newspapers adopted some of the better practices of the "new journalism." While these publications did not emulate the stories of the "yellow press," they did incorporate some of its notions about layout and design. Bold headlines and numerous illustrations became commonplace in the media by the dawn of the twentieth century.

Growth of Magazines

The "new journalism" suffered not only from its association with the "yellow press" but also because of greater competition from other types of media. Magazines expanded their markets in the 1890s through price reductions and changes in content. The style of writing in magazines became lighter and more readable. Specialized periodicals also surfaced. Among them were professional journals for scientists, historians, teachers and medical personnel and less serious organs. Sports magazines were quite popular. Horse racing, the favorite spectator sport in the late 1800s, was the subject of more than one publication. Among others well-received were those for fans of hunting, fishing and boating. Publications for juveniles also flourished as public education presumably trained more child readers. Literary magazines persisted but no longer predominated. Fiction was less popular, replaced by articles on history and politics that audiences apparently preferred. By the end of the nineteenth century, magazines prioritized informing readers ahead of entertaining them. Even the general serials printed more useful information than they had in the past.

Magazines also thrived in the late 1800s for other reasons. Most periodicals switched to the rotary press, which could print larger runs. Further, the latest rotary presses could handle the multicolor reproductions that enhanced the illustration capabilities of magazines. The spread of railroads was likewise important. Tracks made it possible for manufacturers to sell their goods all over the country, and sellers often considered magazines the best place to advertise their wares. The growth in advertising income in turn allowed magazines to invest in new technology that improved their pages as valuable venues for readers and advertisers. And, finally, in 1879 the United States Congress gave magazines the same low postal rate that newspapers had long enjoyed.

A range of magazines succeeded in the late century, but the most spectacular victory came in Philadelphia. In 1883 Cyrus H.K. Curtis and his wife, Louisa Knapp, founded the *Ladies' Home Journal*. Growing out of a column in *The Tribune and Farmer*, the *Journal* rapidly emerged as a leader among women's magazines and then among all. The first magazine to reach a circulation of one million readers in 1904, it was approaching two million by 1912. One of the landmark efforts of the *Journal* was a series supporting sex education, a series which used the word "syphilis" for the first time in an American popular magazine. Having succeeded with a women's magazine, Curtis bought the struggling *Saturday Evening Post*. Intending it as a publication for men, he printed biographies, factual reports and fiction. But the *Post* appealed to both women and men, chiefly of the middle class. Preaching the virtues of this class, the magazine, somewhat by accident, became one of the greatest American press endeavors. By World War I the *Post* had surpassed even the *Journal* in circulation.

Muckraking

The rise in circulation of magazines set the stage for further remodeling of American journalism once a cadre of crusaders moved into that arena, ready to use it to spark reform in the United States. Reformers had long relied on newspapers and magazines to call for change. Abolitionists, women rights advocates, temperance groups, and a host of others had sponsored publications since the 1830s. But these organs, generally read by people who already agreed with the agenda of the reform group, did not typically reach a mass audience. On occasion, newspaper reporters who exposed bad conditions (such as Nellie Bly's story on the Blackwell's Island asylum) or government corruption had spurred improvements. But journalists' primary goal heretofore was upping sales, not instigating reform. What the early twentieth century witnessed was a joining of magazine journalism and Progressive reform that caused actions which made the United States a better place to live.

A reporter and photojournalist of the late nineteenth century presaged what was to come in the first decade of the next. Jacob Riis, a Danish immigrant, was a police reporter for the *New York Tribune*. He saw firsthand some of the problems faced by New York's poor. His photographs reveal the humanity of the people he encountered, even those who broke the law. In 1890 he published many of his photographs as engravings in *How the Other Half Lives*, a book that brought home to many Americans the struggles that poor people faced every day. Riis combined his keen eye for images with a capable literary style that propelled readers to mobilize for reform. In so doing, he was the forerunner of the group of reporters whose journalism was soon dubbed "muckraking."

The reporter-reformers who practiced "muckraking" did most of their work in nationally circulated magazines. These magazines were inexpensive and reached millions of readers. They were well-suited to the goals of reform journalists because the publication schedule of once-a-month gave a reporter the time to develop a story more fully than was possible in a daily newspaper. Relieved of a short deadline, a reporter could research thoroughly the background of a problem and think through its implications. The monthly magazine was also more suitable than the newspaper because many muckraking pieces transcended state and national boundaries. Demonstrating a pattern for an issue and discerning it were simpler in a national publication. Finally, a national audience made it easier to publicize local scandals because it reduced the pressures on local media outlets to keep silent.

Several publishers were ready to take advantage of these circumstances by offering less expensive national magazines that would lure new readers with the different but interesting perspective of social progress. S. S. McClure was one of these publishers, and his new serial was soon the primary forum for the muckraking journalists. McClure launched the magazine that bore his name in 1893. Although *McClure's* initially struggled financially, it stabilized by 1895 after printing biographical pieces that attracted many readers. Its inaugural price was fifteen cents, but dropped to ten cents in 1895. Because the content and writing in *McClure's* outshone its competitors, the magazine garnered more advertising, which further secured its financial position. By 1900 *McClure's*, with a circulation of 350,000, was the leading magazine in the United States. Its articles pointed out both the good and the bad in contemporary society in articles penned by a staff of excellent writers, including some of the best of the muckraking journalists.

McClure's aired the first piece labeled muckraking journalism in 1902. By the January 1903 issue, McClure himself realized that something unusual was happening: "We did not plan it so; it is a coincidence that this number contains three arraignments of American character such as should make every one of us stop and think. 'The Shame of Minneapolis,' the current chapter of the history of Standard Oil by Miss Tarbell, Mr. Ray Stannard Baker's 'The Right to Work'— they might all have been called 'The American Contempt of Law.' Capitalists, Workingmen, Politicians, Citizens — all breaking the law or letting it be broken. Who is there left to uphold it? ... There is no one left — none but all of us." Over the next decade, the magazine printed a variety of investigative pieces. Each one called on American citizens to act. But muckraking was not limited to this one magazine. Others, such as *Cosmopolitan* and the *Ladies' Home Journal*, entered the fray. In *Cosmopolitan*, David Graham Phillips penned an article spotlighting "The Treason of the Senate" because so many members voted to support special interests instead of the wishes of the people. The *Ladies' Home Journal* led the fight against dangerous patent medicines. Between 1900 and 1915, approximately 2,000 muckraking articles appeared in a range of magazines. Muckraking also spilled beyond magazines into other types of media. Probably the most famous example outside a magazine was Upton Sinclair's *The Jungle*, published in 1906. A novel based on Sinclair's probe of the meat-packing industry, the book is generally given partial credit for the passage of the Meat Inspection Act and the Pure Food and Drug Act in 1906.

Very few aspects of American society escaped the muckrakers during this era, but their focus on reform was relatively brief. Muckraking journalists burst on the scene in the early 1900s and were virtually gone by the time World War I began in 1914. Historians have struggled to decide just how much credit to give the muckrakers for reforms that occurred during this Progressive Era. At the very least, the exposés created an atmosphere which legitimized the work of other reformers and thus abetted improvements in the lives of many Americans. For muckrakers, the decade was a journalistic halfway house. It proved the power of facts, but it also underscored their limitations. Many of the muckrakers assumed that reform would automatically follow once a story documented a problem. They were disappointed and disillusioned when reform was not forthcoming. More important for journalism, the muckrakers confirmed the value of gathering and reporting facts in an organized and systematic manner. This value is the basis of the research and writing of news stories today.

In the hundred years after the War of 1812, the American press changed drastically. When that war ended in 1815, journalism was mostly newspapers consisting of four pages of advertisements and news items chunked together with little differentiation in content or format. By the time World War I began in Europe in 1914, multi-sectional newspapers and magazines of all descriptions prevailed throughout the United States. Greater literacy and better technology had encouraged rapid and widespread growth of publications all over the country. The political ties that had dominated gazettes in the early 1800s had disappeared, replaced by a dependence on advertising perhaps equally distasteful. Newspapers and magazines had become a business, designed to make money by keeping people informed. The mass medium of print now constituted the major source of news and information for a large majority of Americans. It would continue so until the alternate media of radio and then television broke its monopoly.

Bibliography

Ames, William E. *A History of the* National Intelligencer. Chapel Hill: University of North Carolina, 1972.

Baldasty, Gerald J. *The Commercialization of News in the Nineteenth Century*. Madison: University of Wisconsin, 1992.

Campbell, W. Joseph. *Yellow Journalism: Puncturing the Myths, Defining the Legacies*. Westport, CT: Greenwood, 2001.

Crouthamel, James L. *Bennett's* New York Herald *and the Rise of the Popular Press*. Syracuse: Syracuse University, 1989.

Dickerson, Donna Lee. *The Course of Tolerance: Freedom of the Press in Nineteenth-Century America*. Westport, CT: Greenwood, 1990.

Hale, William Harlan. *Horace Greeley: Voice of the People*. New York: Harper & Bros., 1950.
Humphrey, Carol Sue. *The Press of the Young Republic, 1783–1833*. Westport, CT: Greenwood, 1996.
Huntzicker, William E. *The Popular Press, 1833–1865*. Westport, CT: Greenwood, 1999.
Juergens, George. *Joseph Pulitzer and the* New York World. Princeton: Princeton University, 1966.
Luxon, Norval Neil. Niles' Weekly Register: *News Magazine of the Nineteenth Century*. Baton Rouge: Louisiana State University, 1947.
Nasaw, David. *The Chief: The Life of William Randolph Hearst*. Boston: Houghton-Mifflin, 2000.
Nevins, Allan. The Evening Post: *A Century of Journalism*. New York: Boni & Livewright, 1922.
Smythe, Ted Curtis. *The Gilded Press, 1865–1900*. Westport, CT: Greenwood, 2003.
Thompson, Susan. *The Penny Press*. Northport, AL: Vision, 2004.
Wilson, Harold. McClure's Magazine *and the Muckrakers*. Princeton: Princeton University, 1970.

Notes on Contributors

Ulf Jonas Bjork is a professor in the School of Journalism at Indiana University-Indianapolis. He has written book chapters and articles on subjects such as early international organizations for journalists, the American media abroad and the American immigrant press. He is working on a book about the impact of United States mass media on popular culture in Sweden in the twentieth century.

Ross F. Collins is an associate professor in the Department of Communication at North Dakota State University, Fargo. He is the author of a book on World War I journalism and has completed a second book on that topic. He has published numerous scholarly articles on aspects of French journalism, European journalism and American frontier journalism. A former journalist and photographer, he has contributed more than 800 articles and photographs to a wide variety of non-academic publications. He serves as treasurer of the American Journalism Historians Association.

Rod Kirkpatrick is the program director, journalism, in the School of Journalism and Communication at the University of Queensland, Brisbane. He is the author of three books on Australian provincial journalism and has completed a manuscript on the history of provincial dailies. A former New South Wales provincial daily newspaper editor, he has published more than ninety history articles in *PANPA* (Pacific Area Newspaper Publishers Association) *Bulletin*, has edited the *Australian Newspaper History Group Newsletter* since 2000, and has co-edited three books published by that group.

Carol Sue Humphrey is a professor of history at Oklahoma Baptist University, Shawnee. She has published five books on the role of the media during the American Revolution and the early years of the United States. She has also written a number of book chapters and articles on topics ranging from the Boston Massacre to the Lewis and Clark Expedition. She is a former

Notes on Contributors

president and the current administrative secretary of the American Journalism Historians Association.

E.M. Palmegiano is a professor of history at Saint Peter's College, NJ, where she received a faculty research award to undertake this project. She has published four books on nineteenth-century British magazines and has another in progress on Victorian journalists' perceptions of journalism. She has also published numerous articles on press treatment of marginalized social groups. She is a past president of the American Journalism Historians Association and is a member of the editorial board of the *Encyclopedia of American Journalism* and two scholarly journals.

David R. Spencer is a professor in the Faculty of Information and Media Studies at the University of Western Ontario, London. He is the author of the book *The Yellow Journalism and the Rise of America as a World Power* as well as numerous chapters in scholarly books and articles in history journals on the nineteenth-century press in Canada and the United States. He has served as president of the American Journalism Historians Association and as chair of the History Division of the Association for Journalism and Mass Communications, is the founder and editor of *The Canadian Journal of Media Studies/La Revue Canadienne d'Etudes Mediatiques*, and sits on the editorial boards of several scholarly publications.

Index

Aberdeen Journal 145
Adelaide Express 31
Adelaide Times 31
advertising 2, 4–5, 8–9, 21, 28, 43, 64, 72–73, 80–81, 88, 90, 95, 102, 104, 128, 132, 136, 142, 144–145, 147–148, 153–155, 163, 170, 178, 187, 190, 197, 199–200; and *Age* (Melbourne) 21–24, 41
agencies 69, 127–128; and corruption 100, 102–104, 142, 160; and press control 22, 49, 120, 124, 136, 141, 147, 153, 189
Albany Argus 174
Albany Evening Journal 174
Albury Banner and Wodonga Express 38
Alexander's East India Magazine (London) 149
Altick, Richard 143, 150, 171
American Farmer (Baltimore) 175
American Review of Reviews 106–107, 138
American Turf Register and Sporting Magazine 175
L'Ami du Peuple (Montreal) 53
Amtsblätter 124
Andrews, Alexander 139, 158
"Annie Laurie" 194
Antislavery periodicals 183
Appeal to Reason (Kansas) 58
Archibald, John Feltham 38
Arden, George 20, 36
Argus (Melbourne) 20–22, 24, 27, 40
Argus of Western America 174
Armidale Telegraph 37
Arnold, Matthew 162
Associated Press (AP) 4, 50, 72, 88, 129, 183–184
Athenaeum (London) 145
Atkinson, Joseph 66
Augsburger Allgemeine Zeitung 110, 112, 114
L'Aurore (Paris) 100–101
Australasian (Melbourne) 22

Australian Associated Press (AAP) 27
Australian Journalists' Association 39, 41
Australian (Sydney) 28
Australian Star (Sydney) 29
Australian Worker (Sydney) 39–40
Australian Workman (Sydney) 40
Authoritarianism, effect on press 92, 107

Bailey, W.H.L. 28
Baker, Ray Stannard 199
Ballarat Times 37
Baltimore Republican 174
Baltimore Sun 184
Balzac, Honoré de 88–89, 91
Banks, Elizabeth 166–167
Banner (Toronto) 46
Barnaby Rudge 54
Barnes, Thomas 144
Barnhurst, Kevin 65, 70
Barrier Miner (Broken Hill) 36
Barrow, George 34
Bartlett, Columbus 62
Beehive (London) 154
Bengough, John Wilson 54, 57, 70
Bennett, Alfred 26
Bennett, Christopher 26
Bennett, George 48
Bennett, James Gordon 9, 50, 178–180, 188, 191
Bennett, James Gordon, Jr. 188–189, 191
Bennett, Samuel 25–26
Bent, Andrew 12–14, 41
Benwell, F.C. 68
Berliner Abendpost 133
Berliner Illustrierte Zeitung 133–134
Berliner Lokal-Anzeiger 132, 134–135, 137
Berliner Morgenpost 133–134
Berliner Tageblatt 126, 128
Berliner Zeitung 122, 133
Berthiaume, Trefflé 66–67, 70

205

Index

Between Caesar and Jesus 59
Le Bien Public (Paris) 100
Birchall, Reginald 67–68
Bismarck, Otto von 8, 106, 119–126, 128, 130–132, 135, 137
Black, Jeremy 142, 171
Black, Winifred Sweet 193–194
Black Dwarf (London) 144
Blackburn, Josiah 50, 70
Blackwood's Edinburgh Magazine 139, 145
Blair, Francis P. 174
Blatchford, Robert 59
Blessington, Marguerite, Countess of 150
Bloomer, Amelia 175
Bly, Nellie (Elizabeth Cochrane) 192
"Bohemian Brigade" 184
Bonaparte, Louis Napoleon (Napoleon III) 73, 92
Bonaparte, Napoleon 73
Boomerang (Brisbane) 39–40
Border Watch (Mount Gambier) 32
Bourbon monarchy 73–74, 79–80, 83–84
Bourne, H.R. Fox 139
Bowles, Samuel 174
Bowles, Thomas Gibson 159
Boys' Friend (London) 164
Boys of England 164
Brady, Mathew 179, 186–187
Bribes of the press *see* Corruption of the press
Brient, L.J. 28
Brisbane, Arthur 193
Brisbane Courier 20, 33
British Colonist (British Columbia) 62
British Mothers' Magazine 149
Brotherhood Era (Ontario) 59
Brown, George 46–51, 61, 70
Brown, Gordon 49, 70
Brown, Lucy 142–143, 161, 171
Brown, Peter 46
Brunhuber, Robert 135–137
Bulletin (Sydney) 38
Bulletin de la Grande Armée (France) 73
Bunyip (Gawler) 32
Bushell, John 42
Bussey, H. Findlater 150
Buzacott, Charles Hardie 33
Bylines 186
BZ am Mittag (Berlin) 134

Cable, Australian 27, 29
Cable, transatlantic 51, 161, 190
Calgary Herald 63
Can West Global Communications 63

Canada Farmer's Sun (Ontario) 59
Canadian Free Press (Ontario) 49
Canadian Illustrated News 53, 55
Canadian Press 50, 69–70
Le Canadien (Montreal) 45
Carey, J.R. 28
La Caricature (Paris) 84
Carlile, Richard 144
Carlsbad Decrees 109–111, 115–116, 119
Carrel, Armand 79, 90
Carter, Henry (Frank Leslie) 53
Cartier, Georges Etienne 48, 67
Cartoons, non-political *see* Comics; Illustrations
Cartoons, political 2, 7, 38, 51, 53–55, 114, 168
Cavaignac, Godefroy 92
Censoriads 114–115
Censorship, government control 4, 11, 19, 71, 73–75, 78–79, 80–84, 84, 87, 94, 97–99, 101–102, 104, 107–115, 117, 119, 121, 125–126, 132, 136, 137, 140, 168, 185
Central Press 160
Century Magazine (New York) 55
Chambers's Journal (Edinburgh) 139, 147, 149, 156, 159
Chapleau, Adolphe 67
Le Charivari (Paris) 84–85
Charles II 60
Charles X 79–81, 111
Charleston Mercury 174
Chateau Clique 44–45, 47
Chateaubriand, François-Réné de 76, 79
Chicago Daily News 189
Chiltern Standard 37
Church, Frank 188
Civil War: French 71, 92, 97; Spanish 45; United States 9, 181, 183–189
Clark, William Nairne 18
Clarke, Marcus 14
Clemenceau, Georges 100–101
Cobbett, William 14, 43, 140
Cochrane, Elizabeth 192
Colburn, Henry 146
Colonial Advocate (Queenston) 43
Colonial Times (Hobart) 15, 17, 30
Colonist (Sydney) 16–17
Comics 65, 192
La Commune (Paris) 98
Commune, Paris 97–98
Conservatives 45–46, 92, 98–99, 163
Constant, Benjamin 74, 76
Le Constitutionnel (Paris) 76, 80–81, 90
Contemporary Review (London) 143, 162, 169

Index

Control of the press *see* Advertising; Censorship
Cook, E.T. 163
Co-operator (Manchester) 154
Cornhill Magazine (London) 159–160
Corruption of the press 8, 103–104, 143, 155, 164, 168, 182, 188
Cosmopolitan (United States) 199
Cosmos, Amor de (William Alexander Smith) 62
Cotta, Johann Friedrich 112
Count of Monte Cristo 89
Courier-Mail (Brisbane) 20, 33
Courier of the Mines and Bendigo Daily Mail 37
Le Courrier de la Nouvelle Calédonie (Vancouver) 62
Cowen, Joseph 154
Crawford, Emily 167
Creighton, Donald 61, 70
Crimes of the press *see* Corruption of the press; Libel
Croly, Jane Cunningham (Jennie June) 180
Croswell, Edwin 174
Crusading journalists 162, 181
Curtis, Cyrus H.K. 197

Dagger (Canada) 53
Daily Chronicle (London) 154, 168, 170
Daily Commercial News and Shipping Gazette (Sydney) 35
Daily Express (London) 170
Daily Herald (Adelaide) 40
Daily Mail (Brisbane) 20, 33, 35
Daily Mail (London) 167, 169, 171
Daily Mirror (London) 169–170
Daily News (Braidwood) 36
Daily News (London) 153, 156–157, 165, 167–168, 170
Daily News (Perth) 39
Daily Post (Sydney) 29, 35
Daily Standard (Brisbane) 40
Daily Telegraph (London) 153, 160
Daily Telegraph (Melbourne) 24
Daily Telegraph (Sydney) 27–28
Daily Times (Geelong) 36
Dana, Charles 9, 188
Darling Act 15
Darwin, Charles 47
Daumier, Honoré 84
Davies, John 30–31
Davis, Richard Harding 195
Dawson Nugget 64

Day, Benjamin 50, 96, 177–178
Debs, Eugene 58
Defoe, Daniel 140
De Gaulle, Charles 104
Delane, John 148, 150
Demers, Modeste 62
Democracy in America 177
Democratic Press (Philadelphia) 175
Democrats 173–174
Derwent Star and Van Diemen's Land Intelligencer 12
Desbarats family 53–54, 70
Detroit News 195
Deutsche Journalistenag 127, 129–130
Deutsche Reichs- und Preußische Staatsanzeiger (Berlin) 124
Deutsche Tribune, 113
Dickens, Charles 54, 151–152
Diogenes (Canada) 53
Direct Action (Sydney) 40
Drotner, Kristen 164, 171
Dublin University Magazine 149
Duels, and journalists 89–90, 104
Duffy, Charles Gavan 145
Dumas, Alexandre 89, 91
Dupuy, Jean 101
Dutacq, Armand 90

Echo (Canada) 58
Echo (London) 162
L'Echo de Paris 101
Edinburgh Review 141, 145
Editorials 14–15, 19, 26, 28, 33, 35, 37, 49, 65–67, 69, 109, 113, 124, 129, 136, 144, 148, 151, 153–154, 156, 160, 163–164, 168–169, 171, 181, 188
Edmonton Bulletin 63
L'Electeur (Paris) 99
Empire (Sydney) 25–26
Empire (Toronto) 47, 49
English Woman's Journal 152
Escott, T.H.S. 166
L'Evénement (Paris) 93
Evening Journal (Adelaide) 31
Evening News (London) 163, 169
Evening News (Sydney) 26, 28–29
Evening Observer (Brisbane) 33
Express (Fremantle) 34
Express (Perth) 34
Eyewash (*bourrage de crâne*), and World War I 104

Fairfax, John 25–26, 28
Family Compact 44, 47

Index

Family Herald (London) 148
Family Visitor (United States) 176
Favre, Jules 94
Fawkner, John Pascoe 19–20
February Revolution of 1848 91, 114
Fetherling, Douglas 50, 64, 70
Fetscher, Elmar 113, 116, 137
Feuilleton 88, 113
Fickler, Joseph 113
Le Figaro (Paris) 86–87, 101
Flaubert, Gustave 93
Forbes, Archibald 157
Force, Peter 174
Forster, Thomas 16
Fortnightly Review (London) 159
Franco-Prussian War 97, 157
Frank Leslie's Illustrated Newspaper (United States) 53, 186
Fraser's Magazine (London) 149
Free Lance (Canada) 53
Free Selector (Tamworth) 37
Freedom of the press 9, 12–14, 41, 71, 78–79, 91–92, 98–100, 103, 106–107, 110–115, 117, 121, 122, 137, 140, 153, 183, 188, 200; *see also* Censorship
Fremantle Observer, Perth Gazette and Western Australian Journal 17
French Revolution 73, 88, 98, 104
Fuller, Margaret 180

Gales, Joseph, Jr. 174
Gambetta, Léon 98–99
Garrison, William Lloyd 183
Garro, Paul de 62
Gartenlaube (Leipzig) 127–128
Geelong Advertiser 36–37
Generalanzeiger 132, 137
Genius of Universal Emancipation (United States) 175
Gentleman's Magazine (London) 140
German Confederation 8, 107, 109–110, 113–116, 122
Germania 131
Gill, André 84, 87
Gillray, James 51, 53
Girardin, Emile de 87–90, 92, 95, 99
Glasgow Herald 16, 145
Gleason's Pictorial Drawing-Room Companion (United States) 175
Globe (Sydney) 28
Globe (Toronto) 46–49, 61
Godey's Lady's Book (Philadelphia) 175
Godkin, E.L. 188–189, 196
Good Words (Edinburgh) 159

Gorgon (London) 57
Görres, Johann Joseph 108–109, 130
Government, control of press *see* Censorship; Libel
Grafton Argus 37
Graham, Hugh 66–67, 70
Grain Grower's Guide (Canada) 59
Grant, James 139
Greeley, Horace 9, 50, 180–181, 188, 201
Green, Abigail 111, 137
Green, Duff 174
Greene, Bartholomew 42
Greenwood, Frederick 160
Grévy, Jules 99
Gridiron (Canada) 53
Grinchuckle (Canada) 53
Grip (Canada) 54, 56–57
Guardian or True Friend of Tasmania (Hobart) 30

Hackett, John Winthrop 35
Hale, Sara Josepha 175
Halifax Chronicle-Herald 43
Halifax Gazette 42
Hall, Edward Smith 13–15
Hamburgische Correspondent 108
Harbor News Association 183
Harmsworth, Alfred (Lord Northcliffe) 8, 163, 167–168, 170–171
Harper's Weekly (United States) 54, 186
Hartung'sche Zeitung (Könisberg) 121
Havas, Charles 4, 72, 87, 102, 128
Haynes, John 38
Hearst, William Randolph 9, 66, 193–196, 201
Heine, Heinrich 111–112, 114
Henriksson, Fritz 134–137
Herzen, Alexander 155
Hillock, William Henry 34–35
Hobart Town Gazette and Southern Reporter 12–14
Hobarton Guardian 30
Hobarton Mercury 30
Hogan's Alley 192
Hogarth, William 52
L'Homme Libre (Paris) 100
Household Words (Britain) 152, 162
How the Other Half Lives 198
Howe, George 11–13, 41
Howe, George Terry 14
Howe, Robert 12–13
Hudson's Bay Company 60–61, 63
Hugo, Victor 91–93
Hummer (Wagga Wagga) 40

Index

Hunt, F. Knight 153
Hunter River Gazette 36

Illustrated London News 148
Illustrated Police Budget (London) 164
Illustrated Post (Melbourne) 24
L'Illustration (Paris) 84
Illustrations 2, 27, 51–52, 55–57, 84–85, 120, 140, 145, 148, 150, 163, 173, 176–178, 186–187, 191, 194, 196
Illustrations, political *see* Cartoons
Industrial Banner (London, Ontario) 58
Industrial News (Canada) 58
Ingersoll, Robert 59
Innis, Harold 60, 70
Inquirer: A Western Australian Journal of Politics and Literature 18, 34
Institute of Journalists 166
Irish Exile and Freedom's Advocate (Hobart) 30
Isis (London) 147

Jackson, Mason 139
Jaffray family 49
"Jennie June" 180
Jester (Montreal) 53, 55
John Bull (London) 145
Johnstone, Christian 149
Jones, Auber George 30
Jones, Kennedy 163
Le Journal (Paris) 101
Le Journal des Débats (Paris) 74, 76–77, 81, 89
Julien, Henri 55
July Monarchy 78–79, 81, 83, 87, 89, 91, 111
Jump, Edward 53–54
June, Jennie (Jane Cunningham Croly) 180
"June Days" 92
The Jungle 199
Junius 140
La Justice (Paris) 100

Kapunda Herald 32
Keil, Ernst 127
Keller, Gottfried 116
Kendall, Amos 174
Kenny, John A. 63
Kerr, William 21
King, William Lyon Mackenzie 43
Kirkland, Charles 32
Kleinstädterei 116, 127
Klondike Miner 64
Knapp, Louisa 197
Knight, Charles 149

Knox, Thomas W. 185
Kölnsischer Zeitung 118
König, Friedrich 116, 145
Konstanz Seeblätter 113, 137
Koszyk, Kurt 107, 137
Kreuz-Zeitung (Berlin) 131

Labor: press of 6, 29, 32, 35, 38–40, 57–60, 148
Labor Call (Melbourne) 39
Labor Union (Canada) 58
Ladies' Cabinet (London) 149
Ladies' Home Journal (United States) 197, 199
Ladies' Magazine (Boston) 175
Lamartine, Alphonse 91
Lambton, John, Lord Durham 45
Lamennais, Félicité de 92
Landor, William 33
Lane, William 39
Lang, John Dunmore 16
Launceston Advertiser 19
Laurie, Patrick 63
Law and the press 4, 13, 15, 19, 45, 52, 73–76, 78–79, 82, 84, 87, 91, 93, 97–101, 106–107, 109–113, 117, 119–122, 126, 136–137, 141, 144, 146–147, 161, 164, 166, 171; *see also* Libel
Lawson, Henry 39
Lawson, Victor F. 189–190
Leader (Melbourne) 22–23
Lee, Alan J. 141, 161, 171
Lee, Robert E. 185
Leech, John 149
Leisure Hour (London) 159
Leslie, Frank (Henry Carter) 53
Lespès, Léo (Timothée Trimm) 96
Libel 4, 6, 14–15, 18, 100, 107, 117, 122, 141, 143–144, 159, 161, 164, 166; *see also* Law and the press
Liberals 14, 16, 25, 45–50, 65, 69, 71, 76, 79, 81–83, 97, 99, 112–114, 118–121, 124–128, 131–133, 141, 163
Liberator (Boston) 183
Lily (United States) 175
Lindsay, Norman 38
Literacy 3, 5, 43, 161, 176–177, 200
Literary Gazette (London) 145
Livingstone, David 153, 189
Lloyd's Weekly Newspaper (London) 154
Lochée, Francis 18
London Journal 149
Lord Campbell's Act 164
Louis XIV 80, 84

Index

Louis XVIII 74, 79
Louis Philippe 83–84, 87, 91
Lovejoy, Elijah 183
Lovekin, Arthur 39
Lucy, Henry 165
Lundy, Benjamin 175, 183
Luxton, William Fisher 63
Lyon, Arthur Sidney 20

Macarthur, James 16
Macdonald, John A. 46–49, 54, 57, 60–61
Macfaull, Charles 17–18
Macfaull, Elizabeth 18
McGarvie, William 15–16
Mackenzie, William Lyon 43–45, 49
Mackinnon, Lauchlan 21, 27
MacMahon, Patrice 98–99
Macmillan's Magazine (London) 159
Madame Bovary 93
Magazines 3, 8–9, 17, 53–54, 68, 110, 126, 139–141, 143, 145–147, 149, 150–152, 154–155, 159, 163–166, 169, 171, 175–176, 183, 196–200
Mail (Adelaide) 32, 35
Mail (Toronto) 47, 49
USS *Maine* 196
Maitland Mercury 36
Manchester Guardian 145, 160
Manchester School 46
Manitoba Free Press (Winnipeg) 63
La Marseillaise (Paris) 98
Martineau, Harriet 156
Marx, Karl 59, 114, 155
Mason, Tony 168, 172
Massingham, H.W. 143, 168
Le Matin (Paris) 101
Mayfair (London) 165
Mayhew, George 32
McClure, S.S. 199
McClure's Magazine (United States) 199, 201
McKim, A.E. 69
Mechanics' Free Press (Philadelphia) 57
Melbourne Daily News 20
Melbourne Morning Herald 20
Mercury (Hobart) 30–31
Merle, Gibbons 140, 146–147
Merrie England 58
Métis 63
Mignet, François 79
Millaud, Moïse 95–96, 101
Millière, J.B. 98
Milton, John 140, 178
Mirror of Literature, Amusement, and Instruction (London) 146

Le Moniteur (Paris) 79
Le Moniteur Universel (Paris) 89
Monitor (Sydney) 13–14, 16
Montreal Gazette 67
Montreal Star 55, 66–67
Moon Hoax 178
Moonta Herald (shipboard) 32
Moreton Bay Courier 20, 32–33
Moreton Bay Free Press 32
Morning Chronicle (London) 140, 144, 157
Morning Herald (London) 144
Morning Leader (London) 167
Morning Post (London) 140
Mosse, Rudolf 128
Muckraking 198–199
Murray, Robert Lathrop 17

Naquet, Alfred 98
Nashville Republican 174
Nast, Thomas 54–55
Nation (Ireland) 145
The Nation (United States) 181, 184, 188
Le National (Paris) 79, 90–91
National Advocate (Bathurst) 36
National Association of Journalists 164, 166
National Intelligencer (Washington) 174, 200
National Union of Journalists 167
"Nellie Bly" 192, 194, 198
Nerone, John 65, 70
New Brunswick News (St. John) 50
New Grub Street 143
New Hampshire Patriot 174
New Journalism: Australia 28; Britain 5, 8, 162–164, 167, 172; France 72; United States 5, 190–191, 194, 196
New Monthly Belle Assemblée (London) 149
New York Associated Press *see* Associated Press
New York Courier and Enquirer 174
New York Daily Graphic 54
New York Evening Post 188, 196, 201
New York Herald 50, 178–179, 185, 189, 200
New York Illustrated News 186
New York Journal 192–196
New-York Mirror and Ladies' Literary Gazette 176
New York Sun 50, 96, 177–78, 188
New York Times 50, 181, 184, 187, 194–195
New York Tribune 50, 180–181, 184, 197–198
New York World 191, 194–196, 201
Newcastle Morning Herald and Miners' Advocate 36–37
Newnes, George 163–164

Index

News, concept of 1–2, 4–5, 7–8, 28, 38, 43, 46, 50–51, 65–66, 69–70, 72, 82, 87, 90, 96, 110, 120, 123, 125–126, 129, 135, 139–140, 145, 149, 154, 157, 166–168, 170, 173, 175, 177–183, 187–188, 190–191, 194
Newspaper Benevolent Association 147, 157
Newspaper Libel and Registration Act 164
Newspaper Press (London) 157–158
Newsprint 23, 100–101, 116–117, 190
Niles' Weekly Register (Baltimore) 175, 201
Norddeutsche Allgemeine Zeitung 123, 125
Normanby, Lord 92
North Australian (Darwin) 32
North German Confederation 122
Northcliffe, Lord (Alfred Harmsworth) 8, 163, 167–168, 170–171
Northern Society of Journalists 167
Northern Star (Kapunda) 32
Northern Star (Leeds) 148
Northern Territory Times and Government Gazette 32
Nor'Wester (Winnipeg) 62–63

Observer (London) 145, 165, 169
Ochs, Alfred 194–195
O'Donohue, Patrick 30
Official Secrets Act 171
Oldenburg, Karl 124–125, 129
Oldenburg Correspondenz 124
L'Opinion Publique (Montreal) 53, 55
Opinions *see* Editorials
Oregon Treaty 61
Outcault, Richard 193

Pall Mall Gazette (London) 160, 162–163
Palladium of Labor (Canada) 58
Palmerston, Lord (Henry John Temple) 155
Papineau, Louis-Joseph 45
Parent, Etienne 45
Parkes, Henry 25
Parliamentary reporters 140, 151, 156, 160–161, 165
Party Press *see* Political parties and the press
Patent medicines 199
Patrons of Industry 59
Paul Pry (Canada) 53
Pearson, C.A. 170
Pellegrini, Carlo 159
Pelletan, Eugène 100
Penny-a-liners 145, 151, 156
Penny Magazine (Britain) 6, 127, 149
Penny press 50, 72, 89, 94–95, 116, 153–154, 156, 177, 180–182, 191, 201
People's Daily (Melbourne) 40

Perry, James 157
Perth Gazette and Independent Journal of Politics and News 18
Perth Gazette and West Australian Times 33
Perth Gazette and Western Australian Journal 17
Peterloo Massacre 144
Le Petit Journal (Paris) 95–97, 100–101, 167
Le Petit Parisien 72, 101
La Petite Republique (Paris) 99
Le Peuple (Paris) 92
Le Peuple Constituant (Paris) 92
Pfennig-Magazin (Germany) 126
Philadelphia Palladium 174
Phillips, David Graham 199
Photography 4, 55, 69, 163, 179, 186–187
Pigeons, as transmitters of news 87, 151, 157
Polignac, Jules de 79, 84
Political Letters and Pamphlets (London) 147
Political parties and the press 8, 25, 32–33, 37, 45–49, 58, 62, 64, 67, 82, 115, 118, 130–131–132, 141–143, 145, 160, 173–175, 177, 179, 182–183, 187–188, 189, 190, 194
Poor Man's Advocate (Manchester) 147
Poor Man's Guardian (London) 146
Port Lincoln Herald 36
Port Phillip Gazette 20, 36
Port Phillip Herald 20
Port Phillip Patriot and Melbourne Advertiser 20
Postal express systems 149, 151, 182
Postal fees *see* Censorship
Press: manipulation of *see* Censorship; power of 7, 13, 23–24, 40–41, 71–72, 82, 84, 87, 91, 99, 101, 104, 125, 140, 142, 153, 169, 171, 176–179, 187, 194, 200
Press Association 160
Press barons 169–170
La Presse (Montreal) 66–67, 70
La Presse (Paris) 88, 90, 92, 95
Printers' Union 47
Printing press, German invention of 107
Prior restraint *see* Censorship
Progressives 198, 200
Proudhon, Pierre 59, 91–92
Provincial Newspaper Society 147, 160
Provinzial Correspondenz (Berlin) 124, 126
Public (Canada) 57
Public Opinion (London) 162
Pulitzer, Joseph 9, 66, 170, 190–193, 195–196, 201
Punch (London) 51, 149, 165
Punch in Canada (Montreal and Toronto) 47, 51–52

Index

Quarterly Review (London) 145, 166
Queensland Free Press 32
Quotidienne (Paris) 76

Radicals 14, 21, 25, 40, 108, 115, 141, 147
Raymond, Henry 181, 188
La Réforme (Paris) 91
Regina Leader (*Leader Post*) 63
Reid, T. Wemyss 154
Remington, Frederic 195–196
Le Représentant du Peuple (Paris) 92
Requate, Jörg 118, 129
Restoration government 74–76, 78
Retallack, James 130, 138
Reuter, P.J. 4, 88, 156
Reuters agency 26, 51, 72, 128, 157, 160
Review of Reviews (London) 164
La Revue de Paris 93
Reynolds's Weekly Newspaper (London) 154
Rheinische Zeitung für Politik, Handel und Gewerbe 114
Rheinischer Merkur 108–109
Richmond Enquirer 174
Riel, Louis 63
Riis, Jacob 198
Ritchie, Thomas 174
Robertson, Gilbert 17
Robertson, John Ross 66–67, 70
Robinson, Henry Crabb 157
Roper, David 176
Ross, James 14
Russel, Alexander 145
Russell, William Howard 157
Rutherford, Paul 64, 70

St. Louis Observer 183
St. Louis Post-Dispatch 190–191
Sala, G.A. 162
Salons, reading 76
Sand, George 91
Saskatchewan Herald (North Battleford) 63
Saturday Evening Post (United States) 175, 197
Saturday Night (Canada) 66
Saturday Review (London) 152, 160, 169
Scandals, and the press 54, 103, 181, 198
Scherl, August 132–135, 137
Scotsman (Edinburgh) 145, 160
Scott, George Byng 32
Scripps, Edward W. 195
Scripps-McRae League 195
Seaton, William W. 174
Security deposits *see* Censorship

Sensationalism 5, 67, 96, 130, 162–163, 181, 191, 194, 196
Serialized novels 22, 72, 88–89, 90, 96, 113, 132, 152, 181
Shaw, Flora 167
Shenton, Arthur 18, 33–34
Sheppard, E.E. 66, 70
Le Siècle (Paris) 89, 90, 96
Sinclair, Upton 199
Sketches *see* Illustrations
Skinner, John 175
Smith, Adam 48
Smith, William Alexander (Amor de Cosmos) 62
Smith, W.H. 149
Social Democrats 60, 131
Socialism, Socialists 58–60, 91–92, 97, 100, 132, 164
Society of Women Journalists 166
South Australian Advertiser 31
South Australian Gazette and Colonial Register 19
Southam Chain 63
Southern Argus (Port Elliott and Strathalbyn) 32
Spanish-American War 195–196
Spectator (London; 18th century and 19th century) 140, 145
Spencer, Herbert 47
Spender, J.A. 163–164
Springfield Republican 174
Sprite (Quebec) 53
Stadacona (Canada) 53
Standard (London) 148, 170
Standard and Port Phillip Gazetteer (Melbourne) 20
Stanley, Henry 153, 189
Stanton, Edwin 65, 186
Star (London) 167
Statham, E.H. 16
Statue of Liberty 193
Stead, W.T. 162, 164
Stephens, Alfred Ward 15–16
Stevenson, George 18–19
Stock, sales of 78, 80, 103, 189
Stokes, Frederick Michael 15–16
Stone, Melvin E. 190
Strachan, John 44
Strode, Thomas 20, 36
Sue, Eugène 90
Sun (Sydney) 29, 35
Sutherland, William 49
Swan, James 20
Swan River Guardian 18

Index

Sydney Evening Mail 25
Sydney Gazette and New South Wales Advertiser 11
Sydney Herald 15–16, 36
Sydney Mail 26–27
Sydney Morning Herald 15–16, 25–30
Syme, David 22–25, 41

Tait's Edinburgh Magazine 149
Tarbell, Ida 199
Tasmanian Daily News 30
Tasmanian Times 31
Tasmanian Tribune 31
Tasmanian Weekly News 17, 31
"Taxes on knowledge" 141, 146–147, 149, 153–154
Taxes, tariffs *see* Censorship
Telegraph (Adelaide) 31
Telegraph (Brisbane) 33, 35
Templar (Hamilton) 60
Le Temps (Paris) 79, 95, 101
Thiers, Adolphe 79, 83, 97
Thomas, Robert 18
Three Musketeers 89
Times (London) 5, 13, 102, 116, 140, 144–145, 147–148, 153–154, 156–157, 160, 167, 170
Times-Colonist (Victoria) 62
Tit-Bits (London) 163
Tocqueville, Alexis de 177
Toronto News 66
Toronto Star 66
Toronto Telegram (*Evening Telegram*) 66
Tory, Toryism 47, 49–50, 52, 141, 145
Towne, James W. 62
Townshend, George 51–52
Traill, W.H. 29
Le Trait d'Union (Canada) 58
La Tribune (Paris) 100
Le Tribune (Paris) 87
Tribune and Farmer (United States) 197
Tribune and News of the Week (Sydney) 28
Trimm, Timothée (Léo Lespès) 96
Troppmann, Baptiste 96
Truth (London) 163
Twain, Mark 64
Type Riot 44

Ullstein family 133
Unions, labor 29, 47, 57–59
United States Telegraph (Washington) 174

Van Diemen's Land Gazette and General Advertiser 12

Vanity Fair (London) 159
Vaughan, John 161
Victoria Gazette and Anglo-America (Canada) 62
Victoria Magazine (London) 159
Vizetelly, Henry 147
Le Voix du Peuple (Paris) 92
Volks-Zeitung (Berlin) 118–119, 126
Vormärz period 113
Vossische Zeitung (Berlin) 118

Wade, John 57
Wage Earner (Canada) 58
Wakefield system 18
Walker, John Henry 46, 51–53
Wallaroo Times and Mining Journal 32
Walter, John, II 140
Walter, John, III 140
War correspondents 157, 182–185, 195–196
Ward, Frederick 28
Ward, Harriet 157
Wardell, Robert 13
Warren, Fred 58
Washington Gazette 176
Washington Globe 174
Wason v. Walter 161
Wasp (Canada) 53
Wayland, Julius Augustus 58
Webb, Bernice 59
Webb, Sidney 59
Webb, James Watson 174
Weber, Johann Jakob 126
Weed, Thurlow 174
Weekly Dispatch (London) 148, 169
Weekly Gazette (London) 147
Weekly Herald (Adelaide) 40
Weekly Sun (London) 166
Wells, Richard 32
Wentworth, William Charles 13
West, John 29, 41
West Australian (Perth) 17–18, 34–35
Western Australian Times (Perth) 33–34
Westminster Gazette (London) 163
Westminster Review (London) 140, 145, 147
Westralian Worker (Perth) 39
Whigs 141, 145, 173–174
White Dwarf (London) 144
Whitehorse Star 64
Whiton, Abe 62
Wiener, Joel 142, 146, 172
Wilhelm I 123, 128, 131
Wilhelm II 130, 137
Wilkes, John 14, 140
Willard, Frances 59

213

Williams, Walter 135–136, 138
Williston, H.C. 62
Wilson, Edward 21–22
Winnipeg Free Press 63
Wirth, J.G.A. 113
Wolfe, James 52
Wolff, Bernard 4, 88
Wolff agency 128–129, 135
Women, and journalism 6, 9, 78, 143, 147, 149, 152, 156–157, 159, 164, 166–167, 169–170–172, 180, 197–198
Women's Suffrage Journal (Britain) 164
Woodfall, William 151
Worker (Brisbane) 39–40
World (London) 163
World War I 8, 40, 68, 70, 72, 84, 90, 101, 103–104, 126, 134, 139, 157, 164–165, 171, 197, 200
World War II 104
Wrigley, George 60
Wynne, Watkin 28

Yass Free Holders' and Free Selectors' Advocate 37
Yellow journalism, yellow press 9, 65, 169, 190, 195–196, 200
Yellow Kid 192–193
"Yes, Virginia, there is a Santa Claus" 188
Young Germany movement 111–112
Yukon Midnight Sun 63

Zola, Emile 101

www.ingramcontent.com/pod-product-compliance
Lightning Source LLC
Chambersburg PA
CBHW032055300426
44116CB00007B/751